LIVING THE MARTIAL WAY

A Manual for the Way a Modern Warrior Should Think

FORREST E. MORGAN, MAJ, USAF

BARRICADE BOOKS

To the noblest warrior I've ever known,
my father

Published by Barricade Books Inc.
185 Bridge Plaza North
Suite 308-A
Fort Lee, NJ 07024

Printed in the United States of America

Library of Congress Cataloging-in-Publication Data

Morgan, Forrest E.
Living the martial way: a manual for the way a modern warrior should think /
Forrest E. Morgan
ISBN 0-942637-61-5
ISBN 0-942637-76-3 (pbk)
1. Martial arts. 2. Martial arts--Training. I. Title.
GV1101.M66 1992
796.8—dc20 92-16969
CIP

15 14 13 12 11 10

ACKNOWLEDGEMENTS

I would like to thank all my friends in the martial arts whose constant encouragement motivated me to write this book. I would also like to thank all my instructors, past and present, for giving me the technical foundation to undertake a project of this nature. Finally, my deepest gratitude goes to my family, Susan, Samuel, and Aubrey, who patiently endured the long months of neglect while I labored over this manuscript.

I would like to express my special appreciation to the following schools for allowing me to photograph their students and instructors: Gokyo Dojo and Sandia Budokan, Albuquerque, New Mexico, Frederick Tart, Head Instructor; Hakkosen Dojo, Aurora, Colorado, Dennis Palumbo, Head Instructor; The Korean Academy of Taekwon-Do, Aurora, Colorado, Jae T. Chung, Head Instructor; Runes Kung Fu Institute, Parker, Colorado, J.T. Runes, Head Instructor.

CONTENTS

PART TWO: THE *WAY* OF HONOR

PART THREE: THE *WAY* OF LIVING

FOREWORD

THE ASIAN MARTIAL ARTS are grounded in a rich heritage of blood and honor, and they have a great deal to offer serious students in today's dangerous world. Unfortunately, in most modern schools that heritage has been lost. It seems that the modern world and the marketing that drives it revolves around sport competition. As a result, students in today's schools are only getting the surface features of a deeply rooted tradition, and even older styles of the traditional arts are gradually losing their historical perspective. Sadly, with each new generation more is lost. This is a bitter pill to swallow for traditionalists such as my teachers and me, who have devoted our lives to preserving those legacies.

Unlike most modern martial artists, Forrest Morgan understands and appreciates the rich heritage of martial arts tradition. When I first met Mr. Morgan in early 1988, he already had more than 15 years of training and experience in a particularly formal style of Asian combat. But he was discouraged that his original system, rigorous as it had once been, had given way to the pressures of modern sport application, and he expressed a desire to study the more traditional styles. I was impressed but a little skeptical of his willingness to begin again in an entirely new form of martial art after having already attained considerable stature in his primary art. But without hesitation, he strapped on a white belt and began scrubbing mats along side beginners half his age.

In the years since our meeting I've watched Mr. Morgan's warriorship mature. He now has more than twenty years of experience in the martial arts, and he applies the principles he teaches in his book both in and out of the training hall. Forrest Morgan is no mere martial artist. He's a warrior, and he truly lives The Martial *Way!*

Mr. Morgan gives aspirants a course to follow for their lives' well-being as well as their martial arts success. This book is long overdue, one that every martial artist should add to his or her library. If, like most students, you have a teacher who does not teach these values, this book will fill the gap. If you're fortunate enough to have one who does, it will surely reinforce how lucky you really are.

DENNIS G. PALUMBO
Kaiden Shihan (8th Dan) of the Hakko Ryu
Director, Hakko Ryu Martial Arts Federation

INTRODUCTION

IN 1981 I ATTENDED a seminar for black belt karate students and instructors directed by a noted master. After a morning of grueling technical drills, he seated us around him on the floor. Given the topic, "When and When Not to Fight in Today's World," he had our rapt attention.

After explaining the standard doctrines of self defense, the master summarized by saying it is appropriate to fight to defend our selves, our loved ones, our country, and our honor. Then he began to address the next topic.

"Sir," I said, shooting up my hand, "can you please define honor? And can you give us some situations in which it's appropriate to fight in its defense?"

Momentarily perplexed, he began to pace as he carefully composed his answer. "When an attacker threatens your safety or that of your family," he said, "you have the right to defend the honor of your physical body or theirs."

"But Sir, how does that differ from simply defending ourselves from physical attack? I've always had the impression the word 'honor' involves some moral code or implied justification for an individual fighting to save face following a public insult. Gentlemen once fought duels to defend their honor. Are we justified in doing the same?"

The master's cheeks flushed, and I could see the muscles in his jaw tighten as he began again, "As I said, you have the right to defend the physical honor of..."

"But Sir..."

"You're nitpicking," hissed a young woman sitting beside me.

Frustrated, I turned, prepared to deliver a terse reply, but, feeling the glares from others in the training hall, I realized I had already overstepped the bounds of courtesy. I settled back and fumed in silence as the master moved on to the next topic.

My experience was not an isolated incident and I was not the only one in the audience whose questions remained unanswered. Today's martial arts students are much more sophisticated than those of the past, and they're asking questions. Unfortunately, they aren't getting answers from their teachers. Most instructors explain how to perform a physical technique very well but respond with only vague platitudes when asked how to apply their martial concepts to daily life.

My experience at the karate seminar launched me on an exhaustive quest to learn what philosophical foundations underpin the martial arts. The search hasn't been easy; hundreds of volumes have been written by modern masters, but most are little more than picture books showing us how to do the various strikes, throws, and holds we learn during the first few months of class. But the foundation is indeed there, and slowly it surfaced.

What emerged was a common way of thinking, feeling, and living among the warriors who developed the various martial arts and among those who still truly practice them today. Of course, there are cultural differences between warrior groups in different parts of the world, but there is also a core attitude, common to these groups, that separates them from non-warrior people within their own cultural strains. Asian warriors and all classical martial artists know of this common bond. They call it The Martial *Way*.

During my years of study, the more I learned about The Martial *Way*, the more convinced I became that a book elaborating its tenets would be helpful—no, invaluable—to other martial artists wanting to follow warrior paths. Not a book telling karate people how to do better karate or aikido people how to do better aikido, but one to teach all martial artists how to integrate their arts into their daily lives. In essence, this is a book not about how to do a martial art but how to live The Martial *Way*.

Sadly, what also became apparent during my study was how little most Western martial artists really know about what is and is not martial art.

BACKGROUND ON THE MARTIAL ARTS

The term "martial art" is used in Western idiom to describe a wide variety of Asian combative systems and sports. Under close examination, however, we find that not all of these activities are truly martial in nature, nor are they all arts. While some have indeed developed as systems of combat used by warriors, many others evolved in religious and civil settings as methods for physical and spiritual development, personal self defense, and sport.

Examples of combative systems actually developed by warriors include those devised by the *hwarang* (literally "flower of manhood"), a warrior society in the 6th century Korean kingdom of Silla, and, of course, the martial systems developed by the *samurai* of feudal Japan. The significant characteristics of these martial arts are that they focused on the use of weapons and encompassed a wide range of other military skills such as horsemanship, swimming, fortifications, and strategy, as well as unarmed combat.

Many other systems evolved in religious environments. Most martial artists are familiar with the story of how the monk Bodhidharma brought Buddism from India to China in the 6th century A.D. and subsequently founded the long combative arts tradition at the Shaolin Temple in Hunan Province. As the legend goes, Bodhidharma was father of the *Ch'an* sect (*Zen* in Japanese) of Buddism, who's practitioners aspire to achieve spiritual enlightenment through meditation.*

Shortly after his arrival at Shaolin, he realized his Chinese devotees lacked the physical stamina required to withstand the long sessions of meditation he prescribed for their spiritual training. So he developed a series of exercises to improve their fitness. In time, this training system evolved into a method of combat, and the Shaolin monks became renown for their fighting prowess. Over the ensuing centuries before the Manchu destroyed the Shaolin Temple in the late 1800s, a number of combative systems originated there and spread across the Orient. Today, arts practiced in several Asian countries attribute their roots to this source.

Then again, a number of combative systems were developed by common people for personal self defense. Karate is perhaps the best example. This unarmed method evolved on the island of Okinawa over a period of centuries as a blend of locally developed techniques and those adopted from the Asian mainland.** Its development accelerated in the 15th century when Okinawa was united under one ruler and possession of weapons by common people was prohibited. By 1609 when the territory fell under control of the rigid Satsuma clan of Japan, all weapons had been confiscated and the populace was left with their empty hands and feet

*Several versions of this story can be found. Actually, Buddism began to filter into China as early as the first century. While the Shaolin Temple did exist and was indeed a center of combative arts development, the Bodhidharma story is largely apocryphal.

**Most accounts name China as the source of *te* (hand) systems developed in Okinawa, often citing the Shaolin Temple specifically. However, some historians believe combative systems were imported from the kingdoms of Silla or Baek Je on the Korean peninsula. Actually, Okinawans probably assimilated techniques from a variety of mainland sources over a period of centuries.

to defend themselves from each other and their sometimes brutal *samurai* overlords.

Each of these environments has produced effective systems of personal combat, but are they all martial arts? Noted martial arts historian, the late Donn F. Draeger, thought not. Draeger's position was that unless a system was developed by professional warriors for use in actual warfare, it is not a martial art. Systems developed in temples or by common people may be effective forms of combat, but their very reliance on and in many cases preference for unarmed techniques made them impractical for battlefields, past or present. He chose to classify these as "civil" arts. Draeger's bottom line was, if an art was not developed for military application, it's not "martial" (1980).

While Draeger was completely correct in the literal sense, I find his definition a bit too constraining. In the first place, while the "civil" arts aren't practical in military combat, neither are the unarmed portions of those arts Draeger considered truly martial; no one would willingly attack an armed soldier with empty hands. Yet several of these "civil" arts are today being taught to military forces. Just as warriors of the past developed unarmed techniques as an auxiliary to arms, some modern soldiers are being taught karate, taekwondo, and other methods as a part of their martial art.

Secondly and perhaps more importantly, many of the "civil" arts, though developed by priests in temples, were practiced purely for military or paramilitary reasons. Many Buddhist temples were centers of political activity, and they frequently fielded their own combat forces. Therefore, the combative systems they developed, as well as those that evolved from them later, should be considered martial. Where I do emphatically agree with Draeger, however, is in his differentiation between martial art and combative sport.

Sport applications of combative systems, such as competitive taekwondo, karate-do, and judo, are not martial arts. Putting a combative system in the competitive arena requires an array of rules to be placed on it, constraining its maneuvers and detrimentally modifying its technical application. In time, as "players" are trained in how to work within the rules to best win the game, the system evolves to fit the framework of those rules. What is effective in the constrained, competitive environment is often worthless in the no-holds-barred world of actual combat, and what is effective in combat, being illegal in sport, gradually fades from the training program and is lost. As Draeger and Smith pointed out in their book, *Asian Fighting Arts*, "the more remote a *budo* (Japanese for martial way) form remains from sportive endeavor, the more positively it identifies itself with combat effectiveness and the classical tradition" (1969, p. 92).

Don't misunderstand me, I bear no ill feelings toward combat sports or those who choose to play them. There are positive features in these activities as there are in all forms of competitive athletics; they promote physical fitness, perseverance, courage, and fair play. And many of these qualities are also valuable in the martial or military context. After all, the famous words of General Douglas MacArther are still carved on the stone portals of the field house at the United States Military Academy at West Point:

Upon these fields of friendly strife
are sown the seeds
that, upon other fields on other days
will bear the fruits of victory.

But players should not deceive themselves into thinking they are practicing martial arts or The Martial *Way* while preparing for or competing on the tournament floor. What they're doing may very well enhance their own personal growth and have a positive role in society, but it isn't martial, it isn't art, and it most certainly isn't The Martial *Way*.

Then, what is?

MARTIAL ARTS, MARTIAL WAYS, AND THE MARTIAL *WAY*

Perhaps the biggest misunderstanding among Western "martial artists" is whether the systems they study are martial arts or martial ways. To best understand this dichotomy, let's turn to Japan.

The Japanese group their combative systems into two distinct categories. Those developed by warrior groups purely for use in combat are called *bugei* or *bujutsu* (both words literally mean "martial art"). Typically, names of those systems end in the suffix *jutsu*. On the other hand, *budo* (martial way) systems all end in the suffix *do* (way). These systems were developed from the *jutsu* forms but are directed toward goals beyond (sometimes instead of) combat effectiveness. Where the *bujutsu* practitioner is concerned first and foremost with learning how to prevail in combat, the true *budo* aspirant devotes himself to a system of physical, mental, and spiritual discipline through which he attempts to elevate himself in search of perfection (Draeger and Smith, 1969, p. 92).

Notice I was careful to say "true" *budo* practitioner. The various *budo* were developed by *bujutsu* masters who aspired to modify and formalize their combative systems into vehicles for leading others in the *Way*. Having lived and mastered the warrior life style, these men and women sought to devise concise systems for training the general public in the virtues of warriorship for the good of society at large. To make their methods both acceptable and attractive, the combative elements were often toned down and sporting applications were introduced. Unfortunately, while the founders and early followers of the various martial ways such as judo and karate-do understood their systems were mere devices for practicing The Martial *Way*, most of their modern day adherents have lost sight of the *Way* itself and instead wander aimlessly amidst the external trappings of ritual and sport.

Although I used Japan as an example, the martial art/martial way distinction can also be applied to arts from other Asian locales. The concept of "*Way*" is a common one in Eastern philosophical thought. In Japanese and Korean it's called "*do*."*

In China, it's "*tao*." In Japan, *jutsu* and *do* systems survive and coexist, but in some other locales, such as Korea, the original martial arts have all but died out while their *do* counterparts, e.g. taekwondo and tang soo do, continue to flourish. But can an individual who studies one or more of the martial arts or ways or even plays at combat sports also study and live The Martial *Way*? Of course.

First, however, the student must realize that any system he or she may practice is artificial. That is to say, mastery of it is not the desired end in itself but only a vehicle towards that end. Second, the individual must be able to subdue the external gratifications of rank, prestige, competitive victory, and ego in general for the truer rewards of personal development. Finally, the prospective adherent must realize that The Martial *Way* does not start and end at the door of the training hall. It is a way of life in which every action, in and out of the training hall, is done in the context of warriorship.

WHY PRACTICE THE MARTIAL WAY TODAY

In America, many students turn to the martial arts to learn how to defend themselves from the bully at school or work, or to feel more confident while out at night. Others belong to karate or judo clubs and follow the tournament circuit collecting as many trophies as their talents can win. Why would these individuals want to learn seemingly complex philosophical concepts or constrain themselves with ethical notions from past warrior societies?

The simple answer is there is much more to be gained from following The Martial *Way* than technical proficiency and the external rewards of athletic success. A true understanding of The

*Actually, "*do*" is the form when "way" is used as a suffix modifying other words. When the word stands alone, "*michi*" is the proper term.

Martial *Way* opens the door to a rich heritage of ethical principles, training approaches, and esoteric capabilities that can enrich an individual's martial arts experience as well as sharpen his ability to defend himself or succeed in competition.

But most importantly, The Martial *Way* is a way of living. It is a holistic discipline aimed at the pursuit of excellence, not just in the training hall, but at life. Its disciples strive to apply the *Way* in every vocation, and its adepts tend to be achievers in any field of endeavor. This is what separates The Martial *Way* from other pursuits and makes it so valuable. Where one may play a sport or have a hobby, one lives The Martial *Way*.

THE DESIGN OF THIS BOOK

Living The Martial Way is a concise manual for training in warriorship. Although it frequently addresses philosophy, it isn't a collection of quaint but vague expressions or anecdotes. Rather, it provides a systematic, step-by-step approach to applying the warrior mind-set to your martial training and daily life.

The material is organized to produce a cumulative training effect. It is divided into three parts, beginning with a topic that the typical student can understand most readily, The *Way* of Training. The five chapters in this section explain how the warrior approaches martial training and what he hopes to gain from it. It focuses on the warrior mind-set and explains how to orient your physical training program around martial concepts rather than sport or hobbyist pursuits.

Part Two, The *Way* of Honor, addresses the warrior's approach to ethics and provides you with a clear-cut guide for developing a powerful sense of character and will. It explains how warrior ethics, rooted in Eastern philosophical thought, parallel Western concepts of morality. You'll learn about the driving force behind the warrior's concept of honor and understand how to apply the concept of honor in your life.

Part Three is entitled, The *Way* of Living, and it teaches you just that. This section offers practical guidelines for living a warrior lifestyle. It address such important issues as fitness and nutrition, religion and mysticism, and warrior bearing. Combined with the foregoing sections, The *Way* of Living gives you all the knowledge necessary to grasp the concept of mastery as it applies to martial arts and The Martial *Way*.

Living The Martial Way is indeed a modern warrior's master text. Its ultimate objective is not merely to give you an intellectual appreciation of martial concepts but to let you taste the rich flavor that comes with living a warrior lifestyle. When you've finished *Living the Martial Way*, you'll have the following:

■ The two steps to getting the warrior mind-set. You'll acknowledge your warriorship and pursue internal objectives (Chapter 1).

■ A road map for determining your own martial destiny. You'll learn how to choose which martial arts to study and how to plan your training (Chapter 2).

■ The incentive to train as warriors train. Although modern warriors focus on life, you'll know that defeat in combat means death. You'll have three instructions for training more effectively and living more vibrantly (Chapter 3).

■ The fundamentals of strategy and tactics. Strategy plays a crucial role in warriorship. You'll use four steps and five elements to develop your own unbeatable strategy and tactics (Chapter 4).

■ Systematic methods for developing the esoteric skills of warriorship. Martial arts are legendary for the seemingly mystical powers they teach. You'll learn what forces warriors really command. More importantly, you'll learn how to develop them yourself (Chapter 5).

■ The foundations of warrior honor. Honor is a word many people use but few understand. You'll learn to apply three tests to any situation you face to determine the most honorable course of action (Chapter 6).

■ Examples of honor in action. With a firm understanding of the basis of honor, you'll see the role honor plays in five moral issues central to warriorship (Chapter 7).

■ The insight to recognize perversions of honor. Revenge can be honorable, but more often it's self serving. Suicide may be noble, but more times than not, it's the act of a coward. You'll learn to recognize circumstances in which revenge and suicide are honorable and those in which they are not (Chapter 8).

■ A practical guide to warrior fitness and nutrition. Don't believe the story of the 90-pound weakling who, after a few months of training, returns to the beach and beats up the 200-pound bully. You'll understand the importance of fitness and nutrition, and you'll learn how warriors achieve superior conditioning (Chapter 9).

■ An understanding of how religion and mysticism relate to The Martial *Way*. Asian religions and mystical practices have often been associated with the martial arts, but they are not part of The Martial *Way*. You'll learn about the principle beliefs of Asia and see how they have and haven't influenced warrior practices (Chapter 10).

■ The dignity and bearing of a warrior. True warriors exude a dignity that non-warriors feel but can't describe. You'll obtain three keys for developing warrior bearing, and you'll learn the secret of personal power (Chapter 11).

■ The wisdom to understand and recognize true mastery. You'll learn the kind of mastery warriors pursue, and you'll discover how to focus your life toward that goal (chapter 12).

In this book I use terms from several languages to explain specific concepts, but most often I rely on Japanese. Students of arts from Korea, China, and other cultures need not be offended or discouraged. This focus is entirely due to my limited knowledge of foreign languages. The concepts themselves are universal.

One final note: to avoid awkward "he and she" sentence structures, I tend to refer to warriors in the masculine gender. I don't mean this to imply women can't be warriors. Some of the greatest warriors in history were women, and there are great ones with us today. Indeed, warriorship knows no boundaries of sex, race, or culture.

PART I

THE *WAY* OF TRAINING

Chapter 1

THE WARRIOR MIND-SET

You must be deadly serious in training. When I say that, I do not mean that you should be reasonably diligent or moderately in earnest. I mean that your opponent must always be present in your mind, whether you sit or stand or walk or raise your arms.

GICHIN FUNAKOSHI'S FIRST RULE
FOR THE STUDY OF KARATE-DO.

Funakoshi was karate's greatest modern master. He was the man who raised the art from its obscure roots in Okinawa to public attention in Japan and eventually the world. As a result, more people are familiar with his name than any other in the history of karate.

Although Funakoshi was a great karate master, the source of his greatness and fame was not his physical prowess. Certainly, having devoted his life to the practice of karate, he commanded all the strength, speed, and technical skill associated with that art's mastery. But he had contemporaries who were stronger, faster, and perhaps, even more skillful than he. No, at barely five feet tall, Funakoshi was never destined to be a great champion in any physical arena.

The source of Funakoshi's greatness was his unwavering devotion to the training principles, ethics, and lifestyle that embody The Martial *Way*.

Gichin Funakoshi was a twentieth century anachronism. Born in 1868 into a noble family in Shuri, Okinawa, he grew up amidst the turmoil of Japan's emergence from feudalism. He and his family were *shizoku*, descendants of a long line of *samurai*. This was a turbulent time for Japan and Okinawa. The last *shogun* had been removed from power the year of Funakoshi's birth, and the young lad witnessed first hand the dissolution of the warrior class. He saw the special privileges members of his caste had previously enjoyed, disappear.

Unlike most of his contemporaries, however, Funakoshi never stopped being a warrior in spirit. He began studying karate

Funakoshi introduced karate to Japan in 1922. There, he founded the Shotokan, or "House of Shoto."

as a child, even though practice of the art was forbidden by the Japanese, and he continued to study under several of Okinawa's leading masters throughout most of the first fifty years of his life.

This was by no means an occasional pursuit or part-time study. For Funakoshi, karate was a part of his daily existence as important as eating and sleeping. Nor should we assume his noble heritage provided him an easy life style with hours to devote to any pastime he fancied. For though the Funakoshi family were *shizoku*, they were poor, and young Gichen felt lucky when he first found work as a school teacher, even though it meant cutting off his queue, a symbol of his warrior heritage.

The fact is, Funakoshi was committed to a lifetime study of karate at all costs and at any risk. He worked long hours teaching school each day, and since karate was forbidden, he trained at night. Every evening he walked several miles to his instructor's house where one or more masters drilled him in *kata* (patterned movement) by the moon's light or that of a dim lantern. Often, he didn't get home until dawn.

Gichin Funakoshi never lost his commitment to training. Even during the last years of his life, while other octogenarians rested, Funakoshi began each day rising early, washing, and then practicing several *kata* before taking his morning tea. How different this is from the attitude of today's martial artists.

Unlike Funakoshi, I haven't yet studied martial arts for fifty years. But the travel associated with my military career has enabled me to meet quite a number of supposed martial artists, and I never fail to be amazed at the things they say:

"I do karate on tuesdays and thursdays; other nights I bowl or play cards..."

"I hate *kata*. It's boring and it doesn't have any basis in reality. After all, you can't do a kata on someone who attacks you..."

"Your class was okay, but I'm practicing with somebody else now. He took second place in the Florida Nationals, so he's gotta be good. Right?"

"You spend so much time on basics and forms. I want to learn the nitty-gritty, down-and-dirty way of fighting."

Or worse yet, "I don't waste your time on all that form crap. I'm only going to teach you the nitty-gritty..."

As you can see, there is a striking difference between the way these folks see their martial training and the way Funakoshi saw his. We Westerners are individualists by nature, and we each perceive the martial arts differently from the next person. Unfortunately, the typical Westerner sees his art as something very different than what it was originally meant to be.

First, there are students who "do" some martial art as a hobby or pastime. These folks come to class a couple of nights a week and usually don't think about martial art on the off days other than to brag about their prowess or complain about their sore muscles. They put their taekwondo night or aikido night in the same category as their bridge night or bowling night, except they are confident (at least outwardly so) that their martial ardor has provided them some secret weapon with which they will one day bring an unsuspecting mugger his just reward.

All too often, people of this ilk are preoccupied with attaining rank. They beg, badger, or pay instructors to test them as often as possible. You can see them strutting around some less reputable training halls as senior students in relatively short periods of time. Once they reach the first *dan* (degree of black belt), however, they usually feel they've "learned it" and drift away shortly afterward.

The second type of student I see is the obsessive tournament competitor. This individual believes the martial arts are a category of athletics and that skill in them is measured in tournament victories. Enthusiasts of this genre are forever looking for ways to "improve their arts" by modifying the techniques to better score points. Later, as instructors, they gradually stop teaching those aspects that can't be applied within the rules of their respective sports. In time, their narrowed and disfigured games bear little resemblance to the noble namesakes from which they descended. Unfortunately, this process has been a driving force behind the evolution of combative systems in the twentieth century.

Combine this with the ever-present financial inducement to attract and please tournament spectators and we see the emergence of musical *kata*, garish costumes, medicine show exhibitions, and theatrics that only look good when compared to professional wrestlers. Whole organizations and even entire combative systems have fallen prey to this lure. As a result, we now have styles that promote on the basis of tournament wins and schools that train students in boxing rings.

Finally, there are those individuals who want to find the "true secret" of deadly combat. These folks don't want to waste their time learning courtesies, fundamental techniques, *kata*, and the other aspects of disciplined training. Instead, they want a short cut. They're certain they can learn a concise series of kicks, gouges, and cat scratches that will make them formidable fighters. They can often be seen drifting from school to school, staying at each only long enough to become bored with the discipline before deciding it doesn't have the secret and moving on.

All of this is in marked contrast to the mind-set of men like Funakoshi. But perhaps we shouldn't judge Western martial artists so harshly. Most of us weren't born into a warrior heritage as Funakoshi was. Many Westerners take up a martial art looking for an interesting pastime or a source of exercise. Others are drawn by the promise of a challenging sport, a method of personal self-defense, or a combination of these offerings. Indeed, martial training can provide all of these things. But where the warrior and non-warrior differ in their thinking is in the way they see themselves and the way they orient and prioritize the art in their lives.

Most Western martial artists don't consider themselves warriors. Certainly, many fantasize and play at being warriors while in the training hall, but once they step out the door they return to their roles as carpenters, salesmen, or college students. They are no more warriors than are arcade game players who fantasize themselves in aerial combat true fighter pilots. Funakoshi, on the other hand, bore no such illusions regarding his warriorship.

He was born into a warrior family. As such, he was trained from early childhood, as were generations of his ancestors, in how a warrior should think, feel, and act in every situation. It didn't matter that there had been no war in Okinawa for over two hundred years. The *Shizoku* were still warriors, the tempered, the polished, the elite. So it's no surprise Funakoshi embraced his training in karate the way he did.

Warriors don't consider martial training a hobby to be done a couple of evenings a week. Nor do they see it as a game. To a man of arms, weapons, natural or manufactured, are tools of his trade. He knows his skill in wielding them can determine whether he lives or dies in battle. To men of warrior heritage and profession, martial arts are a way of life, an unrelenting commitment, a constant struggle to improve.

But the noblest warriors took martial training a step further than just refining their physical skills for combat. Throughout the many years of peace in Tokugawa Japan and Okinawa, warriors of Funakoshi's breed continued to train for war, while many others lost their martial instincts and became warriors in name only. Those who remained true to warrior ideals realized that constant training in the martial arts developed in them qualities that helped them to excel in endeavors totally unrelated to combat. In the extended peace, these secondary products of martial training became primary, and warriors began using their various disciplines as vehicles for personal development. Combine this with the rigid ethical standards that inevitably develop among men who acknowledge the responsibilities of noble birth and power, and we witness the development of The Martial *Way*.

Gichin Funakoshi stood firm amidst the chaos of social change. With the abolishment of the warrior class, he saw the noble qualities of warriorship dissolving into a turmoil of reform; the good was being discarded with the bad. And he reacted the way the noblest warrior would. He loyally supported his government in all the positive aspects of reform—he cut off his queue and embraced the newly declared social equality—but he continued to practice and adhere to the very elements of warriorship that had truly made his class superior. Furthermore, with the caste system abolished, he decided it was time to teach The Martial *Way* to anyone who was willing to learn, believing he could strengthen and improve society at large.

I've used Funakoshi as my model for this chapter because he and Japan provide archetypical examples of the warrior ethos. But

The martial arts are not games, and the most traditional training halls don't teach children. This 15-year-old jujutsu student is the youngest in his *dojo.*

I want to point out that he was by no means the only warrior of this period who tried to formalize The Martial *Way* and bring it to the public. Nor is cultivation of The Martial *Way* unique to Japan or even the Orient.

Martial cultures have developed in widely scattered locales throughout history. And though cultural norms and ethical foundations differ from group to group, there's a core attitude between warrior groups of widely diverse societies that has made them, in some ways, more common to each other than to non-warrior elements of their own cultures.

Indeed, we can see common threads between groups as diverse as Japan's *samurai*, the *hwarang* of sixth century Korea, the warrior caste of India, the chivalric orders of feudal Europe, and even the American Indians. In the late 1960's, when Carlos Castaneda studied the ways of warriorship and mysticism among the Yaqui indians of America's southwest, his mentor once told him, "To seek perfection of the warrior's spirit is the only task worthy of our manhood (Castaneda, 1972, p. 109)." Certainly, Funakoshi could identify with that statement more readily than the non-warrior Yaqui or the typical American martial artist.

Understanding and cultivating the warrior spirit is what true martial training is all about. Without this essential foundation, the martial arts student can develop physical skill but little more. With it, the aspiring warrior can enter a world in which physical skill is just one of many rewards. This chapter is devoted to helping you attain a warrior orientation in your training.

GETTING THE MIND-SET

Before you can take up any study of The Martial *Way*, you have to get the right mind-set. Look closely at Funakoshi and others like him. You'll see two common traits. Those are the common threads that comprise the warrior mind-set. Unlike the hobbyist or athlete, the warrior:

- Acknowledges his warriorship.
- Pursues internal versus external objectives.

ACKNOWLEDGE YOUR WARRIORSHIP

I watched you, Nic San. You fought well. So do not expect us to pander to your weaknesses. We would be very bad senpai if we did that... We are like soldiers. When a soldier puts on his uniform, carries a weapon, and goes to war, he is obviously willing to fight and kill his enemies. If he is willing to kill, then he must be prepared to die. It is only right. We must cultivate spirit.

From Moving Zen, by C.W. Nicol

I don't like the term "martial artist." To me, that expression implies an individual "does" a martial art among his or her other hobbies or recreational pastimes. What's more, the focus of a martial artist tends to be on a given martial art itself. Learning karate or judo becomes an end rather than a means of cultivating the martial spirit. As a result, the student tends to focus exclusively on one discipline and justifies his narrowness by claiming it's superior to all others.

Living The Martial *Way* means thinking of yourself first and foremost as a warrior. Certainly, you study and practice one or more martial arts, but you do so as a vehicle for developing your warriorship and honing your spirit. As you proceed in this book, you'll learn there are many avenues of study that factor together with your martial training to cultivate this spirit. And many other seemingly unrelated pursuits and experiences can enhance your warriorship when approached with the proper attitude.

You might wonder why a waitress, bricklayer, or doctor—individuals neither born into a warrior heritage nor involved in the profession of arms—would want to think of themselves as warriors in today's society. One could have asked Funakoshi the same question. If you recall, the warrior caste in Okinawa and Japan were abolished shortly after his birth. He no longer had any legal status as a warrior. In fact, he was a school teacher by occupation. But that didn't change his identity. He was still a member of an elite part of society.

Warriors are special people. Since they understand the concept of honor, they set their ethical standards above most of the rest of society. Since they pattern their lives around the pursuit of excellence, they tend to achieve in their chosen vocations. Why would people in today's society want to think of themselves as warriors? Because warriorship is an extraordinary and powerful way to live!

These kenjutsu students don't play at their martial art. They've acknowledged their warrior calling.

Warriorship is not for everyone. In past martial cultures the warrior caste was occupied by an elite few, usually chosen by birth. They were admired and respected by the rest of society because of their noble birth. Gone now are the days of inherited status. To achieve admiration and respect today, the warrior must set himself apart from the rest of society by his personal excellence. Where warriorship was once a birthright, it is now a calling.

Start today by thinking of yourself as a warrior. Stop being a dentist or an accountant who does karate as a hobby and become a warrior who practices both his profession and karate to hone his spirit. You'll discover that both your professional competence and your karate will improve.

But true mastery in The Martial *Way* involves more than mere physical prowess and expertise. The master warrior is a man of character, a man of wisdom and insight. These goals are far more elusive than those regarding technical expertise. Elusive they may be, but you can begin the long road towards character development by learning to recognize and pursue internal versus external objectives.

PURSUE INTERNAL VERSUS EXTERNAL OBJECTIVES

He who stands on tiptoes does not stand firm. He who stretches his legs does not walk easily. Thus he who displays himself does not shine. He who vaunts himself does not find his merit acknowledged. He who is self-conceited has no superiority allowed him.

Lao Tzu
(Minick, 1974, p. 88)

Have you ever gone to a karate tournament and seen the guy in the satin costume with a dozen patches and the four inch wide multi-colored belt? You wonder how I saw the same guy you did? Well, I probably didn't, but there seems to be someone like him at nearly every tournament in the United States. These people provide us classic examples of martial artists enslaved to ego gratification from external sources.

The Martial *Way* is a discipline devoted to the perfection of character. It's a very personal pursuit in which the student turns his attention inward. He evaluates the strength of his spirit and sets about polishing those facets that need work. Outward displays of finery expose an individual who needs external reinforcement to reassure him of his self worth. Even public displays of skill and prowess, when motivated by the desire to impress others, demonstrate and intensify fundamental weaknesses within. And there lies the pitfall of tournament competition.

Jigaro Kano introduced competitive *randori* to his newly developed judo in the late 19th century, hoping to generate public enthusiasm for his martial way. Likewise, when Funakoshi brought karate to Japan and began teaching it as karate-do, *kumite* became a principle source of its popularity. Both of these masters were motivated by noble goals: the more people they could attract to their respective disciplines, the more they could lead to the *Way*. But one must wonder if more is always better.

Warriorship is by nature an elite calling. Neither Funakoshi nor Kano nor other warriors of their ilk ever needed to impress others to bolster their own motivation. And when, in order to attract the masses, we have to provide channels for ego gratification, I question whether those masses gain any value from The Martial *Way* and whether they are even aware of it.

Randori, *kumite*, and similar exercises do have merit in The Martial *Way*, but only when approached purely as training procedures with no external reward. The pomp of tournament exhibition, with the promise of prize and public recognition, can actually obscure the *Way* and make it more difficult for an aspiring warrior to find if his character is not yet fully formed.

Another lure that traps many would be warriors is the desire to attain rank. Warriors of the past had very little concern for establishing grading systems within their martial arts. Consider their situation: they were most often soldiers serving in established military organizations. Their motive in studying combative techniques was to help them to prevail in battle, and the proof of their competence was survival and victory, not some artificial system of grade. In fact, a martial grading system would have, in many cases, conflicted with the military ranking system under which they served. That is not to say there were no grades in traditional martial training.

A typical warrior practiced several martial arts for years with no outward distinction or recognition; it was part of his job, just as an engineer uses mathematics and a carpenter becomes skillful at pounding nails. In time, the warrior often found he had a particular aptitude for a certain weapon or a specific skill and he began to specialize. A select few of these specialists would then choose—and more importantly, would be chosen—to master their respective arts and would be tutored in the inner or secret techniques. Only then, after mastering the entire system, did the individual receive any kind of certification or formal recognition. In Japan this certificate is called the *Menkyo Kaiden*, and it traditionally served as both a certificate of mastery and a license to teach.*

Modern ranking systems came about with the emergence of the various martial ways. The *Dan/Kyu* (in Korean, *Dan/Gup*) or "Grade/Class" system with which we are so familiar today was developed by Kano for grading his judo players. It achieved such popularity that it was adopted by nearly all the *budo* systems and even some of the modern *bugei*. Kano's motives were innocent enough; he wanted to provide a yard stick for his students to measure their progress in the art and by implication, their personal development. But here again, we see an example of an artificial

*However, during the extended peace of Japan's Edo Period (1600-1868), schools became much more formal and various grades of student and teacher emerged. The three most common levels of teacher were *renshi*, *kyoshi*, and *hanshi*.

system developed to gratify participants from the general public but for which true warriors had no use.

Ranking systems are not inherently bad, just dangerous. If both student and instructor realize and firmly adhere to the principle that attaining rank is not an objective but only a measurement of technical progress, then the system may not impair the warrior's advancement in The Martial *Way*. But even then, the danger lies in the risk that once having attained rank in a given system, the student, often now an instructor, will assume he has mastered the *Way* itself (if he's aware of its existence). His progress in The Martial *Way* will then stop. Remember, all systems are artificial.

To attain the proper mind-set, it's crucial that you learn to recognize the difference between internal and external motiva-

The Martial *Way* is not a sport, hobby, or casual pastime. It's a way of life. This master of Lun Gar Pai Kung Fu began his training in 1936.

tions. Do you only train when there's someone there to watch you? Do you only practice *kata* to prepare for a test or tournament? And how about competition; why do you do it? Is it for the prize? The recognition? Are you trying to reinforce a macho self-image you've created?

The warrior doesn't train for others to see him. He trains because he is a warrior and perfecting his spirit is his lifetime objective. The master of The Martial *Way* needs no one to reinforce his self-image with praise or reward; he is self contained. As a result, he is just as satisfied to train alone, and he is alone in a crowd.

Start today by examining your own motives, and then begin to pursue internal objectives. Turn your eyes inward, warrior!

POINTS TO REMEMBER: THE WARRIOR MIND-SET

- The Martial *Way* is not a sport, hobby, or occasional pastime. It's a way of life.
- Warriors belong to an elite group—one that knows no cultural boundries.
- Begin by acknowledging your warriorship. Think, feel, and act like a warrior. Set yourself apart from the rest of society by your personal excellence. Where warriorship was once a birthright, it is now a calling.
- Throw away your vanity, and pursue internal objectives. Learn to recognize the difference between internal and external motivations. The Martial *Way* is a discipline devoted to the perfection of character, not the collection of prizes. Beware of rank; train to achieve personal excellence, not certificates and belts. Remember, all systems are artificial. There is one true Martial *Way*.

Chapter 2

YOUR MARTIAL DESTINY

I hope martial artists are more interested in the root of martial arts and not the different decorative branches, flowers, or leaves. It is futile to argue as to which leaf, which design of branches, or which attractive flower you like; when you understand the root, you understand all its blossoming.

BRUCE LEE FROM *TAO OF JEET KUNE DO* (1975, p. 23)

People often ask me which martial art is the best. Knowing I've traveled over the years and worked with students and instructors in a variety of arts, they want to know if I've found one superior fighting system that beats all others.

But more often, people are anxious to tell me which martial art is the best. Be it Shorin Ryu Karate, Tomiki Aikido, or any of a hundred other styles; if they study it, then it's the best. After all, their instructors told them so and gave them scores of reasons to believe it.

I usually try not to argue with people of this ilk; it's as fruitless as debating politics or religion. But occasionally I take the time to pass on an old expression, one familiar to most people who've studied the arts long enough to understand it: "There are no superior martial arts, only superior martial artists."

But there's a greater truth here, one more relevant than the merits of specific arts or the skills of those who practice them. When it comes right down to it, there are no superior or inferior martial arts, there are only warriors and non-warriors.

Every society throughout history has been comprised of essentially two classes, one consisting of those who were warriors and one composed of those who were not. You could argue that various cultures have had numerous classes—peasants, merchants, aristocrats, etcetera—and that modern society is composed of a multitude of strata. But the fact remains, all of these elements can be categorized as either warrior or non-warrior groups. The reason our civilization has evolved to this condition is simple: life revolves around struggle.

It's this very struggle that has led to the development of the warrior class. For not everyone is fit for combat, and as each society develops and its culture diversifies, the onerous task of defense is eventually delegated to that select group of individuals most suited for it. Those individuals then proceed to prepare themselves for their assigned role, protecting their society.

Warriors don't quibble over which system of fighting is the best. For them, the relative strengths and weaknesses of specific methods are of less concern than the overall objective of survival and victory. I'm not saying the quality of a given system isn't important, I'm saying any real warrior knows that no one system fits everyone's needs in all situations.

All systems are artificial. They are codified methods of teaching and practicing given sets of skills. A typical martial art was born when a skilled warrior discovered a set of moves that worked particularly well for him in a crisis. Wanting to preserve that experience, he then refined those moves and developed a system to practice them. If his system had merit, it drew the interest of other warriors and the founder soon had a following.

In each instance of an established style of fighting, what went into the system at inception was based on what worked for the founder and what he believed would work for others in similar circumstances. The founder and his warrior followers practiced the system for what it was, a specific method of combat they believed would work in circumstances similar to those that spawned it.

Though some warriors specialized, they all practiced more than one art. They had no illusions that there was any single best style of fighting that worked in situations other than those for which it was designed. Given a choice, they never used an unarmed method against a swordsman or a pole fighting style against an archer. When your ultimate goal is survival, there's no room for foolish notions of one superior weapon or one unbeatable style of fighting.

As time passed, many martial disciplines eventually fell into the hands of non-warriors who practiced them for sport, fitness, or

When your goal is survival, there's no room for foolish notions of one superior weapon or one unbeatable style of fighting.

personal self-defense. Unlike their warrior forebears, these individuals usually studied only one art. Unfortunately, that led to confusion in times past, and it's even worse today.

People who study a single martial art tend to focus exclusively on the beliefs or "doctrines" of that art. They often don't understand that those doctrines, valid though they may be, were developed in response to specific threats and for fighting in specific situations. These disciples of a single doctrine tend to shut out ideas from other sources and convince themselves that their's is the one true way of fighting, the ultimate in armed or unarmed combat. As a result, they become slaves to the very doctrines they profess.

This is quite unlike the warriors who founded the arts these individuals practice, for warriors never tolerate enslavement to anyone or anything. They are masters of their own destinies.

This chapter will teach you how to master your own martial destiny. It will explain the role of doctrine in the development of the various methods of combat and show you how martial doctrines guide the development of strategy and tactics. You'll learn the pitfalls of narrow doctrine as you discover how to dissect and analyze each art. Most importantly, you'll learn to choose wisely those martial doctrines that guide your training—you will master your own martial destiny.

DOCTRINE, STRATEGY, AND TACTICS

All martial arts are based on doctrines developed by those who founded them. The term "doctrine" can best be described as a set of broad and general beliefs. For our purposes, I'm referring to martial doctrine—the doctrine of personal combat—rather than the many others such as religious or political doctrines.

The concept of martial doctrine is closely related to strategy and tactics, but the terms aren't synonymous. Strategy consists of the general or "broad brush" plans for fighting, developed according to the beliefs of a chosen doctrine. Tactics, on the other hand, are the specific techniques and maneuvers employed to carry those plans out. Although doctrine, strategy, and tactics are different concepts, the warrior's choice of a doctrine has a very direct effect on the strategies he will develop and the tactics he will use in combat. Let me draw on some 20th Century military history to illustrate this point.

One of the better known strategies the allies employed in World War II was that of strategic bombing in Europe. This strategy came about as a result of a doctrine developed by army fliers at the Air Corps Tactical School at Maxwell Field, Alabama, in the early 1930s. Those men were fascinated with the many possibilities of employing in war that new technological marvel, the airplane. Planes had been around since before World War I, but only in the late 1920s had powerful enough engines been developed to build large planes able to carry heavy loads.

In 1933, the first true "bombers" entered the Air Corps inventory, and the officers at Maxwell were inspired. They developed the theory that given a fleet of huge aircraft carrying tons of bombs, one nation could pound another into submission by bombing its industrial centers to rubble. They supposed that with sufficient air power, ground forces might not even be needed. The bomber force would pound and pound the adversary until its industrial base was destroyed and with it, its ability and will to wage war. This theory became the Army Air Corps' strategic bombing doctrine.

As their ideas took shape, the boys from Maxwell took their show on the road. They presented a series of papers and lectures designed to convince the military and political establishments of the efficacy of strategic bombing. And, despite stubborn resistance from the Army general staff, they succeeded. At least enough so that by the end of the 1930s we were producing the famous B-17 "Flying Fortress," a heavy bomber like the world had never seen before.

World War II set the stage to put the strategic bombing doctrine into practice and gave us a classic demonstration of how a doctrine—nothing more than an unproven set of beliefs—can drive the development of strategy during war. With the Germans controlling nearly all of Western Europe, the allies were left to fighting them from England. Doctrine became strategy as plans were drawn to bomb Germany into submission. Reconnaissance and intelligence provided detailed information on German industrial centers, and the allies resolved to bomb them around the clock—the Americans by day and the British by night.

As the plans were put into effect, tactics were developed to support them. Tight formations were employed to make the best use of the bombers' heavy armament and prevent German fighters from singling out and swarming on lone planes. When low level bombing proved too vulnerable to anti-aircraft fire, new bombsight technology was developed and high altitude bombing was employed. With the demands of war, heavy bombing strategy and tactics advanced years beyond what they would have in peace, and by 1945, millions of tons of high explosives had been dropped on German factories.

But what has all that to do with martial arts? Well, let's examine a popular martial art and see if we can identify some of the doctrines, strategies, and tactics associated with it. Perhaps then we can draw some comparisons.

Tang soo do (literally, China hand way) is a Korean martial art practiced around the world. Like its sister art, taekwondo, it's similar in technique to Japanese karate, but due to doctrinal differences, its strategies and tactics are very different. According to the martial doctrines common to both Korean arts, the foot is a far better weapon than the hand. A small man's legs are longer than a large man's arms and stronger than arms of even the largest man. A man's hips are located near the center of his body, providing a centered pivot around which the legs can swing. With proper training, the Korean masters reasoned, a man can learn to use his feet against any target on an attacker's body, as quickly and even more powerfully than with the hands.

This kind of doctrine leads to some very distinctive strategy. Attempting to capitalize on the length of his legs, a Korean strategist sets his fighting range at the length of his longest kick and often resolves to keep opponents at that distance, out of arm's reach. The longest, most powerful kicks in the Korean arsenal are side kicks and round kicks, both thrown from side-facing stances. So Korean fighting stances tend to be side-facing from the onset, unlike the more front-facing stances usually used in Japanese karate. A side-facing orientation leads to spinning attacks, making it possible for a fighter to use both feet from either direction. These stances also lead to some very specialized tactics.

Tactics in personal combat, like those for forces at war, are the specific techniques and maneuvers needed to apply a strategy successfully. Our Korean stylist has developed a general strategy for employing his feet effectively; he'll fight from a distance, using side-facing stances, so he can strike with his longest kicks from either foot. Now he must develop the tactics to employ that strategy.

Since his strategy makes him primarily a foot fighter, his tactics will often involve feinting attacks with his hands, designed to distract the opponent, while he strikes decisively with his feet. He may also use exotic foot combinations, snapping kicks at several targets in one step, before striking the intended vital area. All these maneuvers are devised to employ the strategies of foot fighting, based on the general belief or doctrine that the feet are superior weapons to the hands.

In both of these examples, we see broad and general beliefs forming the basis of strategic plans. The Army Air Corps believed the heavy bomber was the ultimate weapon, and Tang Soo Do masters believe feet are better weapons than hands. These beliefs drove plans for the air war in Europe and the Korean fighter's strategy in unarmed combat. Finally, tactics were developed in each case to carry out the plans most successfully and with the least risk of loss.

So how do we use this knowledge to make us better fighters? How do we use this understanding to master our own martial destinies? Well, we start by choosing the best doctrines on which to base our strategy and our entire approach to training.

CHOOSE YOUR STRATEGIC FOUNDATIONS

Now that we know that doctrinal beliefs form the basis of all methods of combat, it follows that in order to master our martial destinies and become truly formidable warriors, we must start from the beginning; we must apply a sound doctrine.

Committing to a given doctrine will determine the art we will study and the strategies and tactics that will follow. But how

Korean foot-fighting doctrine focuses on the belief that the feet are better weapons than the hands.

do we go about selecting a doctrine to embrace? Well, a fundamental element of strategy is analysis, and the warrior approaches this problem, like all others, strategically. To select a martial doctrine, you must:

- Analyze the threat you're most likely to face.
- Evaluate your physical and emotional assets.
- Select a doctrine that best fills your needs.

ANALYZE THE THREAT

What enables the wise sovereign and the good general to strike and conquer, and achieve things beyond the reach of ordinary men, is foreknowledge.

Sun Tzu from *The Art of War*
(Clavell, 1983, p. 77)

The starting point for you and every warrior must be a frank analysis of the threat you're most likely to face. We live different lives, and the threats to our safety, as well as the constraints on our behavior, vary widely. A soldier preparing himself for the field of battle sees a far different threat than the executive preparing to cross a parking garage at night. A police officer may face conditions as lethal as the soldier, but the ways in which he is allowed to respond to those conditions are much more limited.

Most women face different threats than men. Where a man attacking another man is most likely to strike with crushing force, he may be more likely to grab, subdue, and intimidate a woman or simply take her belongings from her. But women must also be prepared to face male attackers as brutal as if they were men.

So the first step in choosing a doctrine is to analyze the threat you expect to face. Will it most likely be life threatening or merely harassing? Will your attacker be apt to strike you, or will he try to wrestle you to the ground? And what can you do? Might you face criminal or civil penalties if you brutalize your attacker, or can you leave him with his body broken and bleeding? All these questions must be addressed and answered honestly before you can select an appropriate doctrine for self defense.

Equally important, you must evaluate your own physical and emotional capabilities.

EVALUATE YOUR PHYSICAL AND EMOTIONAL ASSETS

> *First see that you, yourself, are all right, then think of defeating an opponent.*
>
> From *The Way of the Spear*
> as cited in *Fighting to Win*
> (Rogers, 1984, p. 70)

Each of us is an individual with different physical and emotional capabilities. This is critically important to remember when selecting a doctrine to follow and, subsequently, a martial art to study. A 90-pound woman may not be up to the contact and rigors of training in judo or a hard style of karate. She might not even be able to generate enough force to make those systems effective in combat. On the other hand, very few ex-football players will have the patience to study the soft, esoteric applications of tai chi.

Body type is a crucial factor in selecting a martial doctrine. When I began studying martial arts, I was tall and lanky, I sought an art best suited to my body type. Taekwondo, with its long range foot fighting approach, fit my needs. Using my long and relatively powerful legs, I reasoned I could best hold stouter, more muscular men at bay. But had I been a short, powerful man, I might have chosen judo. That art would have taught me to quickly close with an opponent and throw him to the ground where I could use my superior strength and the leverage of my short limbs to wrestle or choke him into submission. The key is fitting the belief system and, in turn, the method of combat to your strongest physical assets.

For any martial art to be effective it must be right for you. You need the capability—or at least the potential for developing it—to perform all the physical techniques with speed and power.

But just as importantly, you must have the fortitude to carry out the violent acts on your adversary that your chosen art may call for. For instance, if you can't stomach the groin-kicking and eye-gouging responses called for in karate, maybe you could better defend yourself with the blending, controlling, and throwing techniques of aikido. What's important, is you must have both the will and ability to do in a crisis what you're art attempts to teach you in the training hall.

Once you've settled these issues, you're ready to select a doctrine.

SELECT A DOCTRINE

Follow what is right and you will be fortunate.
Do not follow what is right and you will be unfortunate. The results are only shadows and echoes of our actions.

From *Counsels of the Great Yu*, 2255 B.C.
(Minick, 1974, p. 115)

Armed with a frank analysis of your abilities and an honest appreciation of the threat at hand, you're prepared to select the appropriate doctrine to follow. But unfortunately, it's not that easy. Schools don't advertise by publicizing their doctrines, and most instructors wouldn't be able to explain their systems' doctrines if you asked. So how do you select from the myriad of martial arts available? You do it by looking for and learning to recognize the doctrinal tenets of the arts you survey.

Most martial doctrines are easily recognizable in the arts that profess them. You don't have to watch a shotokan karate class long to realize their doctrines focus on forging the student's hands and feet into weapons and delivering them in powerful, frontal attacks.

Likewise, it's just as apparent that the beliefs behind modern aikido discourage meeting force with force, preferring instead to blend with and redirect an attacker's strength against him. Some arts, however, aren't so easily analyzed.

The very soft arts, such as some of the Chinese systems, are based on subtle and esoteric doctrines, not easily recognizable to the eye. One might watch tai chi practitioners for hours without even realizing those slow, graceful movements comprise a martial art, much less determine their doctrinal basis. So how do you evaluate the doctrines of these systems? Well, the easiest way is by reading.

Lots of articles and books have been published on most martial arts, and although few come right out and state their doctrines, reading with an objective eye and an open mind can lead to a pretty sound understanding of the beliefs put forth by the founder of each art.

Another source of information lies with the masters in your local area. Although the most traditional masters may not answer many questions, some will take the time to talk with a potential student.

So now you've used the methods I've described and chosen a doctrine. Or perhaps you've applied these principles to confirm the art you've studied for years is really right for you. You're all set, right? Well, maybe not. What if the doctrine you've chosen is too narrow? What if it's the best system you could find but isn't up to all the threats you expect to face? Now that can be a dangerous situation!

THE PITFALLS OF NARROW DOCTRINE

To explain the concept of doctrine and how it guides the development of strategy and tactics, I used two examples: the development of strategic bombing and Korean foot fighting doctrine. Both seemed to be based on sound, logical principles, and both have enjoyed a degree of success. But have these doctrines really proven valid? More importantly, at least to the air crews over Germany and the fighters in the street, how successful have they really been in combat?

Both the strategic bombing doctrine and the Korean foot fighting doctrine have valid points. Bombing the Germans around the clock forced them to tie up millions of *marks* in air defense. The repeated destruction of factories caused a scarcity of some strategic materials and put strains on every facet of Germany's economy. Likewise, competition in the ring and the streets has demonstrated that Korean stylists can be formidable fighters; many an attacker has lost his teeth trying to close the distance to strike or grab a tang soo do or taekwondo practitioner. But the principles professed in these two doctrines aren't the universal truths their exponents would have you believe.

Strategic bombing didn't win World War II. Despite the millions of bombs we dropped on German factories and cities, we failed to cripple the German war effort and we failed to break Germany's will to wage war. In the end, conventional armies still had to defeat and occupy Germany, street by bloody street.*

Nor is Korean foot fighting doctrine the panacea of unarmed combat. While legs are longer and stronger than arms, for most people they're also slower. Exotic, multiple, high kicks leave the defender standing on one leg, dangerously exposed. And focusing one's strategy and tactics on one set of weapons often produces fighters who haven't learned to use their other weapons effectively. Many Korean fighters have fallen to attackers who've managed to close the fighting range to fight in close or grapple on the ground.

*As I wrote the first draft of this chapter, Operation Desert Storm was underway. I watched with interest as once again, despite the most concentrated aerial bombardment in history, allied leaders were disappointed to find they still had to employ ground forces to defeat the enemy.

Having concentrated their training on kicking tactics, they discovered themselves vulnerable when fighting nose to nose and all but defenseless when tangled up with their opponents in the dirt.

The fact is, no one doctrine is universally true. While most martial doctrines are based on sound principles, they are by definition beliefs, not facts. The beliefs which comprise martial doctrines, just as in religious or political doctrines, all contain elements of truth. Therefore, they work in certain situations. But the key here is each doctrine works in certain situations, not all. No one martial doctrine deals effectively with all threats.

Warriors of the past knew this. You wouldn't have seen a *hwarang* warrior of ancient Korea practicing kicking and punching at the exclusion of grappling. Nor would you have seen a *samurai* studying jujutsu while ignoring swordsmanship, archery or horsemanship.

Modern soldiers are just as pragmatic. Have you ever heard of a soldier bent on mastering hand grenade throwing while disdaining riflery, camouflage, and the many other arts of modern warfare? Of course not.

So the problem with most martial doctrines isn't that they aren't valid—they usually work within the context for which they were designed—the problem is that no one of them works in all situations. Therefore, if we are to be warriors and not just martial artists, we need to pursue a variety of doctrines and skills. Does this mean I endorse the approach of those individuals who flit from school to school, staying but a few weeks or months at each? Absolutely not!

There are few people martial arts masters and instructors think less of than those who move from school to school, sampling the systems taught but never staying long enough to develop any true skill in them. Not only does this behavior demonstrate a profound lack of self discipline, it insults all the instructors involved.

You should never enter formal training in any martial art without making a sincere commitment to learning that art thoroughly. Then how do you accumulate skills in more than one art, and how do you organize this varied approach to training? You do it by selecting a core art to study, then building around it.

BUILD YOUR SKILLS AROUND A DOCTRINAL CORE

As I explained, the genesis of warrior training involves finding the martial doctrine most suited to your needs, based on your ability and the threats you may face. That belief system will become your doctrinal core, and the art it employs will become your core art.

Throughout the course of your life, you should devote the most time to mastering your core art—it's the one that best fulfills your strategic requirements—and the master you train under should be your principle instructor. But now you realize no one doctrine is complete. So once you reach the black belt level in your core art (never, before then), you need to critically examine the holes and weaknesses in it and find other disciplines to fill those gaps.

For instance, a stout, powerful man may first practice judo to take advantage of his strongest assets, then take up karate to defend against attackers who won't let him close and grapple. A woman may first study jujutsu to learn to defend against grabs, then a kung fu system to develop striking power. A long, lanky taekwondo enthusiast may learn to kick well, then study Japanese karate tactics to learn to fight with his hands at close range, and finally judo to defend against grapplers who manage to wrestle him to the ground.

The first art each of these individuals chose to study becomes his or her core art, and each will remain loyal to that art, devoting a lifetime to mastering it. However, each also recognizes there are other skills he or she needs to fight effectively in some situations, skills not provided by the individual's core art. The true warrior pursues those skills, sometimes formally, sometimes informally.

Our taekwondoist saw value in the doctrines of Japanese karate and decided to study those strategies and tactics. Since the techniques employed in karate and taekwondo are very similar, he may not need to seek formal instruction. The analytical ability he developed while evaluating doctrines will enable him to develop the strategic skills he seeks by observing Japanese stylists train or working with them informally. But when he takes up judo (likewise, when the judo man studies karate or the jujutsu woman, kung fu), he'll need formal training. That will require serious commitment.

Never join a martial arts training hall on a whim, even if you don't intend that system to be your core art. Consider seriously whether you really need to add that art to your strategic arsenal. If you decide you do, then devote your energy to reaching the black belt level before starting any other art. From then on, be loyal to that master and plan to spend at least some of your training time developing skill in that art.

One might watch tai chi practitioners for hours without even realizing these slow, graceful movements comprise a martial art.

By now you've realized I'm talking about an enormous amount of time and effort. The years it takes to earn a single black belt once seemed like an eternity to you. Now, I'm asking you to master one art and earn black belts in others. But that's what warriorship is all about; it's a lifelong commitment. But hold on, there's more yet!

The final ingredient is integration. As you begin developing skills from a variety of doctrines, you must learn to integrate them into an effective personal arsenal. Our taekwondoist should learn to blend his Korean tactics with those from Japanese karate. The judo man should learn to blend punching and kicking with the grappling techniques of his core art. The final product should be a smooth fighter, effective at all ranges, in any situation.

Don't get me wrong, I'm not advocating you develop your own system and teach it to others. Remember, all systems are artificial. What I'm saying is you must not let your own fighting ability be limited by any one's narrow doctrine. You must choose to be a warrior, not a martial artist.

You must master your own martial destiny.

POINTS TO REMEMBER: YOUR MARTIAL DESTINY

■ There are no superior or inferior martial arts, there are only warriors and non-warriors.

■ Warriors don't quibble over which system of fighting is the best. They know no one system fits everyone's needs in all situations.

■ Each martial art is based on doctrine, a set of broad and general beliefs. People who study a single doctrine tend to shut out ideas from other sources and convince themselves that their's is the one true way of fighting. They become slaves to the very doctrines they profess.

■ Choosing which doctrines to follow not only determines what arts you will study, it drives how you'll develop your strategy and tactics.

■ Choose each martial doctrine by analyzing the threat you're most likely to face, evaluating your physical and emotional assets, then selecting the doctrine that best fills your needs.

■ Relying on one narrow doctrine is dangerous, so build your skills around a doctrinal core.

■ The final ingredient is integration. As you develop skills from a variety of doctrines, you must learn to integrate them into an effective personal arsenal. The result should be that you become a smooth fighter, effective at all ranges, in any situation.

Chapter 3

TRAIN AS WARRIORS TRAIN

If someone asked me what a human being ought to devote the maximum of his time to, I would answer, "Training." Train more than you sleep.

KARATE MASTER MASUTATSU OYAMA
(1979, p. 19)

The warrior is always in training, and to some extent, at some level of consciousness, training is always on his mind. Each morning when he climbs out of bed, he inventories his physical resources—notes the fatigue, stiffness, and pain remaining from the previous day—and weighs them against the training day ahead of him. As the fog of sleep clears from his head, he begins to review the day's obligations to his superiors, family, and friends, then schedules his training time around them. At some point, from some level of mind, memory of his weaknesses returns and with it his goals to overcome them. Then, the warrior calmly plans the specific exercises he will use that day to continue his slow, steady progress towards obtaining those goals.

To non-warriors, Oyama's words and mine in the foregoing paragraph sound irrational and fanatic. Let them think so. Warriors are distinctly different from the rest of society. Where the typical man in today's culture fills his spare time pursuing entertainment and pleasure, the warrior entertains himself cultivating his spirit. That is his pleasure. In fact, his very survival depends on it.

Warriors of old had two ever-present goals in life: to serve valiantly and to die well. Death was their profession and their constant companion; it hung over each of them like a specter, waiting for an unguarded moment to snuff out his existence.

This was never more true than in the case of Japan's *samurai*. For these warriors wielded razor-sharp swords, and each confrontation inevitably resulted in the death of at least one of the combatants. As the *samurai* faced his enemy, he expected one of only three possible outcomes. If he was significantly more skilled than his opponent, he would find *katsu* (victory) and the enemy would die. If, on the other hand, the opponent was the superior swordsman, our *samurai* would face *make* (defeat) and die himself. Often though, they were of relatively equal skill and *ai uchi* (mutual killing) would result. In these circumstances, each warrior knew he had at best a one in three chance of surviving combat. Given these odds, you'd better believe he took his training seriously, and so should you.

You probably won't have to face a sword-wielding enemy, but your potential attackers today can be every bit as dangerous. We warriors rarely have to face one another in actual combat. Nor do we have much to fear from the other gentle folk of society. The threats we face are from the gun, knife, and club toting degenerates who thrive by preying on the weak. Fighting is still a life and death proposition. Even an unarmed man can injure you with every blow, and your attacker won't stop after he bloodies your nose. Once enraged, the alley mugger or the parking lot rapist will keep brutalizing you until you're completely helpless. Then, only if he's merciful, will he let you live. I don't trust his mercy. Do you?

Today, warriorship focuses on life. Where warriors once trained to die, we now train to live. Nonetheless, you should never lose your ties to those noble warriors of the past, because people die just as easily now as they ever did. Burn that fact into your psyche. If you never forget that defeat in combat means death, you'll train more effectively and live more vibrantly as well.

If you want to learn to win in mortal combat... if you really want to be a warrior... you must put aside the ways of the hobbyist and the game player. Instead, you must study and follow the ways of the classical warriors, the men and women who lived in paths of service and died in the name of honor.

But what if your's isn't a classical martial art? What if the system you study focuses on dance-like grace or the competitive arena? Well, don't dispair. You don't necessarily have to abandon the art you've invested your time in and grown to love for a clas-

As anyone who has faced the army of the Republic of Korea can testify, taekwondo can be a devastating method of unarmed fighting. But to learn true combat, students must practice without the constraints of tournament rules.

sical fighting system. Any martial art can be studied and practiced in the traditional way. This chapter will teach you how. This chapter will teach you to train as warriors train.

There are three essential elements in true warrior training. If you want to train as warriors do, you must:

- Make training a daily regimen and improvement a constant preoccupation.
- Make *shugyo* a part of your training.
- Take a *jutsu* approach to training.

MAKE TRAINING A DAILY REGIMEN

The warrior trains daily. Physical conditioning, technical proficiency, tactical fluency, spiritual strength, emotional control—these are the substance of his goals and the weapons of his arsenal. Every day he devotes some amount of time to honing and polishing at least one of them. Some days he pushes himself to the limits of his capability in one or more to test his progress.

Friends, acquaintances, even family often think warriors are obsessed or compulsive, but that isn't true. Obsessive and compulsive behavior are, by definition, traits of individuals who are unable to control themselves. The warrior is just the opposite; he is the model of control. The warrior doesn't seek pain, fear, fatigue, and the other unpleasant byproducts of constant training because he likes them. But he knows they are obstacles between him and his objectives. His goal is to overcome them, and he knows that to defeat an enemy, he must attack. It isn't that the warrior is driven. He is the driver.

Do you train daily, or does your training consist of going to class two or three evenings a week? You say that's the only time your class meets? Well, who says you have to be in class to train? Warriors hone their skills constantly, and if you've achieved the warrior mind-set, you're looking for ways to fit some sort of training into every day.

That doesn't mean you have to suffer through a gut-wrenching workout each day. Proper martial training isn't brutal or relentless with only weaklings stopping to rest and heal. In fact, the warrior way of life isn't completely physical; a significant portion involves academic study. Warriorship demands a never ending balance. Exertion is followed by rest. Physical development is tempered by intellectual growth. Even work and discipline must be balanced by play and release.

As the non-warrior rests and plays, the warrior does as well. You'll often see them together. But the difference between them lies in discipline. The non-warrior rests and plays out of habit; it's what he does to fill his spare time. Warriors, on the other hand, have very little spare time. They lead goal-oriented lives, and their goals demand dedication. But warriors also know they must balance work and training with rest and play. They do so by choice, as a part of their training. Warriors are always under control.

Having studied and taught martial arts for a number of years, I can usually spot those beginners who won't last six months. They come in two varieties. First, there's the individual who didn't realize martial training involves hard physical work. He or she goes into shock the first week of training and is usually gone before the end of the first month. But then there's the other extreme, the beginner who becomes so enthused he drives himself relentlessly day and night.

Since over-training is as counterproductive as under-training is unproductive, a student of this sort often sees his peers advancing ahead of him. Frustration leads to more over-training which, in turn, leads to more frustration. Eventually, the fellow gives up and quits.

As a warrior, one of the first things you decide is that you're here for the long haul. Reckless training will lead to exhaustion, injuries, and discouragement. To avoid those setbacks, follow these simple guidelines:

1. Vary the focus and intensity of your training from day to day.
2. Get an adequate amount of sleep every night.
3. Schedule rest into every training day and at least one rest day into each week.

Only balanced, disciplined training will condition your body and harden your will so you can withstand the rigors of *shugyo*.

EMPLOY *SHUGYO* IN YOUR TRAINING

I attended my first martial arts seminar as a 19-year-old taekwondo student. It made a dramatic impression on me, one I'll never forget.

This Chung Do Kwan master and ex-Green Beret demonstrates a side of taekwondo you will never see on the tournament floor. This is martial art.

We all arrived at the dojang (training hall) on a friday evening, and after a light workout and a slide show of the master's training in Korea, we made our beds on the floor and stretched out for the night. This weekend's going to be a lot of fun, I thought.

Clang! Bang! Clang!

It was five the next morning, and I sat bolt upright to the sound of sauce pans banging together as several black belts walked among us demanding that we get to our feet. My hands were shaking with nervous shock as we quickly stowed our bed rolls and dressed. "Hurry," yelled the senior student, "or you won't have time for breakfast!"

It must have been several degrees below freezing as we ran through the dark, Michigan morning, dressed in *dobok* (training uniforms) and sneakers. The coffee shop was only a half mile away, and we got there quickly. We crammed down toast and orange juice—the black belts wouldn't let us eat anything heavier. Soon, we found out why.

We were back in the *dojang* well before six, and after some brief formalities, we began marching through the fundamental walking exercises typical of formal taekwondo training. Up and down the length of the *dojang* we went, snapping out repetitions of *najunde makgi* (low block), the first basic technique, as the senior black belt barked a quick cadence in Korean. The other black belts milled among us, occasionally yelling things like, "more power," to one student or another and kicking student's legs to tell them they were improperly bent.

Up and down. Low blocks and more low blocks. My breathing became labored, and I was sweating freely. Still, the cadence didn't slow down. Occasionally, a student was caught looking around or stretching his fingers to relieve the strain. "Give me twenty, Mr. Smith!" and Smith would drop to the floor, pumping out twenty quick, knuckle push-ups before springing back into stance. I kept my eyes straight ahead.

Just when I was sure the entire seminar was going to be devoted to practicing low block, the instructor commanded us to begin *najunde jirugi* (low punch). And so it went. Minutes became hours, and sunlight streamed into the *dojang* before we worked through the designated fifteen basics.

Following the last basic technique, we finally heard the commands, "*pahdo, shult*," return to ready position and stand at ease. I turned around and adjusted my sweat-drenched *dobok*. Looking down the ranks, I saw wet, matted hair over haggard faces. Many students were bent over, hands on their knees, trying to catch their breath. Thank God I got through that, I thought. But then I heard the shrill command, "*Comault*!" I wheeled around and snapped to attention, only to find the master had stepped onto the floor.

"Are the students warmed up?" he said, turning to the senior black belt.

"Yes, sir!"

"Then, let's begin."

I couldn't believe it. Let's begin? To my shock, we were starting basic drills all over. But this time was different. Instead of simple basics, we were to do each one as a jumping technique, requiring twice the energy!

Under the master's ear-spitting cadence, we felt a new surge of strength, but that didn't last long. Soon we were stumbling with exhaustion, only to be driven harder by the master's verbal and physical jabs. One by one, students began breaking ranks and running for the back door. I fought to control my stomach as the sounds of their heaving gripped me. "Get back in line," was all the master said as each stumbled back in, pasty white.

Basic techniques were followed by combination drills. I thought it would never end, but finally it did.

"*Pahdo*!" I stepped back to ready position, waiting for the command to stand at ease. As I stood there swaying, the master said something about how proud he was of us... that we had earned the right to be called Chung Do Kwan... I couldn't concentrate on what he was saying. All I caught for sure was the order to take a 30-minute break and return in a fresh *dobok*. Finally, "*shult*!"

We stumbled out the door and gasped in the crisp, November air. I felt as though I weighed a thousand pounds. I looked around and saw steam rising from the bodies of my friends. They saw it too, and we began to laugh. Our laughter rose out of control, and feeling the tears streaming down my face, I realized we were all laughing and crying at the same time. Suddenly, I felt as though an enormous weight had lifted off my shoulders. I was completely exhausted, but in an odd way, I felt as though I could overcome anything put before me. I felt cleansed, purified. I had survived.

This was my first encounter with a ritual observed in some way, shape, or form by every warrior society in the world. It involves hardening the spirit through severe training or some extreme physical test. The ritual takes different forms in different cultures, but they all have a common element: the warrior drives himself, or is driven, to a level of endurance beyond what he previously believed possible. The experience is both grueling and frightening, but the warrior emerges from the ordeal feeling purified. One who has experienced this kind of training is never quite the same afterwards.

The *samurai* called this regimen of severe training *shugyo*, and one's very survival depended on his discipline in it. This truth is reflected in the maxim, "Tomorrow's battle is won during today's practice."

But why would modern men and women, who probably won't have to face someone trying to cut them down tomorrow, submit themselves to *shugyo* today? Psychiatrist and jujutsu adept, Dr. Alan Hasegawa, explained it best when he wrote:

> *Paradoxically, in many respects, the need for* shugyo *is even greater in an affluent society. The poet Berryman noted that "...the trouble with this country is that a man can live his*

> *entire life without knowing whether or not he is a coward." He saw a society of complacency and ennui, which was a result of a life of shallow distractions and luxuries. In an affluent society, it is necessary to purposely seek out the challenges which were once a part of the daily life of the warrior. This drive to test the limits of one's own potential is universal (1987).*

How many Americans know the limits of their physical and emotional capabilities? Do you? Do you know how fast you can run a mile, or how many miles you can run before you have to stop? Do you know how much weight you can lift or how many minutes you can spar against multiple opponents before you can't fight any longer? Do you know if you can climb, rappel, or even stand at the edge of a shear cliff without freezing in panic?

The warrior who applies *shugyo* in his training knows these things if they are related to his personal goals. Furthermore, if he senses weaknesses in these or any other areas, he may add them to his goals or log them away for future challenge.

Shugyo isn't a routine part of training; it isn't something you do daily, weekly, or even monthly. Most traditional training halls pick special occasions for the ritual, such as annual seminars or New Year's Eve training sessions. The idea is to find a memorable occasion that will have emotional significance to those taking part. Then the *shugyo* serves as a cleansing, a rite of passage. But what if your school doesn't use *shugyo*?

Shugyo doesn't have to take place in the training hall, and if your spirit is strong, you don't need someone else to drive you on. In fact, undergoing *shugyo* alone, with no one else to motivate you or look after your safety, can temper your spirit like nothing else can. And there's no warrior ritual more traditional than solitary *shugyo*.

So pick a special date, one with personal significance such as your birthday or the change of a season. Then plan a project that will truly test your physical and emotional limits, an obstacle you previously believed insurmountable. When the day comes, leave alone without fanfare and vow not to return until you've overcome your limitations and met your goal. What better way to close one chapter of your life and find yourself reborn to another level of warriorship?

Stop! Don't go out and run until you drop or injure yourself with some severe physical test you haven't properly prepared for. Warriors condition themselves for a strenuous activity before pushing toward their limits. After all, senseless injuries mean lost training time. Neither do warriors, smart ones anyway, embark on dangerous projects such as mountain climbing without proper training and equipment.

But you do need to carefully and intelligently push yourself to the edge of your limits and then beyond. Only by knowing where you are today can you determine where you want to be tomorrow.

One more point: always follow severe training with disciplined rest and release. Apply *shugyo* with determination and enthusiasm, but plan a specific stopping point. Then, reward yourself! This is an important detail. Always reward yourself with some form of social or recreational activity that will enable emotional release following *shugyo*. It will relieve the tension you've generated and help prepare you to embrace shugyo enthusiastically the next time around.

TAKE A *JUTSU* APPROACH TO TRAINING

The essence of life is struggle and its goal is domination. There are higher goals and deeper meanings, but they exist only within the mind of man. The reality of life is war.

From The *Way* and the Power
(Lovret, 1987, p. 1)

Martial arts can be broadly categorized as *bugei* systems, those who's central purpose is to win in combat, and *budo* systems, those aimed at developing character.* Living The Martial *Way* involves pursuing the ideals put forth by the warriors who founded the various *budo*—living powerfully and honorably. However, the problem with many of the modern *budo* systems, with their emphasis on sport play or on spiritual development, is that they've lost touch with the reality of combat. And some of the modern *bugei* have fallen into the same trap. This is unfortunate, because while real warriors are ever mindful of developing character, they never forget that warriorship involves combat.

When it comes right down to it, martial arts are about one thing, fighting. And regardless of how much one philosophizes about developing character and walking in peace, if he's a true warrior he began by learning to fight, and he will spend the rest of his life honing his combat skills. That's not to say peace and character development aren't important parts of The Martial *Way*, but strength and confidence are its foundations, and the warrior must learn to walk without fear. As a warrior, you will strive to live a life of *budo*, but you should train in the ways of *bujutsu*. You must always strive to master the arts of personal combat.

Too often, today's martial artists forget this fundamental principal. I once sparred with a black belt who had never been struck because his instructor didn't allow students to make contact while sparring. Imagine his surprise when I began kicking and punching him.

I also enjoy sparring with some of today's taekwondo students. Since rules for sport taekowndo now prohibit hand attacks to the head and any attacks below the belt, many instructors don't permit their use in sparring during class, and some don't even teach them any more. As a result, the typical student who doesn't

*The *bugei* are also called "*bujutsu*" systems. Both terms literally mean "martial art." For a better understanding of how martial arts and martial ways differ, refer to the introduction to this book.

know me and my disregard for such contrary rules, strides forward standing upright with hands held low. Even the gentlest foot sweep or punch to the face destroys his composure and disrupts his ability to fight effectively.

Jujutsu provides another example. This art concentrates heavily on escapes from grabs and holds. To learn the various techniques, or *waza*, the student first works against only mild resistance. *Uke* will grab lightly and allow himself to be moved as *tori* executes the defense and counter. However, as *tori* improves, *uke* should attack with ever-increasing vigor. The final stage and ultimate goal of this practice sees tori attacking with full speed and power, forcing *uke* to defend himself.

You must train as warriors train. This jujutsu master leaves no doubt in the disciple's mind that he has control of the situation.

But too often, a student becomes complacent during the learning stage and never attacks more than half-heartedly even later, after his partner masters the mechanics of the technique. This cheats *tori* of effective training because he never really experiences a serious attack. Problems can be even greater in aikido training.

Aikido is similar to jujutsu, but there is much more emphasis on employing *aiki*, united or dominating spirit, in its various *waza*. An aikido master's demonstration is a study in grace and beauty. He glides effortlessly among multiple attackers, using the force of their own attacks to send them flying through the air or crashing to the mat. Unfortunately, learning to employ physical *aiki* is such a subtle skill that training in this art requires *uke* to cooperate with *tori* in an almost dance-like ritual for years. Once again, students can become complacent or misled into believing they can defend themselves long before they really can.

Don't misunderstand me; I'm not attacking any of the martial arts cited here. What I am saying is, regardless of what martial art you study, if you truly want to learn to win in personal combat—and warriors are bent on learning exactly that—you eventually have to train against unrestrained, realistic attacks. Street fighters won't refrain from punching you in the face or kicking you in the knee. Muggers won't grab your purse half-heartedly and then wait for your counter. Rapists won't offer you a slow, exaggerated lunge for you to redirect, then smoothly roll out.

Today's warriors must train as did the warriors of the past—as if their lives depend on it. True warriors must retain a *jutsu* orientation in their training. To achieve a *jutsu* orientation in your training, follow these simple guidelines:

1. TRAIN AGAINST SERIOUS ATTACK.

This point seems almost too obvious to mention, but as I've already explained, too many of today's martial arts students are playing at combat. There's a time to learn form and technique, a time when attacks must be measured and restrained. But once the mechanics of a given defense are learned, you must test and refine that defense against serious attacks.

A serious attack is, to the greatest extent safely possible, an attack done full strength and full speed. As unsavory as it seems, you must learn what it feels like to defend against a man trying his best to punch you in the face or kick you in the groin. You need to experience the difficulty of breaking a bear hug when a stronger attacker refuses to let go until the pain or leverage you apply forces him to. And notice I said, a stronger attacker.

Often students will develop a false confidence while working with smaller training partners, and sometimes they'll shy away from working with big men because "they don't make good *ukes*." But the simple truth is, on the street, little people don't attack big people; it's always the other way around. Until you're certain your techniques work against a larger, stronger man who's really trying to hurt you, you haven't learned self defense. Learn to appreciate the biggest men in your school and seek them out as training partners. After all, you're the one getting the greater training value.

As your training progresses, you must learn to handle multiple attackers and attacks with weapons. Once again, a cycle emerges. First work against slow, restrained attacks until your defenses and counters become second nature. Then, increase the intensity until you are really defending yourself. These principles are central to learning true self defense.

2. MAKE FREE SPARRING AN IMPORTANT PART OF YOUR TRAINING.

At this point, you probably believe I have no regard for modern *budo* systems with all their emphasis on sport play. But that isn't entirely so. While I generally consider combative sports to be a negative and eroding influence on the traditional Martial *Way*, there have been some twentieth century innovations that I believe enhance sound warrior training. One of those innovations is free sparring.

In past centuries, there was no such thing as free sparring. Warriors learned the various techniques and practiced them in choreographed, controlled sets with a partner and in solo patterns the Japanese called *kata*. Since there was little or no concept of controlled contact, controlled locks, and safe break-falls, the dynamic, rough-and-tumble sparring we use today would have then resulted in serious injury or death. We can thank the early twentieth century *budo* masters such as Funakoshi who introduced *kumite*, free-style karate, and Kano who introduced *randori*, free-style for the grappling arts such as jujutsu, judo, and aikido, for providing these excellent methods of training.

Physical *aiki* can be deceptively graceful. Here, an aiki-jujutsu practitioner redirects an attacker's force.

Free sparring, done as a training exercise rather than as a contest, is an essential part of the modern warrior's regimen. It provides you a forum in which you can develop the strategies and tactics you will use during actual combat, and it enables you to test the effectiveness of your attacks against a partner determined not to let them succeed. But for free sparring to be an effective method of training, it must be realistic, and that rules out "point sparring."

Realistic free sparring is, to the extent safely possible, unconstrained by rules. We warriors aren't concerned with scoring points, we're concerned with learning to win in actual combat. And combat has no target area restrictions. Never constrain your sparring by not punching to the face or kicking to the groin. More importantly, don't constrain your partner from doing so, or you'll never learn to defend against those attacks.

Of course, safety compels us to have some limits in training. Attacking the eyes must be taboo, and all contact must be controlled and even more limited on vital areas and fragile targets (head, throat, groin, knees, etc.). But contact is a must.

You'll never learn to fight until you know the feel of hitting and being hit. That doesn't mean you need to climb into a ring and bash it out. Nor do I suggest women learn to absorb even moderate blows from gorilla-sized men. But fighting is a brutal experience, and you'll never be physically or emotionally prepared for it unless you've tasted some amount of contact. For white belts, contact can amount to little more than touches on the target areas. But as you progress in rank and skill, you should learn to dish out and take blows of increasing force in sparring. And above all, always aim your strikes at specific targets.

Often, while sparring with a student, I'll stop him and ask what target he was trying to hit with that last side kick or reverse punch. And all too often I'll get the response, "the face" or "the body." That answer is unacceptable. There are more than half a dozen separate targets on the face and a score of them on the body. Never strike without knowing exactly what you are trying to hit. A strong man can take quite a blow on his pectoral or abdominal muscles, but a small woman can drop him to the ground with a well placed strike on his solar plexus. Aiming the blow an inch higher can drive his xiphoid process into his chest causing serious injury or death.

The ability to hit small, moving targets can only be developed by constant practice. But you also need to know what those targets are. You need to become a student of anatomy.

3. BECOME A STUDENT OF ANATOMY.

In old China some of the greatest physicians were kung fu masters. They knew exactly how to strike a body to break bones, but they also knew the herbs that would help mend those bones most quickly. They knew the locations of all the organs, understood their functions, and administered treatments to fight disease and improve general vigor, but they were also thoroughly schooled in how to strike or press targets to damage those organs causing illness or death. As knowledge of martial arts spread from China, knowledge of human anatomy, physiology, and the healing arts traveled with it.

Today, serious jujutsu students still study the complex system of meridians that distribute *ki* (spirit, or vital energy) throughout the body, knowledge evolved from chinese medicine. And they learn, perhaps better than other martial artists, exactly how each joint in the body articulates. A jujutsu master can press points along the meridians in ways to cause excruciating pain and disrupt organic function, or he can manipulate the points in other fashions that promote relaxation and health. But knowledge of anatomy should not be limited to *jujutsuka*.

Well trained students of the striking arts know which side of the body holds the spleen and what effect they can achieve by striking it. They know the exact locations of an opponent's kidneys, temples, solar plexus and other vital targets. They learn the most effective strikes for each and practice hitting the square-inch-sized targets with precision. Even the most casual student knows how easily a clavicle (collar bone) or knee breaks and understands the devastating effect well placed strikes to those targets have.

If you're a serious warrior, you'll become a student of anatomy.

4. PRACTICE FORMS WITH UTMOST SERIOUSNESS.

Forms practice is probably the one feature of martial arts training most disliked by Americans. Let's face it, it's repetitive, it's boring, and most students don't see any point in it. "You can't do a *kata* on

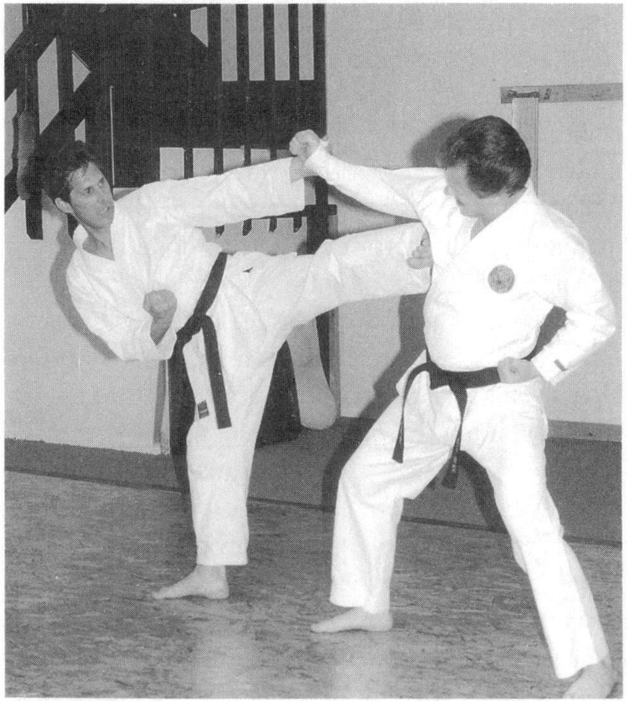

Free sparring can be an important part of your training—but not the kind seen on the tournament floor.

someone who attacks you," is a common expression in American training halls. These same students aspire to be great masters like Myagi or Funakoshi, but what they don't realize is *kata* is what made the great masters great.

In times past, *kata* was the core of martial training, particularly in the striking arts. Before the advent of controlled sparring and sport karate, forms training was how warriors learned to assemble the various blocks, strikes, and kicks that comprised their arts. Controlled sparring, as I've said before, is a definite improvement in modern martial arts training, but it will never replace proper training in *kata*.

No, you can't do a *kata* on someone who attacks you. But you can learn to execute classical combinations with the speed, power, and balance essential to effective combat by practicing forms. More importantly, proper forms training will condition and harden your body for combat and instill in you that steely discipline that separates the warrior from the brawler. But the operative word here is "proper."

Simply walking through a *kata* without applying power, focus, and the necessary attention to detail will not advance your efforts toward being an effective fighter. Forms, done the way most students do them, really are a boring waste of time. For forms training to be effective, it must include several essential elements.

First, you must execute each technique as if your life depends on it. That means a hard stylist, one who's art relies on forceful striking, will pump all the power he can generate into every strike and kick in the *kata*. Those students whose arts rely on more esoteric concepts such as internal energy or blending spirit will concentrate on executing those principles so thoroughly they can actually feel the energy move through their bodies and in essence, become one with the form. In either case, focus is essential.

The word focus (*kime* in japanese) takes on special meaning in the martial arts. Not only does it refer to the ability to hit a target with precise aim and range, it also implies concentrating all of one's strength, internal or external, on the point of impact or leverage at a precise time. Concentration is the keynote here, for without absolute concentration, proper focus is impossible.

Attention to technical detail is nearly as important as concentrated focus. One of the hallmarks of a traditional school is the instructor's uncompromising demand for technical perfection. He'll roam the ranks during *kata* practice, taking students through their forms step by step, correcting even the smallest flaws in stance, posture, and position. A traditional student learns to discipline every bodily detail from the direction of his gaze to the angle of his toes. He knows without looking whether his wrist is straight or his back leg is locked. It's this kind of discipline that makes the difference between two otherwise evenly matched fighters. And it's this kind of discipline that leads to mastery.

There is one last kind of *kata* training that provides a crucial element in a warrior's preparation. That is learning the *kata* in *bunkai* or application. Too many western students and, I'm sorry to say, even some instructors never learn what they are actually supposed to be doing as they wave their arms around and snatch at the air in *kata*. Not only does this cheat those would-be warriors from realistic training, but it leads to more serious implications when these individuals make up new forms, incorporating pretty moves they don't understand, into senseless, impractical patterns. To be effective, forms training must employ sound, practical techniques and combinations, and students must be taught exactly what they are doing in every move. Only then will they really learn to defend themselves using the combinations taught in *kata*.

Begin now by making forms a central feature of your warrior training. Practice daily. Execute your forms with total concentration and proper focus. Learn the *bunkai* of each form you know, and practice its application with a partner so you'll be confident you can defend yourself when it counts. Then, you'll really develop a *jutsu* orientation in your training, and you'll start down the road to mastery.

POINTS TO REMEMBER: TRAIN AS WARRIORS TRAIN

■ Warriorship focuses on life, but never forget that defeat in combat means death. You'll train more effectively and live more vibrantly as well.

■ Make training a daily regimen and improvement a constant preoccupation. You don't have to be in class to train. If you've achieved the warrior mind-set, you're looking for ways to fit some sort of training into every day.

■ Warrior training isn't completely physical; a significant portion involves academic study. Rest is an essential element in

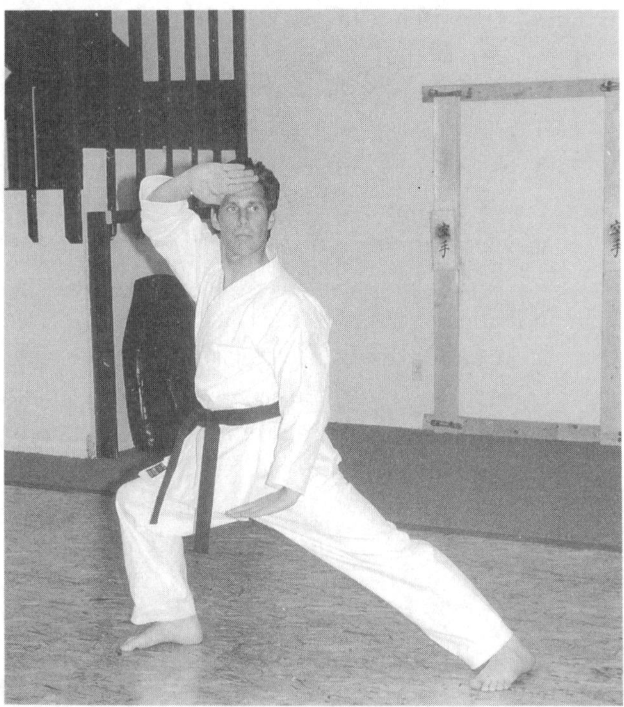

In most traditionally-oriented arts, *kata* is the single most important element of training.

warrior development. Warriorship demands a never ending balance. Warriors are always under control.

■ Employ *shugyo* in your training. Tomorrow's battle is won during today's practice. Condition yourself thoroughly, determine the limits of your capabilities, then exceed them. Afterwards, balance severe training with disciplined rest and release.

■ Take a *jutsu* approach to training. Whether you practice a *bugei* or *budo* system, train against serious attacks and make sparring a key feature of your training. Become a student of human anatomy, and always aim your strikes at precise targets. Most importantly, practice forms with utmost seriousness.

Chapter 4

THE WARRIOR'S *WAY* OF STRATEGY

Those who are certain to capture what is attacked,
Attack locations that are not defended.
Those who are certain to secure what is defended,
Defend locations that cannot be attacked.

Thus, an opponent does not know what location to defend
Against those skilled in attack.
Nor does an opponent know what location to attack
Against those skilled in defense.

Subtle! Intangible! Seemingly without shape.
Mysterious! Miraculous! Seemingly without sound.
They master the destiny of their opponents.

FROM *THE ART OF STRATEGY**
(Wing, 1988, p. 83)

Strategy is the essence of warriorship. It lives in the heart of everything the warrior studies, practices, and does with his life. When the warrior chooses an art to master, a career to follow, or a place to live, strategy lies at the root of his choice. The warrior strives to

*This is Wing's new translation of Sun Tzu's *The Art of War*, written approximately 300 B.C.

keep up with the latest tactical developments, but strategy itself is a timeless commodity.

Sun Tzu wrote *The Art of War* over twenty centuries ago, but its principles are just as valid today as when he used them to become the most effective general in early China. And he has a greater following now than he ever did during his lifetime. Not only is his work an important part of the curriculum of every major military academy in the world, but he's studied by international negotiators and board room executives as well. But Sun isn't the only classical strategist modern warrior chieftains study. Another is Miyamoto Musashi.

Musashi was a master swordsman who lived in seventeenth century Japan, and he's become the most famous *samurai* in history. He began his career in 1600, when less than twenty years old, on the losing side in the Battle of Sekigahara. That was the conflict in which Tokugawa Ieysu defeated all opposition and became *Shogun*, and although Musashi escaped the episode with his life, the peace that followed left him unemployed.

Unlike many other *ronin* (unemployed *samurai*) of the period, Musashi chose neither to become a bandit nor to lay down his arms for another line of work. Instead, he devoted his life to mastering the sword. He trained relentlessly and soon realized that swordsmanship wasn't merely an art of physical prowess but one of cunning as well. Along with this realization came an enlightenment to the *Way* of Strategy, a *Way* which would lead to victory in any kind of combat.

Like Sun, Musashi wasn't merely a philosopher. He set out to test his strategy in the traditional manner—by seeking out and dueling with his country's most skilled swordsmen. Over the remaining years of his life Musashi fought and defeated sixty opponents, killing most of them. His strategy proved so effective that during the later portion of his bloody career he disdainfully felled fully armed adversaries using only his wooden practice sword.

Then, shortly before his natural death in 1645, he retired to a cave and wrote his *Go Rin No Sho* (*A Book of Five Rings*), concisely detailing his strategy. His book, like Sun's, is a standard text for modern strategists. So why aren't more martial artists reading it?

It's remarkable how few martial artists study the art of strategy or are even familiar with these fundamental texts. Somehow, they fail to make the connection between military strategy and martial arts. They don't realize that strategy and tactics aren't just topics of interest for the aspiring martial artist but should actually become the focus of his training as he advances in the black belt ranks. Unfortunately, few modern martial artists can even define the terms "strategy" and "tactics", much less differentiate between them.

Ask the typical martial artist about his strategy and he'll try to explain it by citing examples of "kick low, then punch to the face" or "fake with a quick back fist, then shoot a reverse punch into the opponent's solar plexus." Well I'm sorry fellow warriors, but those are examples of tactics, not strategy. True, the word "strategy" is used loosely to cover a wide range of skills when speaking in broad terms, but warriors should know the differences between the specific concepts of strategy and tactics. Most modern martial artists don't. And some don't have the first clue as to how to use these essential skills in fighting.

One hot Saturday in the summer of 1988, I took part in a special class at a jujutsu school involving black belt students from a variety of arts. During the workout, I was particularly impressed with the skill displayed by a fellow wearing a black belt in jujutsu, and I stayed behind afterward to talk with him. He was flattered by my interest and enthusiastically agreed to discuss some of his techniques in more detail. "That's impressive," I said following one of his explanations, "but what's the tactical application of that technique?" I got only a blank stare. "What tactic would you use to get *uke* into a position in which you could capture his arm and apply that technique?" I persisted.

His face reddened, and after a moment's hesitation he innocently asked, "What do you mean by tactic?"

What indeed.

This chapter will teach you the fundamentals of strategy. No, I'm not going to tell you when or where to punch. Nor am I going to teach you the specific strategies or tactics from any particular martial art. Instead, I'll teach you what strategy is all about. I'll give you the tools to develop your own strategies—plans for fighting and beating all kinds of attackers in all sorts of environments. Then I'll teach you how to develop tactics, the specific manuevers necessary for carrying those plans out. With some forethought, discipline, and a lot of practice, the methods I'm

Judo can be an effective method of self defense, but how would this judo man handle his opponent if he wasn't wearing the stout jacket? He must plan for that environment and train accordingly.

about to show you will start you on the road to becoming a formidable fighter, a warrior strategist.

Let's begin with the four phases of strategic planning.

PLAN YOUR STRATEGY IN FOUR PHASES

You already understand the role doctrines play in fighting systems, so it's time to look at the basics of strategy. As you recall, strategy consists of the general, or "broad brush" plans to put one's doctrines into action. Just believing your feet are superior weapons or that grappling is the best method of fighting for a stout man to use won't get you very far on the street. You also need a plan—actually, a set of plans—to turn those beliefs into reality.

Planning your actions and reactions for the myriad of situations you could face can be an imposing task. Strategic planning is much easier and more effective if you break it into four phases. To develop your own personal strategies, you should:

- Identify your strategic objectives.
- Collect intelligence.
- Plan for environment.
- Program for engagement.

IDENTIFY YOUR STRATEGIC OBJECTIVES

"Focus on your one purpose."

Japanese motto

As I explained earlier, different people face different situations. A soldier's objectives on the battlefield are quite different from a police officer's objectives, or even the objectives of the soldier when he's confronted on a street of his hometown. So a warrior needs to plan his responses—taking into account the threats, his capabilities, and the moral and legal constraints he may face—to achieve a variety of goals.

By now you may have realized this sounds a great deal like selecting a doctrine, and so it is. Strategic objectives are the bridge between doctrine and strategy. But where it differs is while in selecting a doctrine we're weighing and choosing beliefs that will guide our training, in identifying strategic objectives we are planning how we'll use our capabilities in combat; we're deciding just exactly what we want to achieve in battle.

So this is the first step in strategic planning. If you're a soldier, your objectives are pretty clear cut when it comes to practicing your profession. In fact, they're usually decided for you. But if you strive for those same objectives in a bar fight, your going to get into a lot of trouble. So if you frequent taverns, you'd better plan how you're going to defend yourself in those places without landing yourself in prison.

Take some time right now and think. What do you want to achieve if you're attacked in a dark alley? Do you want to escape your attacker, bust him up, or subdue and hold him for the authorities? Will your objectives differ if there's more than one aggressor? What about age? Do you react differently if your antagonists are adolescents rather than adults?

A warrior should consider all these things in advance—not just for the dark alley situation, but for all the circumstances he's most likely to face. I don't mean you need to make detailed plans. Real life rarely obliges you by happening according to plan, nor would you have the time to draw from a large data bank for the appropriate strategy in a crisis. But you do want to consider, in general terms, what you want to achieve in the various situations you're most likely to face. Decide in advance. That way, when the threat materializes you won't hesitate in your response. The goal isn't to clutter your mind with detailed scenarios but to free it for the task at hand.

With your mind clear of debate over how strongly to respond, you're free to read the intentions of your attacker, free to move smoothly and thoughtlessly into defense and counterattack.

Where non-warriors tend to freeze at the onset of conflict, you're prepared for confrontation. And you're even better prepared if you've already collected intelligence on your adversaries.

COLLECT INTELLIGENCE

> *It is only the enlightened ruler and the wise general who will use the highest intelligence in the army for purposes of spying, and thereby they achieve great results.*
>
> Sun Tzu from *The Art of War*
> (Clavell, 1983, p. 82)

The outcome of war is often determined by which side has the more effective intelligence network. In 1967, Israel was surrounded and vastly outnumbered by saber-rattling Arab neighbors. But due to her superior intelligence service, Masad, she knew her enemies' war plans in detail and even knew the hour they planned to attack. With this information in hand, the Israeli military mounted a massive preemptive strike just hours before the Arab attack was to begin.

Detailed intelligence on the Arab force deployment enabled the Israeli Air Force to deliver a devastating first strike, destroying most of her enemies' air forces on the ground and giving her command of the skies within the first hours of the war. This highly coordinated onslaught helped Israel turn the tables and achieve a resounding victory in only six days.

Intelligence is a crucial factor in all levels of conflict, whether between armies or individuals. In medieval Japan, strategists in martial *ryu* (schools) maintained meticulous records on the techniques and strategies used by rival groups. Often, these records were so detailed they even addressed specific strengths and weaknesses of key individuals in opposing clans. As a result, each *ryu* was very secretive about its own techniques, strategies, and tactics.

When lives depended on knowing which cut an enemy tended to open with, warriors took intelligence very seriously in their strategic planning and so should you.

The more you know about your adversary, the better you can prepare to fight him and the better you can handle yourself once combat has begun. If you have a specific enemy, gather all the information you can about him. You want to know everything there is to know about the fighting systems he studies and his physical and technical skills. Consider his size, strength, and physical fitness. Is he right or left handed? Does he favor attacking from a particular side? Does he tend to rely on certain favorite techniques or combinations?

What's more, you want to learn about his personal life. Find out everything you can about his habits and life style. Does he drink or smoke? Learn his typical daily routine.

Finally, you want all the information you can get about his plans to attack you or do you harm. The more you can find out about your adversary, the better you can prepare to preempt or defend against his attack.

Of course, today we often can't identify our enemies in advance as did members of the medieval *ryu*. Most of us face a greater danger from the random violence of thugs and muggers than we do from an enemy trying to carry out a vendetta. But we can anticipate what our attacker may be like and plan accordingly.

Begin by becoming as familiar as possible with the various combative systems available to potential aggressors. Most schools are not nearly so secretive today as they were when personal combat ruled the streets, so some disciplined research will provide you the basic principles used by most systems taught today. You've probably covered a lot of this ground already if you conducted a thorough study as part of the process of choosing your core doctrine, but don't forget to study the disciplines you may not have addressed back then, such as Western boxing and wrestling. Also, get familiar with the typical methods armed and unarmed street fighters employ. If you have no knowledge or experience in this area, someone in your training hall probably does. Tap his expertise.

Once you've gathered and analyzed your intelligence, you know your enemies, but are you prepared to face them on any terrain, day or night, in any weather? It's time to plan for the environment.

PLAN FOR ENVIRONMENT

> *Examine your environment...Always chase the enemy into bad footholds, obstacles at the side, and so on, using the virtues of the place to establish predominant positions from which to fight. You must research and train diligently in this.*
>
> Musashi from *A Book of Five Rings*

I once visited a judo dojo where the *sensei* conducted an interesting experiment with his students. Toward the end of a tough practice, he picked several of his burliest and most aggressive black belts and paired them with brown belt students. Then he asked the black belts, "If these guys grabbed you in the street, are you sure you'd be able to defend yourselves?"

"Of course, *Sensei*!" they said immediately.

The brown belts began to squirm as their indignant seniors scowled at them. Everyone anticipated what was coming. But then the instructor did something that surprised us all.

"Take off the jackets of your uniforms," he said. They hesitated in puzzlement, but they removed their jackets. "Now, *randori*!"

What happened next was a lesson for all of us. As the *sensei* watched with a grim smile, the students attempted to engage in freestyle. They were tentative at first, without their familiar sleeves and lapels to grab, but soon they launched into spirited matches. The results, however, were nothing like the *senpai* (senior students) expected.

Their bodies were slick with sweat from the workout that had gone before. One senior, catching his opponent over-extended, attempted an *ippon seoi nage* (one-arm shoulder throw), but as he turned, the brown belt's glistening arm slipped from his grasp and fell conveniently around the senior's waist. The junior capitalized on this and half tackled, half fell on his opponent, both of them crumpling to the mat. Another *senpai* tried a *tai otoshi* (leg drop), with similar results.

Before long, all the students were grovelling on the mat, slipping in and out of each other's grasp. Classical judo was out, and each found himself struggling with maneuvers more akin to those used by high school wrestlers. The lesson so dramatically demon-

An impressive technique—but how effective on an icy street? Plan for the environment.

strated here is clear: you can't expect combat in the street to go as it does in the training hall. Therefore, you must plan and train for fighting in a variety of environments.

I can't overemphasize how important this point is. What happens when a taekwondo stylist is confronted on an icy street? How does the karate man cope with mid-winter confrontations, when his attackers are wearing multiple layers of heavy clothing? Are you prepared to fight on a snowy hillside, in a heavy rainstorm, or in thigh-deep water? What do you do if you're blinded by blowing sand?

Plan and train for these environments in advance, even as you collect your intelligence. Know your enemy, know how you'll fight in a variety of environments, and you'll be ready to program for engagement.

PROGRAM FOR ENGAGEMENT

Nothing is as difficult as engaging the force.
The difficulties in engaging the force
Are those of making the indirect act directly
And adversity act as an advantage.

Sun Tzu from *The Art of Strategy*
(Wing, 1988, p. 93)

The ground work is done. Now you need to begin planning how you'll defend yourself against various attackers. Once again, I'm not talking about writing down detailed scenarios that will only confuse and frustrate you in a time of stress. I'm talking about conscious, strategic programing to smoothly react to a variety of attackers in a broad range of environments.

Fantasize. Sit back and imagine yourself in one place or another and "create" an attacker. Imagine him in detail. Give him a specific age, size, appearance, and disposition, then see him attacking you using a given set of skills. How will you react, defend, and counter?

This process is a kind of mental programming. Done right it will establish certain pathways in your mind that will lead you to the appropriate strategies in crisis situations without employing the cumbersome, inexact mechanics of conscious thought. This simple exercise will enable you to automatically respond to any threat with the correct strategy. What's more, it will free your conscious mind to read your opponent and apply the best tactics to defeat him.

Repeat the exercise often. Develop general approaches for how you will fight boxers, wrestlers, karate men, foot fighters, etcetera. Consider how you'll handle attackers of all sizes, armed and unarmed, and in all types of terrain and situations. Most of all, you want to anticipate how the unpredictable street fighter might attack and have a general but confident feel for how you'll respond. Forearmed with this conditioning, you can then structure your practice, in and out of the training hall, to best prepare you for the threats you may face.

Mental programing is an excellent tool for developing conceptual responses, but effective strategic planning isn't a head game alone. You have to translate those mental programs into physical reactions. That requires dedicated, repetitive practice.

The starting point, of course, is a thorough command of the various techniques and combinations that make up your core system. Since you chose your art by fitting the most appropriate (for you) set of doctrines to a style of combat, the methods of that art will serve you in meeting your strategic objectives, in most cases. In those situations in which they don't, you'll draw from the various other disciplines you study to fill the gaps.

Practice diligently. Use as many training partners as you can, and train in all kinds of environments. In time, not only will you develop the confident reactions that come from sound strategy, but you'll develop a definite fighting savvy, provided you train methodically to develop your tactics.

The following section will teach you how.

HOW TO DEVELOP TACTICS

If you've done all the exercises I've described in this chapter, you've already become a more effective fighter. You've thoughtfully developed your strategy around a core doctrine. You've developed mental programs for fighting all kinds of adversaries in all kinds of situations. Having practiced with various training partners in differing environments, you've begun to build the conditioned responses necessary for translating strategy into ability. No doubt, your confidence has grown with your newfound ability, but don't start issuing challenges. For until you master tactics, you'll never become a truly formidable warrior.

Tactics are the nuts and bolts of fighting. They are the means by which you "fool" your adversary into defeat. Tactics are the tools the karate man uses to get his fist on his opponent's chin or solar plexus despite that man's overwhelming objections. Tactics make it possible for the judo man to convince his *uke* he's trying to throw him in one direction while he applies *kuzushi* (off-balances) and throws him in another. You must develop tactics to be an effective fighter.

Developing tactics can be as confusing and overwhelming as developing strategy unless you approach the process in an organized fashion. Unfortunately, I can't teach you specific tactics, because they differ dramatically from art to art; your tactics will grow from your own doctrines and strategies. But I can give you a step-by-step approach for developing the tactics that are right for you. Like strategy, tactics can be learned most easily by breaking them into their principal elements. To understand and develop tactics, you must learn to:

- Read Your Opponent
- Control Fighting Range
- Feint Effectively
- Use Rhythm and Timing
- Avoid, Evade, and Intercept

READ YOUR OPPONENT

See first with your mind, then with your eyes, and finally with your body.

Master swordsman Yagyu Munenori (1571-1646)

Imagine playing a game of chess and each time you moved, your opponent knew exactly what you were thinking, what you were planning, what trap you were trying to set for him. What would happen? Well, there would be no contest, of course. You wouldn't stand a chance. Now imagine having that very skill when facing an opponent in the training hall or an attacker on the street. Wouldn't it be marvelous knowing exactly what he was trying to do the moment he moved? How about knowing it before he moves? You can learn to do it.

Reading opponents is a skill all capable warriors have, and it's essential for mastering The Martial *Way*. Skilled warriors know at a glance whether you are close enough to kick, punch, or grab them. They know which leg you are going to kick with before your foot leaves the ground, and they can tell whether you are going to try and close or open your fighting range before you move. You can develop these skills too. Let's use a striking art as an example.

Start by studying the way your training partner stands and moves. Does your partner use a squared-in, front-facing stance when he spars, or does he stand side-facing? What does either situation tell you about which hand or foot he can attack you with before changing his stance?

Now look at his weight distribution. Is his weight divided evenly between his feet? If so, what will he have to do before he kicks with one foot or the other? If he's standing with his weight on his back foot, as many styles teach, what can and can't he do with his front foot, and what does it tell you if he quickly shifts his weight forward?

How about his toes; which way do they point? If he stands in a side-facing, straddle stance, what does it tell you when his front foot suddenly pivots so that his toes face you? What is he up to when his front foot pivots so that his toes point away from you?

Watch your partner as he spars and learn to spot the telltale clues he drops before he kicks or punches. Sometimes a fighter will "telegraph" his intentions by dropping his front hand slightly or taking a tiny step with his front foot just before he attacks. With practice, you can learn to read most fighters' body language as surely as if you could read their minds, and this skill carries over into the street.

As you become more attuned to reading opponents, you'll find yourself reading the potential attackers you see in the street. Hone that skill. Pay attention to the group of youths you see in the parking garage and "feel" whether or not they're taking notice of you. Learn to evaluate the people you pass. Seeing a man near you with his hands in his pockets, sense immediately what kind of weapon he could be holding there and whether or not he intends to use it.

When confronted, measure your adversary by sizing up his weapon, how he holds it, and his ability to attack, based on his reach and balance. Watch for his weight to shift and sense his attack before he moves. With serious training, you can be the chess player who knows exactly what his opponent intends to do before he does it.

But knowing what your enemy is going to do isn't enough. You have to keep him from doing it to you. Either you need to preempt the attack you know is coming or defend against it. You may have to stay out of your attacker's reach until you can carry out a successful attack of your own. To do any of these things, you need to control the distance between you and your adversary. You must control the fighting range.

CONTROL THE FIGHTING RANGE

The maintenance of proper fighting distance has a decisive effect on the outcome of the fight—acquire the habit!

Bruce Lee from *Tao of Jeet Kune Do* (1975, p. 139)

There are masters in every martial are who completely confound their junior sparring partners. Each seems to float effortlessly, always looking like he's in reach. But when his opponent strikes at him, he finds only empty air. The student tries again and again, vainly flailing himself out of breath. Then, when it seems the junior can be humiliated no further, the master calmly steps in and strikes—or worse yet, gently touches him just to show how easily he can do it.

This kind of skill comes from long and determined practice at reading one's opponents and controlling fighting range. The master knows exactly what the junior is trying to do from the moment he begins to shift his weight. But just as importantly, he knows exactly how far his opponent can reach with either hand or foot and with any technique. He floats calmly at the very edge of that range and watches the student struggle.

Each time the junior shifts his weight to attack, the senior either glides back with him, maintaining exactly the same range, or smoothly steps to the side, letting his energetic opponent rush past him. Often, warriors of this skill level won't even bother to put their hands up in defense, knowing the juniors can't touch them. This kind of tactical mastery seems almost mystical, but you can learn it just as they did.

You begin by knowing your own reach, then learning to judge an opponent's reach very precisely. You need to know exactly how far you can reach with any technique in your arsenal. Moreover, you have to be able to look at your opponent and know exactly how far he can strike. From that point, it's a matter of learning to read your opponent's attack and moving with it so you're in control of the range instead of him. You want to be able to keep the range open any time your opponent is strong but close it at will once he's overextended and vulnerable.

There's a very good exercise for developing this ability. Choose a partner and each of you take fighting stances at the proper range. Have him move about, trying to either get closer to you or farther apart than the set range. You, in turn, will move with him, trying to maintain the distance.

At first you'll find this very difficult. Your partner will step in or away from you at will. But things will start to fall into place once you learn these secrets: First, don't watch your partner's feet or any other one part of his body. Instead, let your eyes fall over his whole being without resting on any one aspect. Second, sense the distance between the knots on your belts, and feel his knot pull or push you about as he moves. Before long, he'll find it very hard to close or open against you; you'll be in control of the fighting range.

Once you get good at this, you can try a more advanced variation. Start as before—*uke* tries to change the fighting range and *tori* tries to maintain it. But this time, every so often when you sense *uke* about to try to close, turn the table and close quickly against him, trying to catching him off guard.

There are several other variations to this exercise, and maybe you can come up with some of your own. The important thing to remember is, in combat, you, not your enemy, must control the fighting range. You must stay just out of reach when he's strong, yet close with him at will when he's weak.

Once you can close with the opponent on your terms, you're ready to move in and end the encounter. At this point, feinting becomes an important tool. So you must learn to do it well.

FEINT EFFECTIVELY

Feinting is an essential part of attack. The more the opponent can be caught off guard, or more important still, off-balance by means of feints, the better.

Bruce Lee from *Tao of Jeet Kune Do*
(1975, p. 126)

Feinting is simply convincing your opponent you're trying to do one thing, while you're really setting him up for something else—in essence, "faking him out." As I said early in this chapter, feinting is usually about as far as most martial artists have gone in their strategic and tactical thinking. Actually, there isn't too much to be said about it—not much on the surface, that is. It's mostly a matter of faking high and punching low, *kuzushi* in one direction and throwing in another, etcetera. But some students have trouble making their feints work. They never seem to be able to fool anyone. Well, there are some basic principles they may be ignoring.

First, for a feint to be believable enough to get anyone but the most raw beginner to react, it must be thrown from the proper distance. No one is going to be intimidated by a fake back fist thrown from side kick range.

Next, you must throw the feint with commitment. Half-extended, milk-toast feints don't fool anyone. Throw the feint with commitment and heart. Ideally, if your opponent doesn't react to your feint, it should hit him as if it were the intended technique.

Finally, feint in combination with a series of techniques instead of in singles or pairs. There's nothing that screams novice more loudly than students who "hunt and peck" with their feints and jabs.

Feinting can be developed into a fine art, but it can only take you so far, used alone. To make your feints most effective, you need to learn to use rhythm and timing.

USE RHYTHM AND TIMING

> *There is timing in everything... You win in battles with the timing in the Void born of the timing of cunning by knowing the enemies' timing, and thus using a timing which the enemy does not expect.*
>
> Musashi from *A Book of Five Rings*

Our universe and everything in it is composed of a series of endless cycles. Planets revolve around the stars, and as our planet orbits the sun, we experience the cycle of seasons. Spring brings life, and summer, vitality. In time, that vitality wanes with autumn, and winter arrives with the cold, stillness of death, only to give way to the rebirth of spring.

There are cycles within cycles. During each season we witness the cycle of day and night, and every creature experiences recurring periods of strength and repose as each day passes. Within those periods, each warrior's strength cycles from strong to yielding to strong again as he breaths his millions of breaths until the larger cycle of his life completes its revolution.

Asian philosophers have observed the universe's innumerable cycles since before history was written. All things have shown them unending circles of hot and cold, light and dark, hard and soft, strong and yielding. The Chinese call this dualism *yin* and *yang*. *Yin* represents all the soft, dark, yielding, or female characteristics of the universe and *yang* the hard, strong, male attributes of creation. Likewise, the Koreans know the relationship as *um* and *yang* and the Japanese as *in* and *yo*, confirming the far-reaching acceptance of this universal principle.

Recognition of these natural rhythms has profound implications for you, the warrior tactician. For not only does the strength of your own body and spirit cycle endlessly, but the strength of your adversary does as well. Each breath you take, each technique you attempt, virtually every time you take a step, you go through one or more cycles of *yin* and *yang*. An essential step to mastering tactics, then, is to learn to feel your own rhythms and hide them from your opponent, while sensing and capitalizing on his.

This isn't as hard as it sounds. If you're a serious student under capable instruction, you've already begun to learn the basics of *yin* and *yang*, although your instructor may not have used just those words. You karate students already know each punch or kick starts out weak, grows strong at mid-range, then dissipates near the point of full extension. You're also taught to exhale on impact, adding *yang* to your strikes. Students of judo, jujutsu, and the *aiki* arts know very well that an antagonist can push you strongly only so far before he overextends and his *yang* condition shifts to *yin*. But this is only the start.

Learn to feel your strength cycle with your breath. Inhaling puts your body in a *yin* condition, while exhaling exudes *yang*. Each time you lift your foot to step, you shift to *yin*, and as you shift your weight downward over the foot you're stepping, you return to *yang*. Learn to sense these rhythms within you, and learn to read them in your adversary.

Develop the ability to feel and exploit the rhythms of your opponent. Some breath loudly or snort with their techniques. Others step or dance rhythmically or even bounce up and down, their patterns virtually yelling out when they're strong and when they're vulnerable. Learn to time their cycles, yielding to their *yang* and attacking with your *yang* just as they return to *yin*.

Feel your enemy's rhythms; time and disrupt them. Just as he exposes his *yin*, feint vigorously, throwing him off balance and out of cycle. Then, drive over him before he can recover.

If he openly exposes his rhythms, he's an inferior tactician. If you choose, you can safely set up an obvious rhythm of your own and he'll fall into pattern with you. When he does, disrupt the pattern suddenly, disorienting and throwing him into *yin*. Then, crush him.

Learn to conceal your own cycle when facing a dangerous foe. Breath silently and evenly. If you have to jockey with him for strategic position (remember to use your environment), move at the edge of his fighting range, stepping smoothly and keeping your feet close to the ground. Don't overstep. Keep your feet beneath your center of gravity to minimize the shift to *yin* each step brings. Don't establish a rhythm with your steps, and whatever you do, don't bounce!

Learning to use rhythm and timing effectively is a long, painstaking process. My words can point the way, but you must make the journey yourself. As Musashi said, "You must study this well."

If you've learned to read your opponent and apply the principles of range, rhythm, and timing, you've already begun to become a tactician. The next step is learning when and how to avoid, evade, and intercept your enemy. So press on!

AVOID, EVADE, AND INTERCEPT

If the opponent is ready to challenge:
*When equally matched, we can offer battle;**
When fewer in number, be ready to evade them;
When unequal to the match, be ready to avoid them.

Sun Tzu from *The Art of Strategy*
(Wing, 1988, p. 47)

Long ago, an old warrior taught me there are only three ways to deal with an attack; you can avoid it, evade it, or intercept it. He

*This line was omitted in Wing's translation. I've inserted it from the Clavell version to preserve continuity.

Yin and Yang (Chinese)

Um and Yang (Korean)

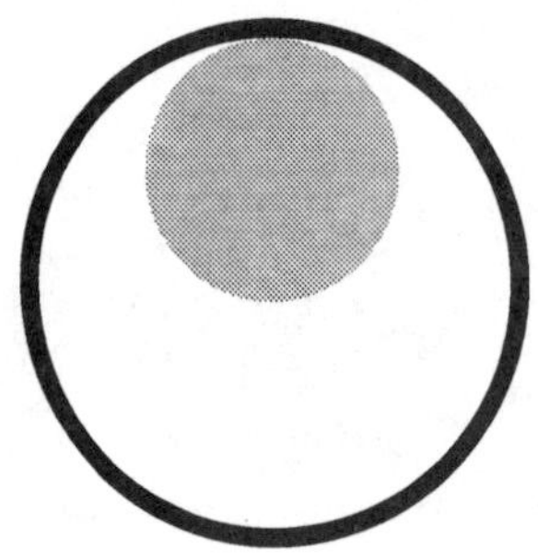

In and Yo (Japanese)

Illustrations by
Michael Dolce

Symbols from several nations testify that the duality of opposites is a concept common throughout Asia.

explained, "Avoiding an attack means to stay just outside the opponent's fighting range and maintain that distance no matter what. As he advances, you retire. If he lunges, you leap back. As long as you keep the distance between you exactly the same, he can't hurt you.

"Evading the attack is more sophisticated. Like avoiding, you move to keep from being hit. But this time, instead of moving back, you move inside his fighting range but just out of his line of attack. You can step to either side, drop under, or leap over him.

"With a good evasion, your adversary's attack will miss you, and he'll overextend before he even realizes you're gone. Then he's ripe for a counter and right in range. As you can see, evading requires being able to read and time your opponent carefully. What's more, you have to read his feints well enough not to evade a false attack while moving straight into the real one. This takes a great deal of practice.

"But if you sense your *yang* is clearly stronger than his, you may want to intercept his attack. You simply overpower his force with yours. Slam straight into his line of attack and stop him cold. Crush him suddenly, decisively. Of course, this isn't merely a matter of brawn over brawn. As you know, there are *yin* and *yang* phases to every attack. The key to intercepting successfully is to catch his attack in *yin* with a well timed *yang* block or counter."

As the older man lectured, I began to look for holes in his approach.

"What about parries?" I asked. "Are they evasions or interceptions?"

"Depends," he said calmly. "If you stand in place and parry, it's an interception. But if you step out of the line of attack, it's an evasion. You're simply redirecting his attack while you evade his line of force."

"What if I step to the side and round kick him as he goes by?" I said, struggling to tangle the old warrior in his own definitions. "That must be an interception, but I'm stepping out of the line of attack."

The old man chuckled patiently.

"It's an evasion," he said. "You're simply countering at the same time instead of afterward."

That old tiger had a lot of patience with me, and I'm glad he did. I finally accepted his approach to tactics, and it's never failed me. Combined with the ability to read my adversaries, I learned to sense the rhythms of each attack and control the fighting range, choosing to avoid, evade, and intercept opponents on my terms. You can too.

When you're clearly stronger than your attacker, intercept his attack with crushing force. Break his attacking arm or leg with your block. Smother his attempts to throw. Even preempt his attack with a feint and vicious barrage of your own. But don't underestimate any opponent; close only when you have the upper hand.

When he's clearly stronger, you can still command the fighting range, so avoid. Remember, if he can't reach you, he can't hurt you. So, let him expend his energy flailing vainly. But I'm not suggesting you run from him. Instead, you maintain the precise distance, just at the edge of his fighting range, waiting ever ready for an opportunity to evade and counter.

As your adversary lunges and swings about, relax and feel the cycle of his *yin* and *yang*. Soon, he'll over-commit his attack. His awesome *yang* will deflate, and for a brief moment he'll be helpless as a baby. When that moment arrives, you'll want him within your fighting range. Therefore, you'll want to have seen it coming and evaded well.

As Musashi said, "Study this deeply."

FINAL THOUGHTS

You now understand the principles of strategy far better than most martial artists anywhere. And the five tactical elements I've given you will take you a long way towards being a formidable fighter.

These simple concepts apply to literally every martial art in some way or another. So, study them well and learn how to apply them in the systems you practice. Use them to develop your own strategies and tactics.

But don't think these specks of knowledge have made you a master strategist or even a competent warrior. For I've only scratched the surface of each of these principles, and for each one I've mentioned, another lies in the shadow, one which I won't tell you about.

Such is the nature of strategy and the final principle I'll divulge. Never teach anyone you don't know your strategies and tactics. A casual acquaintance today may be your enemy tomorrow. Teach only those whom you trust the basics of your strategy and only those whom you trust with your life, the details. When it comes to the art of strategy, secrecy is a time honored tradition.

Study diligently!

POINTS TO REMEMBER: THE ART OF STRATEGY

- Strategy is the essence of warriorship. As you progress, it should become more and more the focus of your training.
- Develop your strategy in four phases: First, determine your strategic objectives, then collect intelligence on your adversaries. Be sure to plan for fighting in a variety of environments. Then, program yourself for engaging your enemy.
- Learn the essential elements of tactics. Develop the ability to read your opponent, and use that skill to help you control the fighting range. Learn to feint effectively, and use rhythm and timing—yours and his. Finally, put it all together as you avoid, evade, and intercept your opponent.
- Keep you own strategy secret. A casual acquaintance today may be your enemy tomorrow.

Chapter 5

THE WARRIOR'S SPELL BOOK

"It is said, a Shaolin can walk through walls," said Wu.

"It was not a Shaolin who said that," said Kwai Chang.

FROM *KUNG FU, THE MOVIE.*
(ABC Studios, 1987)

For many Westerners, the most fascinating aspect of the martial arts is the seemingly magical abilities some adepts command. Even the most mechanical demonstrations of mastery are almost mystical in the layman's eyes, let alone those skills that supposedly reach beyond the physical realm. To the uninformed, the martial arts master seems to have a veritable spell book at his bidding.

Of course, these topics are prime fodder for novelists and movie makers who weave fiction from fact, embellishing each seed of truth to entertain their public. Unfortunately, while martial arts-oriented fiction is entertaining, it misleads the public and students alike as to what is real and what is made up. And the situation is made worse by those who claim powers and abilities that didn't exist before being born of a scriptwriter's pen.

Of all aspects of the martial arts, none are so romanticized, so misunderstood, or so abused as *ki*,* the internal energy some practitioners claim to have and control. Self-proclaimed masters have made hundreds of claims concerning this supposedly mysterious force.

There are those who say *ki* gives them super-human strength. Others claim it makes them heavy as lead or light enough to leap like gazelles, as the situation demands. *Ki* is credited with making arms unbendable and bodies immovable. Proponents have crushed objects, absorbed blows, and even claim to have repelled bullets thanks to their mastery of this elusive force.

To many, *ki* is a commodity they can move about. They send it to their feet or draw it upward. They extend it before them, pull it back, and direct it into their hands. Some claim they can send their *ki* into another body to hurt or heal or even project its force against or into inanimate objects. For others, *ki* is the source of their intuition. It enables them to sense what can't be seen, know events to come, and read or even command the minds of others.

Indeed, the list goes on and on. But what has all this to do with warriorship? Damn little, unless you're a warring magician in a carnival side show!

Ki does exist. It is quite simply the life force that all living things have. There is nothing mystical about *ki*. If you're alive, you've got it. That means if you are a living polliwog, you have *ki*. And if you are a healthy baboon, you have as much *ki* as any karate or aikido master in the world.

We all have physical bodies and living spirits. So having *ki* isn't a relevant issue for the warrior, other than in his need to stay strong and healthy. What's important to the warrior—what does

---

* *Ki* means spirit or breath in the Japanese and Korean languages. In Chinese it's called *chi*. In this chapter, I rely heavily on Japanese terminology, but the principles I explain apply to all traditional martial arts, regardless of national origin.

give the true warrior almost magical powers—is the ability to coordinate his body and spirit and focus those entities so effectively during combat. It's the focused application of *ki* that gives the adept such amazing abilities and makes him or her so formidable. And yes, this precise coordination and focus does, in some cases, produce abilities that can't be fully explained by the physical sciences.

Unfortunately, most modern instructors don't understand these talents, much less use them. As a result, they invent the nonsense we see offered the public today. Even the few who really have the skills—those legitimate teachers of the classical martial arts—rarely comprehend their own capabilities well enough to pass them to others. Instead, they continue the time-honored tradition of repetitive physical drill, year after year, until some small percentage of students intuitively grasp and apply the skills of their forebears. Most students never catch on.

Don't misunderstand me; I'm not criticizing the repetitive nature of traditional martial training. That process lays the essential foundation for properly learning any martial art, and I'm a true believer in the traditional way. But there are better approaches to teach the esoteric skills than simply waiting for students to figure them out for themselves.

There are precise methods for developing the esoteric skills used by traditional warriors. This chapter will explain what each of the internal skills are and how they function. Then it will teach you those methods for developing them. Let's start with the most direct manifestation of *ki*: *kiai* and *aiki*.

KIAI AND *AIKI*

Kiai and *aiki* are Japanese terms describing abilities used at the higher levels in all traditional martial arts. You've probably noticed these two words are *anagrams* of each other. This is no coincidence, for their functions are closely related. Each is a combination of the words *ki*, or life force, and *ai*. *Ai* means to blend, harmonize, or dominate in some contexts, and in others, the existence of something in concentration.

Kiai literally means to concentrate or focus the life force. I know you've heard the word *kiai* defined as a "spirit shout." Indeed, the spirit shout is an important tool for learning to develop *kiai*, but like so many other aspects of modern training, the outward, physical trappings of *kiai* practice have become confused with the internal function itself by those who don't know what *kiai* is. The fact is, exponents of some classical martial arts such as kenjutsu (Japanese swordsmanship) don't shout at all as they *kiai*, focusing their spirits and their blades into their targets. Masters of *kiai* sometimes project it without even moving, much less shouting.

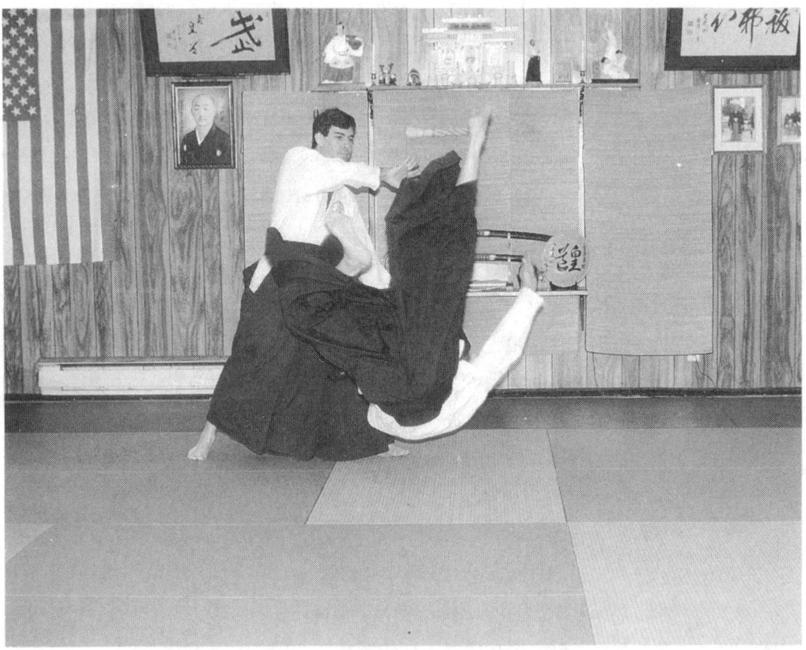

Aiki is an impassive state of mind without a blind side, slackness, evil intention, or fear.

Aiki means united life force or spirit. This union refers not only to the act of coordinating one's own body and spirit but to blending with and dominating an opponent as well. In the modern interpretation, *aiki* usually refers to the act of physically blending with an opponent's attack, then using leverage to upset his balance and dominate him. But there is much more to *aiki* in the classical sense.

Around the turn of the century, Takeda Sogaku, headmaster of Daito Ryu Aikijujutsu, said, "*Aiki* is the art of defeating your opponent with a single glance." This manifestation of *aiki* can be seen as the effect on the opponent of projected *kiai*. In fact, *aiki* and *kiai* are two sides of the same coin. The *Jujutsu Kyoju-sho Ryu no Maki* (*Textbook of Jujutsu, Volume on Ryu*), published in 1913, explained this point when it said, "*Aiki* is an impassive state of mind without a blind side, slackness, evil intention, or fear. There is no difference between *aiki* and *kiai*; however, if compared, when expressed dynamically *aiki* is called *kiai*, and when expressed statically, it is *aiki*." (Draeger, 1974, p. 142)

Whether this phenomenon is actually the product of some projected energy or merely the psychological result of concentrating one's will on a weaker ego can only be answered by those who have experienced it. In any case, *kiai* and *aiki* do exist, and their effects are the same whatever lies behind their function. The story about a 19th century karate master in Okinawa who was challenged to a duel by another karate adept illustrates this fact.

They met at dawn in a field outside the village where they lived, and each expected a fight to the death. As the master approached the field, the other man readied himself and assumed his fighting stance. The master, however, approached the scene standing relaxed with his hands at his sides. As the master came within fighting range, the challenger suddenly felt ill, and his knees nearly buckled. He quickly excused himself for a moment and sat down to regain his composure.

After several minutes, the master asked him if he was ready to get on with it. The man decided he was and got up to take his stance, but as soon as he looked into the master's calm face and firm gaze, he felt ill again and had to sit to keep from falling. "Sir, I withdraw my challenge and apologize," he said. "I can see I am no match for you, and fighting would surely cost me my life."

This story may sound farfetched, but anyone who has developed *kiai* or has felt the effect of one who has can identify with it. I had a similar experience a few years ago.

I was vacationing in a rural part of Michigan with my wife and in-laws. My 14 year-old brother-in-law had been riding his bicycle but came in crying because some young men had pelted him with rocks. There were four or five of them at the end of a dirt road drinking beer outside their cars, and it seems they thought throwing rocks at the boy as he rode his bike down the road was great sport.

I was outraged when I heard about this, and I set out to ask these guys what kind of men they thought they were. As I started down the road, I could see several cars about 200 yards out, and around them, the men. One of them noticed me coming, and seeing my brother-in-law following sheepishly behind, realized I was coming to confront them. They all began to taunt.

Perhaps it was righteous indignation, but as I walked down the road, I felt my sense of purpose focus like a steely blade. I wasn't looking for a fight. I intended to talk to these men, to humiliate them into facing their own cowardice. On the other hand, I was well aware a fight would probably break out, and I wasn't worried. I had confidence in my own abilities as a warrior, and I knew my cause was just. Whatever happened, I would win. The only questions open were how many of them might escape and how badly I would hurt the others.

I walked steadily ahead, never taking my eyes off my enemies. They continued to taunt, but as I closed the distance, their demeanor gradually changed, becoming ever more subdued. By the time I was within 100 yards, they were standing completely silent, shifting from foot to foot and whispering nervously to one another.

Suddenly, one panicked and they all bolted for their cars. They roared out in a cloud of dust, racing toward me and the only outlet to the main road. When the first of the three cars came within twenty yards of me, it was as if something leaped out in its path—the man slammed on his breaks and swerved to the far side of the road. I stood and watched defiantly as each car pulled as far to the other side of the road as possible and crept past, careful not to throw any gravel my direction. Each of the men stared rigidly ahead, refusing to meet my glare. I could plainly see the fear on their faces.

Was this episode a demonstration of my *kiai* or merely a display of their cowardice? You can decide for yourself, but I've experienced *kiai* on many other occasions, and I know what it feels like. I've sparred with partners who were technically and tactically superior to me, but I could clearly sense they had inferior *kiai*, and I willfully dominated, rendering them totally helpless. On other occasions, I've faced opponents who exuded a powerful energy and dominated me as easily as I did the others.

True *kiai* and *aiki* take years to develop. I can't give you a formula for instant success. But I can give you clear-cut instructions that will begin your internal development and take the hit-or-miss guesswork out of this part of your warrior training. To develop *kiai* and *aiki* you must:

- Find *kokoro*.
- Practice *haragei*.
- Develop *kokyu chikara*.
- Apply *kime*.
- Practice *kata* with utmost seriousness.

FIND *KOKORO*

Fast as the wind, quiet as the forest, aggressive as fire, and immovable as a mountain.

Samurai battle banner

The starting point for developing *kiai* is to find *kokoro*, or heart. *Kokoro* is a mental attitude that Korean stylists call "indomitable spirit," and it simply means to refuse to accept defeat.

Of course, refusing to back down from a challenge or threat isn't easy. Too often, we go through life seeking the course of least resistance, the easiest way to get by. But in some situations there just isn't any way to compromise. Sometimes we have to fight; figuratively or literally, we just have to slug it out. *Kokoro* is something we all have within us. We simply have to reach down deep and drag it up. That's why I say you have to find *kokoro*, rather than saying you must learn it.

Traditional teachers have various ways of forcing their students to draw on their own *kokoro*. Some have them train barefoot in the snow or wade waist-deep into a freezing river in January. Others use various forms of *shugyo** to drive students into embracing their *kokoro*. But none of these methods work unless the student truly commits to conquering the situation. That means he doesn't just endure, he throws his entire spirit into the effort of defeating the challenge. Survival isn't enough; he must triumph!

Over the course of my life, I've seen several people close to me demonstrate true *kokoro*, and I'm always struck with awe. Often, these folks are not martial artists, but I think you'll agree, they are warriors nonetheless.

One such case involved a middle-aged engineer I had the honor of working with. Let's call him "Tom." Earlier in his life, Tom was a hopeless drunk. For years he hid his addiction, but eventually it got so bad that he was drinking away his entire paycheck each week. In a short time, he lost his job, his house, his friends, his family, and everything he owned.

Then something happened. Tom suddenly realized that no one was going to save him from destruction but him. He reached

**Shugyo* is an excellent method for discovering *kokoro*. Refer to Chapter 3.

deep inside and found a strength he never thought he had. That day he got up and walked into Alcoholics Anonymous, and he never took another drink again. But that's not the end of Tom's story.

Life wasn't easy for this fellow, but he refused to give up. In time he found a good job and married a wonderful lady. They bought a fine home in the country, and he managed to rebuild the relationships with his children he had lost. But at 50 years old, when everything finally seemed to be going well, Tom's doctor told him the years of drinking and smoking had destroyed his body. He was a physical wreck. His weight, cholesterol, and blood pressure were so bad he would surely die within five years.

"Walking the stick" is good exercise for developing awareness of your *itten*, or one point.

This news would have crushed other men, but not Tom. Life had taught him that only he was the master of his own destiny. Right away, he quit smoking and went on a rigid diet. But what shocked his friends and family most was the running program he began. He started off just going a mile a day—part running, part walking. Within six months this 50-year-old, reformed alcoholic was running five miles a day and leaving men half his aged exhausted behind him. Within a year, he was 30 pounds lighter and his blood pressure and cholesterol were in normal ranges for a 20-year-old.

Just the other day, I saw Tom for the first time in years. I was disappointed to see some of his weight had returned, so I asked him about it over lunch. "No I haven't stopped running," he said. "My thyroid's gone crazy. Started putting fat on my gut, and I was exhausted all the time until the doctor put me on medication. Now I'm back on track, but I've had to cut back to three or four miles a day. I'm not as young as I used to be, you know." He flashed me a mischievous grin.

Tom is nearly sixty now. He's never studied any martial art, but Tom has found *kokoro*.

Another example is a retired Air Force colonel I knew named Jack. At 49, a few years before I met him, Jack had a mountaineering accident that crushed his right ankle. The surgeon told him it would never mend, and the foot would be useless; he ought to let him take it off. But Jack would have nothing of that. He belligerently told him to fix his ankle, his walking days weren't through.

To the doctor's disbelief, Jack was right. After weeks in a cast and months of physical therapy, he walked again. But Jack wasn't satisfied. His game leg made it nearly impossible for him to stay in aerobic condition. "If I could only run," he said, time and again.

Jack ran! He hobbled longer and longer distances each day until, little by little, he began running.

When I finally met Jack, he was a 55 year-old marathon runner. He was gaunt—all skin, bones, and wiry muscle. He always beamed me a warm smile, but in his deep-set eyes I saw a spirit I'd never want as an enemy.

The last time I saw Jack, he was limping again. He showed me his ankle, inflated like a water balloon. "It always swells like that the day after a hard race," he said. Jack was a master of understatement. He had just run one of the hardest races in the world, the "Leadville 100," a 100-mile race, high in the Colorado mountains. Jack wouldn't know a reverse punch from a back fist, but Jack knows *kokoro.*

To develop *kiai*, you must first find your own *kokoro.* Make never giving up a habit. Always attack a challenge; never avoid or simply endure it. As the cliché goes, "you only live once." Only you can decide whether you will live in triumph, whether facing an opponent or meeting the gut-wrenching challenges of life. And only once you've found *kokoro*, can you properly employ technical principles, such as *haragei.*

PRACTICE *HARAGEI*

> *If this sphere that is the universe is condensed, it becomes the one point in the lower abdomen.*
>
> Aikido Master Koichi Tohei

The technical foundation of *kiai* is *haragei*, or "belly art." You must learn it and practice it in everything you do, especially your martial arts. If you're studying under a competent instructor, you are already learning *haragei* as a part of every technique he or she teaches. Whether they be stances, strikes, throws, or holds, they employ the belly when done properly.

Haragei has both physical and spiritual qualities. Asian cultures believe a man's soul resides in the *seika tanden* (lower abdomen) at a point about three inches below the navel called the *itten*, or "one point". Indeed, there is a certain logic to this line of thought. This point is the physical center of our bodies. And while we relate rational thought to our heads, we tend to associate intuition and strong emotion with our guts. We've all felt fear, shock, and grief gnawing there, and what person hasn't had a "gut feel" for something he knew but couldn't quite rationally explain?

In the Japanese language, the word "*haragei*" is, in one sense, synonymous with intuition. This is a very real quality, and applies directly to the martial arts. By focusing attention on their abdomens, adept warriors are better able to tune out conscious thought, thereby freeing their minds to recognize the sensations produced by very subtle physical and emotional changes in their opponents. Actually, there is nothing mystical or supernatural about this skill; it's an advanced extension of the tactical function of reading your opponent I explained in chapter 4. It's root is *haragei*, but in application it requires you to enter *mushin* (mind-no-mind), so I'll explain it in more detail later in this chapter.

Whether or not the soul of man really lives in the *hara*, the source of all proper martial arts technique does. What's more, development of *kiai* and subsequently, *aiki* cannot begin until your sense of *hara* is strong. To begin developing your *haragei*, simply incorporate these three principles in your training:

1. MAINTAIN THE ONE POINT.

Maintaining the one point means to become conscious of your *itten*. More importantly, it means to put strength in your lower abdomen and generate power for all your techniques from there. Remember, the *itten* is the physical center of your body. When you move your body, if you move properly, you move your point to the new location and the rest of your body follows.

Often, I train with jujutsu students who forget this simple principle. They try to execute a *waza* by grabbing my hand or wrist and trying to twist it with arm strength. Usually, I can ignore the minor pain of this weak approach and just stand there looking at them. On the other hand, when I return the *waza*, I grip my *uke's* wrist and turn it just enough to secure the bind and "take up the slack" in the joint. Then I move my entire body smoothly and gently from the center. *Uke* suddenly slams to the mat in pain!

There is a simple exercise for learning to maintain the one point. Choose a partner and select a three-foot staff. Each of you take a front-facing stance (front stance, fighting stance, or whatever) facing each other, and suspend the staff between you with the ends pressed against your abdomens at a point two inches below your navels. Then, without touching the stick with your hands, step forward in stance, your partner stepping back, holding the stick on your abdomen with gentle pressure from your bodies. Walk across the training hall in stance. Maintain proper form throughout. Once you reach the other side, start back with your partner going forward and your retreating.

Done correctly, this exercise will train your mind to always be aware of the *itten*. In the beginning, it will be a conscious process. Later, you won't think of it, but your subconscious will always ensure you maintain and move from the one point in everything you do. And you will learn this principle even faster if you learn to relax completely.

2. RELAX COMPLETELY.

Relaxation is a fundamental principle in all martial arts. You may not think so if you study a hard style that stresses power and flexibility, but even in those systems, relaxation at key points in each technique facilitates the speed and flexibility essential for true power.

For most people, learning to relax is harder than it sounds. We live in a stressful society, and the tension that comes with stress accumulates in our bodies, eroding our *haragei*. So we must all learn to truly relax.

There are relaxation exercises in many disciplines, ranging from yoga to biofeedback. All of them are good, and I recommend you find one you like and practice it daily. But you need something more. Most of the relaxation techniques available are stationary exercises—you sit or lie down and concentrate on removing tension. These are good for you, but you must also learn dynamic relaxation. You must learn to relax while practicing your martial art.

In soft systems such as tai chi, students practice relaxation throughout. In hard styles such as karate, you relax while in stance and in the execution of each technique but flex your entire body as the technique makes impact. Whatever system you study, get in the habit of checking your body from time to time for unwanted tension, then consciously relax it. In time you will relax out of habit. Then, you'll naturally start keeping your weight underside.

Like many Chinese systems, Lun Gar Pai emphasizes health, spirit, and discipline. Its forms invigorate the *chi*, or vital energy.

3. KEEP WEIGHT UNDERSIDE.

When you maintain one point and relax, you get a feeling of your weight settling to the lower part of your body. You feel rooted, yet agile. You feel powerful, yet calm. This is the essence of *haragei.*

Any fluid naturally settles to the lowest point its container will allow. Your body is mostly water, and when relaxed, the weight of all parts of your body will naturally settle to their underside. In this state, you are very stable and therefore, very rooted and powerful. Tense up and you drive your weight upward, above your *tanden.* In this condition, your center of gravity is high, and you are unstable and weak.

People with highly developed *haragei* seem extremely strong, and they are very difficult to move or throw. Some will tell you it's a mystical demonstration of their *ki*, making their bodies heavy as lead. Actually, it's simple physics.

I once demonstrated *haragei* to a fellow Air Force officer without even trying. We were clowning in the office and exchanging verbal jabs. I put in a good zinger and laughing, turned to leave. As I turned, he put both hands on my shoulder to shove me playfully out the door. Sensing the coming push, I simply relaxed and stopped mid-step. He shoved hard, but instead of me springing forward, he flew back, stumbling into a cabinet and nearly falling to the floor.

What I had done was completely unconscious, and its effect seemed magical. It wasn't. I was relaxed; he was tense. My weight was beneath my *itten*, my center of gravity. His was high. Therefore, he was unstable.

To get into the habit of keeping your weight underside, just consciously relax from time to time and *feel* your weight sinking into your pelvis and thighs. Maintain one point while doing this and you are practicing *haragei.* Learn to breath powerfully at the same time, and you have *kokyu chikara.*

DEVELOP *KOKYU CHIKARA*

If you know the art of breathing you have the strength, wisdom, and courage or ten tigers.

Anonymous Chinese Adage

Kokyu chikara, or "breath power," is a basic element of every traditional martial art. It involves using your breathing to coordinate the contraction of your muscles so you can use your physical strength most effectively.

Most people use only a small percentage of their total strength as they move about trying to accomplish their daily tasks. This is because, in part, they tend to only use isolated muscle groups, those they have become conditioned to think are the only ones required to perform the work. To lift a heavy object, the typical man will bend his back and pull with his arm and shoulder. Actually, the man could lift more efficiently (and safely) if he would use the powerful muscles of his thighs to do most of the work. The man who uses *kokyu chikara* knows this and more. He uses his legs to lift, but he uses the internal muscles of his diaphragm and abdomen as well—he uses his *hara*!

Another reason most people use only a small portion of the strength they actually have available is the muscles they do employ tend to fight against one another. A man will flex his arm to make it strong, when actually, flexing pits the strength of his biceps against that of his triceps. The overall result will be less strength exerted no matter what the intended action. The man who uses *kokyu chikara* focuses his efforts most efficiently. He uses all the muscles—but only the specific muscles—required to accomplish the task at hand.

Kokyu chikara works with *haragei* to provide the warrior with extraordinary strength. To develop *kokyu chikara*, relax and breath deeply into the abdomen, not the chest. Of course, the air really goes into your lungs, no matter how you breath. But if you concentrate on putting it in your *hara*, you'll fill the lower portion of your lungs and bring your abdominal muscles into action.

The traditional method of breathing involves inhaling through your nose and exhaling with your mouth. In most arts, you coordinate the delivery of a technique with exhalation. However, in some systems, such as Uechi Ryu Karate (from Okinawa), practitioners inhale as they strike. Actually, whether you should inhale or exhale while executing a technique depends on the nature of the technique. Based on my experience, I believe *kokyu chikara* works most effectively on inhalation if you are directing force upward or drawing it in. If you are striking outward or driving down, strength is enhanced if you exhale in coordination with the movement.

Traditional *kata* training is the single most important exercise for developing esoteric warrior skills.

However you do it, there are two cardinal rules for breathing in combat: first, never empty your lungs completely. Breath is strength; always maintain a reservoir of it. Second, don't puff or snort. The Okinawan *kata* you may have seen or practiced (such as *Tensho* or *Sanchin*) which employ loud, constricted breathing are merely exercises to teach breath control and power. In sparring or combat, don't expose your rhythm to your opponent, letting him time your shifts from *yin* to *yang* and back.* Keep your breathing silent.

Practice diligently. As your *haragei* and *kokyu chikara* develop, you'll begin to apply *kime* effortlessly.

APPLY *KIME*

> *The fighter is to be always single minded with one object in view: to fight, looking neither backward nor sidewise. To go straight forward in order to crush the enemy is all that is necessary for him.*
>
> Daisetz Suzuki
> (Rogers, 1984, p. 35)

Kime, or "spiritual focus," is probably the most important element in the development of *kiai* and *aiki*. It's the gel that brings all the other facets together. Indeed, *kime* is the focus that literally defines *kiai*'s "focused life force."

The word *kime* has physical, mental, and spiritual connotations. It's *kime* that, working with the rooted leverage of *haragei* and the coordinating strength of *kokyu chikara*, concentrates the crushing power of a hard stylist's strike. It's *kime* that directs the warrior-strategist's mind during conflict, giving him or her the tactical advantage over a less refined fighter. And it's *kime* that

*Remember the tactical principle of rhythm and timing. Refer to Chapter 4 to learn more about this.

fuses the warrior's will, giving him the *kokoro* to achieve the impossible, whether in combat or facing the challenges of life.

As in most aspects of The Martial *Way*, the starting point for developing *kime* is in practicing its physical applications. To develop physical *kime*, apply these three principles in your training:

1. FOCUS YOUR ENTIRE BEING ON ACHIEVING THE OBJECTIVE.

The central principle of *kime* is to focus your entire being on achieving your objective. When you apply *kime*, there is nothing else in your world but the task at hand, nothing but destroying the target, defeating the enemy.

This level of commitment must be physical as well as mental. For a hard stylist, that means putting every bit of speed and every ounce of strength possible into each strike. To achieve speed you must completely relax the antagonistic muscles, those that would work against moving your weapon in the desired direction, and focus your energy into the protagonists, those muscles projecting the blow towards the target. Then, to generate power you must drive every protagonistic muscle in your body into the blow in one precise instant. Done correctly, your entire body snaps like a giant spring, levering against the ground and producing explosive force. Aim and timing must be precise. When it is, the resultant *kime* produces a sharp, audible crack* and a remarkable amount of energy is released into the target.

Physical *kime* is different for the soft stylist. Here, the warrior must focus on feeling and blending with the opponent's energy. As he attacks, whether it be a strike or a grab, you must

*Many people measure a student's *kime* by listening for this crack; however, this method isn't foolproof, as many learn ways to pop their uniform sleeves without employing it.

focus every fiber of your attention on sensing the flow of energy and moving with it, not against it. Maintain your *haragei*, your center, and smoothly blend with the force your enemy is projecting until he overextends and you sense his *yang* energy shift to *yin*. At that point you add energy to your opponent's and your passive blending turns to domination, directing him into the strike, hold, or throw of your choice.

In the hard style, *kime* is a critical ingredient of *kiai*; it's the focus that concentrates *ki*, the energy produced by the life force. In soft styles, on the other hand, *kime* more directly facilitates the sensing, blending, and dominating forces of *aiki*. In the first case, the force is linear and the *kime* explosive, as are the characteristics of *kiai*. In the second, the force is circular and the *kime* grows throughout the flow of the arc, drawing energy from the opponent until it turns against and consumes him. This is the essence of kinetic *aiki*.*

In both cases, the so called "spirit shout" is a key tool for training warriors to develop *kime*.

2. MASTER THE "SPIRIT SHOUT."

A pathetic trait of most modern schools is the feeble, patronizing grunts each of their students pass for spirit shouts. The casual "huhs" and "oohs" those students mechanically mouth demonstrate how little their instructors know of *kiai* and *aiki*. And since so few modern martial artists understand the importance of the true spirit shout, its use has all but disappeared from sport competition, as has any semblance of *kiai* and *aiki*.

The spirit shout is one of the most valuable tools for developing *kime* and subsequently, *kiai* and *aiki*. A well trained hard

*While generally correct, this explanation is somewhat simplistic. Actually, no style is completely hard or soft. Each employs both *kiai* and *aiki* and therefore, has elements of both linear and circular *kime*.

stylist will explode with a deafening roar at the crucial point of *kime*, the point of impact with his target. The shout will erupt from his abdomen, ensuring *haragei* and *kokyu chikara*, and it will help him focus that simultaneous burst from all his muscles, essential for generating the crushing force he desires.

The soft stylist's spirit shout is different but no less important. Instead of a sharp, piercing scream, he'll emit a low, accelerating growl from deep within his *hara*. It will grow in intensity as the energy flows through its circle, climaxing as the *aiki* turns against and dominates the opponent.

In both instances, the spirit shout is a tool; it's an audible device the warrior uses to coordinate and focus his physical, mental, and spiritual energies. If you like, think of it as a lens, or a set of lenses, that focus three different portions of the light spectrum onto a single point. The single, intense, cutting spearhead is *kiai*, and it is *aiki*.

3. FOCUS YOUR SPIRIT THROUGH YOUR EYES.

Another telltale sign of whether or not a school is teaching *kiai* is how the students, or instructors for that matter, use their eyes.

A principle often taught to sport competitors is to keep your eyes on the opponent's chest or belt. The rationale being that with your eyes pointed to his center, you can best watch his entire body and see any attack coming, whether it be from hand or foot. Students are also told that, as in basketball, an opponent can "fake you out" if you watch his face, but he can't move his center without committing himself to the direction of movement.

Well that's all fine for competitive sports, but combat isn't a game, and there are forces involved that don't come into play in the competitive arena. Fighting isn't merely a physical contest. It's a battle of wills, a deadly struggle of one spirit against another.

There's a lot of truth in the old saying, "the eyes are a window to the soul." And whether you believe it's metaphysics or simply psychology, you can read the strength of a warrior's spirit in his eyes. A student who watches his opponent's center while sparring probably hasn't focused his spirit to his one purpose. If he has, he's missing the opportunity to use his greatest weapon to defeat his opponent.

I'm not saying you should stare into his eyes or even watch his face; as the famous swordsman Miyamoto Musashi said, you should keep your gaze large. But your spirit must focus on dominating his, and to do that, the center of your gaze should rest gently on the portal to his spirit. That portal is his eyes.

As for the mechanics of vision, you can still see your opponent's feet while pointing your eyes at his, and with your spirit focused, you can tell a feint from a real attack even before he starts it. So keep your gaze broad. your face and eyes must be relaxed but firmly committed. If you go into the fight resolved to destroy your opponent no matter what the cost—if you go into battle truly committed to die for the opportunity to kill your enemy—his spirit will read it in your eyes and he will be crushed, *even if he's watching your chest.* That is the essence of spiritual *kime* and the heart of *kiai*.

PRACTICE *KATA* WITH UTMOST SERIOUSNESS

> Kata *in classical swordsmanship is the discipline of disciplines. It steels the nerves and balances the emotions so as not to disturb the serenity of mind that is so essential in swordsmanship.*
>
> Martial Arts Historian Donn Draeger
> (1982, p. 44)

If you remember, I pointed you in this same direction in Chapter 3, "Train as Warriors Train." Well, once again I'm preaching the old ways, harping on the traditional methods. Of course, modern martial artists know better than to listen to an old fool like me.

They can teach a student what fighting is really all about by showing him a few punches and kicks and throwing him into a boxing ring to spar. Others, the more artsy ones, make up their own pretty patterns and dance them to music to entertain and win prizes. It's enough to make a hardened warrior vomit!

Kata is the purest form of *kiai* training. No, I'm not talking about the flashy forms you see in tournaments or in most training halls. I'm talking about forms taught in the classical manner.

Proper, traditional *kata* training provides a distillate of all the essential elements for developing *kiai*. It emphasizes the solid stances and correct movements that build *haragei*. A qualified instructor will always stress moving from the one point, relaxing at key points, and lowering your center of gravity. With this kind of practice, you can't help but build a strong *hara*. Breathing in *kata* always centers in the *tanden*. It is properly coordinated with the techniques, so *kokyu chikara* grows as each day passes.

But most importantly, *kata* is the quintessential exercise in *kime*. It emphasizes coordinating and focusing physical energy in each technique, and teaches a student to concentrate his mental energy and focus it into the physical movement. Properly disciplined, traditional *kata* training even conditions the warrior to commit and focus his spirit through commanding the directions in which he points his eyes.

No, you can't use a *kata* on someone who attacks you, nor will a properly executed, traditional form do much to win you trophies. But if you want to develop *kiai*, if you want to learn to destroy attackers utterly and completely, if you want to learn to defeat an enemy with a single glance, you'll practice *kata* with utmost seriousness.

MUSHIN—MIND WITHOUT THINKING

Although it does not
mindfully keep guard,

In the small mountain fields
the scarecrow
does not stand in vain.

Haiku by Bukkoku, c. 17th Century

If there is a single trait most characteristic of classical masters it's the ability to enter *mushin*, or "mind-no-mind." This mental state is the principle source of the traditional warrior's quick reactions, extrasensory perception, and steely calm. In fact, *mushin* is probably the biggest discriminating factor between modern martial artists and true warriors of the past and present.

Although the effects seem mystical, *mushin* is actually a very simple concept—just don't think. Well it may sound simple, but unfortunately, it's one of those ideas much harder to apply than to understand. Try it. Put this book down for a moment and see how long you can stop your thoughts.

Didn't last long, did it? But difficult as it may be to stop thinking, those who practice true warriorship learn to do just that. And the skills they command are most remarkable.

Thinking interferes with fighting. Crazy as it seems, thinking gets in the way. Of course, we all have to think to learn. Whether it be a new stance, an advanced kick, or a new *kata*, we all have to think it through to internalize the correct form and function of the movement as we practice it the hundreds of times it takes to learn it. But there comes a point when conscious thinking interferes with our ability to do the technique and slows down our reaction time.

Picture for a moment the processes that occur when a thinking student has to block a kick: The opponent begins the kick, and the student's eye sees the movement. As his eyes gather information, his mind struggles to interpret what he sees and select the proper response with which to command his body. This action involves not only conscious interpretation of sensory signals but a decision process as well. As a result, the student probably isn't going to get the right block up in time to stop the kick. And his performance will be even worse if his mind is on another train of thought—anticipating a different attack or planning an attack of his own—when the opponent launches his kick.

Now imagine the same student sparring while in *mushin*. The opponent launches his attack, but this time, instead of waiting for his mind to think the situation through, our student's body moves spontaneously, not only to defend against the attack but to intercept and counter as well. One smooth, fluid movement. No thought—just action.

Actually, *mushin* is a little harder to describe than this account would lead you to believe. Conditioned response plays an important role in its development, but one in *mushin* isn't an automaton reacting without volition. Quite the contrary, a warrior in *mushin* is in complete control of his actions. Without all the mental chatter most people endure, he freely senses his enemy commit to an attack even before the man moves. Then, he absorbs the tactical situation and reacts—all without thought. It's not that the warrior in *mushin* has no mind. Without interference from his consciousness, he's free to act from another level of mind. The warrior in *mushin* acts directly from will!

Developing the ability to enter *mushin* is a long process. The first step is to build conditioned responses for all your techniques. This is the same process every athlete goes through as he masters the mechanics of his chosen sport. Next, you must internalize your strategies and tactics as I taught you in Chapter 4. To reach this point, you've spent at least five years of dedicated training. Now the most important work begins; you must learn to stop your internal dialogue.

Conscious thought is a never ending stream of self talk. We are conditioned from infancy to use language to express ourselves. Long before we reach adolescence, we learn to do all our conscious thinking in words—a constant process of discussing with ourselves the world around us and our actions in it. To our rational minds, these discussions seem very necessary and important. But what our conscious minds strive to deny is that there is another level of mind that operates much more directly. To enter *mushin*, we must learn to stop the internal dialogue of verbal thought and allow that inner mind to function.

Disciplines that can teach you to turn off your verbal thoughts range from the mystical to the scientific—from yoga to biofeedback. The method most popular with classical martial artists is called *zazen*, the form of meditation done in the Soto sect of Zen.

In *zazen* the aspirant sits or kneels, maintains one point, controls his breathing, and concentrates on emptying his mind. The goal of the Zen practitioner is to achieve a *satori* experience, a spontaneous enlightenment, by stopping his rational thought processes. Typically, the devotee spends weeks, months, or even years consciously struggling to keep his mind quiet, while waiting for enlightenment. Finally, through resignation or fatigue, the mind gives up and stops talking. Then intuition takes over and enlightenment occurs spontaneously... *satori*!

Most martial artists, however, aren't concerned with reaching enlightenment. For them, the *mushin* that leads the zen student to *satori* is the end in itself. Therefore, they don't wait the long years for enlightenment but simply focus on stopping conscious thought.

Zazen and the other various methods for teaching *mushin* are effective, but they all have one major drawback: they are static exercises. Too often, students learn to achieve *mushin* easily while in stationary meditation, but fail to reach it while practicing their art. What they need is a moving, dynamic form of *zazen*, a drill that employs *haragei*, *kokyu chikara*, *kime*, and subsequently, *kiai* to develop their *mushin*. That dynamic *zazen* students need is... you guessed it... *kata*!

Once again, we're back to the old standard, that archaic exercise so many modern martial artists have shunned as unrealistic and useless. For centuries classical warriors have practiced *kata* to master their arts. All the great masters trained using *kata*. You would think modern students would realize how very valuable a tool it is.

Kata is the single most important facet of warrior training. It builds and coordinates the three elements of your being. Initially, it builds your body as you develop the strength and flexibility to execute the various techniques. Then, as you develop your *haragei*, *kokyu chikara*, and *kime*, it hones your spirit and your *kiai* grows. Finally, using *kata* as a dynamic form of meditation, you learn to discipline your mind and achieve *mushin*.

Likewise, you should practice each *kata* you learn in three stages. In the first, learn the pattern thoroughly, paying strict attention to proper form, speed, and power. After hundreds of repetitions, turn your attention to developing *kiai*; concentrate on your *haragei*, *kokyu chikara*, and *kime*. Finally, when you can always feel the *kiai* surging within you when performing any of your *kata*, start practicing the forms without thinking.

By then, it won't be hard. Maintain your one point, breath from the *tanden*, and just stop talking to yourself. The *kata* will happen by itself. You will have learned it so well your body will do it without conscious thought.

Once you can consistently execute your *kata* in *mushin*, start trying to employ *mushin* in all aspects of your training. Train your mind to enter *mushin* whenever you take a fighting stance, execute a technique, and of course, whenever you sense danger.

When *mushin* becomes a part of your art, you'll discover you have remarkable speed and reactions. You won't feel fear or self consciousness. Most importantly, you'll find you can sense a great deal more from your opponent than you ever dreamed possible. Not only will you read his attacks more quickly, but you'll sense his emotions and feel his decision to attack even before he moves.

Once you reach this point you will begin to discover an alertness that verges on dominance. You will be at the threshold of *zanshin.*

ZANSHIN—SO ALERT YOU DOMINATE

But the warrior might also choose to crouch down on his left knee in iaigoshi posture. This posture announced his mistrust of the person or persons whom he faced and served as fair warning that his zanshin was unbroken.

Draeger

One of the most advanced skills in the martial arts is the ability to enter *zanshin. Zanshin* is a Japanese word that has no direct translation into English. Roughly speaking, it means alertness, but there is much more to it than that. *Zanshin* is alertness distilled to its essence. Martial arts historian, Donn Draeger, called it "the ideal of alertness" (1982, p. 56). But a definition that is even more descriptive is "alertness-remaining-form."

As a student develops, he first notices the onset of *zanshin* during practice with a partner. Sometimes it's while practicing individual techniques, more often it's during sparring or *randori*, and in some rare instances, a warrior will first discover *zanshin* immediately following actual combat. Notice I said, "immediately following."

Usually, *zanshin* first occurs right after an individual has scored a perfect technique, or a series of techniques, and has brought his opponent under complete control. At that instant, if the individual has developed his abilities of *kiai* and *mushin*, a primordial instinct will kick in. The fighter will feel a sudden rush of energy and strength. He'll feel every fiber of his attention focused on his opponent, and his entire body, mind, and spirit will be set to trigger and explode back into combat if the opponent moves, *or even decides to move* in any way that would show he is resuming the fight.

This is absolute, focused alertness. This is total dominance. This is *zanshin*!

Zanshin is an instinct we all have buried within us. Warriors don't learn it, they remember it. By building our *kiai* and training our minds to enter *mushin*, we strip away the conditioning modern civilization has put upon us, impeding our access to this basic fighting instinct. Once we remove those blocks to our natural fighting skills, *zanshin* emerges for us to discover.

Zanshin is a core instinct in all predatory animals. You can watch a domestic house cat demonstrate it after killing a mouse. Notice how she focuses her attention on her prey and sets to pounce. She carefully prods it with her paw, then leaps back to stance again. What happens if the mouse moves?

Wolves perform a ritual that clearly demonstrates *zanshin* as they compete for bitches and leadership of the pack. A strong male will stake his claim only to be challenged by another, and they'll fight. Eventually, one will dominate and pin his weaker opponent on his back. With the stronger fighter astraddle his victim, teeth bared and ready to rip out the loser's throat, the vanquished animal will freeze in admission of defeat. At that point, the wolf on top is in complete *zanshin*. Every fiber of his being is focused on the animal beneath him. But rather than kill him, he'll begin to back off, still growling and snarling, still poised and triggered to resume battle should the opponent flinch.

Developing *zanshin* is more a process of discovery than learning. If you've developed *kiai* and *mushin*, then *zanshin* will follow naturally, on its own. But there are things you can do in your training to focus its development, that is, to make it less haphazard and erratic, thereby honing your skills more quickly.

First, start practicing alertness, and make it a habit. I'm amazed at the mental fog in which most people walk. When I walk in a crowded shopping mall, I see people completely oblivious to others around them. People walk one direction with their heads turned in another. Often, I stop dead-still to avoid collision with someone who walks past, missing me by a hair's breath while looking the other way. The individual doesn't even know I'm there.

Consciously practice sensing who is around you. Learn to pick up telltale sounds, smells, and even feelings that tell you someone is around a corner, behind you, or any other place where you can't see him (don't forget above and below). I always teach these skills to my senior students, and I once had an interesting experience with one of them.

Keith and I worked in the same building. One day, coming out of my office, I saw him heading down the hall about twenty yards away and decided to play a game. I silently fell into step behind him, maintaining the same distance between us. For a few moments I could tell he didn't know I was there. But suddenly, though he didn't move his head or change his stride, I *felt* his attention focus on me, and I knew he knew I was following. Even stranger, I could sense Keith knew that I knew he knew I was behind him.

We proceeded down the hall until he came to a corner. Keith turned right, but just before he disappeared, he stopped and slowly turned his head my direction. Our eyes met and he smiled.

My experience with Keith was one of alertness, sensitivity, and maybe even telepathy, but it wasn't *zanshin*. *Zanshin* is a state that goes far beyond just being sensitive to your surroundings. It's a condition in which you are entirely focused and triggered to react. The mental exercises I described above won't develop *zanshin*, they will just help you refine and apply it once it begins growing within you.

The way you develop *zanshin* is to experience it, then internalize the feeling. I know that sounds impossible—to learn how to do something by experiencing how it feels to do it—but it's really not. If you remember, *zanshin* begins to happen naturally, once you've developed *kiai* and *mushin*. When it does occur, you'll feel it. You'll feel the energy surge within you. You'll pounce on your opponent and snuff his every attempt to defend himself. He'll be helpless to your domination. The experience is unmistakable!

When that feeling comes, savor it. Feel it to your core. Let it sink into the deepest recesses of your spirit. As you develop your skills over time, you'll be able to call up that feeling on demand. Then, you'll be able to enter *zanshin* before the fight. That's when the sensory exercises you'll have been practicing will pay off.

At that point, you will learn to enter *zanshin* anytime you sense a threat—walking down a dark street, entering an unfamiliar place, or any other time you feel danger. You'll feel energized, focused, and poised to strike. You will be ready to seize the initiative. The *samurai* called this state "*happo zanshin*," eight-directional awareness.

When you reach this point in your training, you'll be a very formidable warrior indeed.

FINAL THOUGHTS

Martial artists love to debate whether the amazing skills I just described are rooted in mysticism or mere physical science. To the romantically inclined, the force one projects in *kiai* and *aiki* are the supernatural extensions of his or her spirit. But from the realist's point of view the physical effects are demonstrations of leverage, and the ability to dominate an opponent from afar is nothing more than applied psychology.

Likewise, students with a metaphysical bent see *mushin* as a direct channel to the spirit, bypassing the conscious mind. Conversely, doubters believe it is nothing more than conditioned response resulting from the thousands of repetitions one does over years of training.

But the most hotly debated issue is *zanshin*. The warrior with highly developed *zanshin* can sense his enemy's decision to attack even before he moves. While the nonbeliever insists that masters with this skill merely key on the subtle nuances of body language, the more mystically oriented individual believes *zanshin* provides a direct link to his opponent's spirit, not only to read his intentions but to snuff them out before his enemy can act. He sees *zanshin* as direct evidence of extrasensory perception and the practical application of it in combat.

Actually, there is a common thread in the esoteric skills warriors possess and mystical teachings from some cultures. Breath control, focus, and centering are central principles for developing spiritual strength in systems ranging from yoga to Sufi mysticism. Furthermore, mystics from most disciplines believe the conscious mind is an obstacle between an individual and his or her connections to the spirits of others and a universal intelligence. Therefore, they teach their disciples to stop thinking so they can sense more from other people and the world around them. But all this debate is unimportant to warriors.

Warriors are pragmatists. When you're fighting for your life, it doesn't matter whether the sudden impression that your enemy is about to strike comes from sensing his change of spirit or from seeing his subtle change of expression. As you focus your gaze on him, you won't care whether his sudden loss of nerve happened because of the *kiai* you projected or because his will to fight didn't match yours. To warriors, only one thing really matters—defeating the enemy before, during, and after combat.

So practice the skills I explained in this chapter, but don't worry too much about why they work. Master the esoteric ways of warriorship, and you'll truly have a warrior's spell book at your bidding.

POINTS TO REMEMBER: THE WARRIOR'S SPELL BOOK

■ *Ki* exists, but there is nothing mysterious about it. It's simply the life force that all living things have. What's important to the warrior is the ability to coordinate his or her body and *ki* and focus those entities during combat.

■ *Kiai* means to concentrate or focus the life force. *Aiki* means blended life force or spirit. These are related concepts that involve focusing one's *ki* to crush or blend with and dominate an opponent's spirit.

■ You can develop *kiai* and *aiki* by first finding *kokoro*, the warrior's heart. Next you practice *haragei*, moving from your physical and spiritual center. Develop the breathing power of *kokyu chikara* and apply *kime*, or focus. Finally, put these methods together and practice *kata* with utmost seriousness.

■ *Mushin*, or "mind-no-mind," is the mental state that is the principle source of the traditional warrior's quick reactions, extraordinary perception, and steely calm. Learn to enter *mushin* by turning off your internal dialogue. Once again, the most important exercise to practice *mushin* is *kata*.

■ *Zanshin* is alertness distilled to its essence. If you are developing *kiai* and *mushin*, *zanshin* will eventually follow on its own. However, you can focus its development by practicing alertness and savoring each onset of *zanshin* as it occurs. Your goal is to achieve *happo zanshin*, or "eight-directional awareness" at will.

■ Many martial artists debate whether the esoteric skills in warriorship are mystical or physical. To a real warrior, it doesn't matter why they work. The only thing that really counts is defeating the enemy.

PART II

THE *WAY* OF HONOR

Chapter 6

THE FOUNDATIONS OF HONOR

Mine honour is my life; both grow in one;
Take honour from me, and my life is done.

RICHARD II, SHAKESPEARE

The morning air was cool and damp as the two men eyed each other from across a meadow. The sun had risen barely an hour before, and the dawn mist hadn't yet burned off the glade.

Thomas Mackay watched his adversary through reddened eyes. Beside him his second, Richard Carlton, drove a ramrod down the barrel of his pistol, seating the ball snugly against its powder charge. Thomas' cheeks burned again as he remembered the humiliation he'd been dealt the evening before—humiliation at the hands of Geoffrey Harrington, who now watched him from across the glade. For a moment, he experienced again the satisfaction he had felt when he slapped the bastard with his gloves, but it was different now. After a sobering, sleepless night, his yearning for revenge had dulled. Thomas now struggled to contain his fear.

"Ready!"

Thomas jerked back to the present as Richard called to the men across the meadow.

"We're ready," came the reply.

As the two groups began walking towards one another, the air was electrified. Horses snorted and shifted nervously. There was no other sound but that of the grass rustling beneath their boots. Thomas fought back a wave of nausea.

The men came to about thirty paces of each other and stopped. The seconds met in the center, and each examined the other's pistol. Satisfied, they returned to their groups. Next, the mediator, a portly, well-dressed man, stepped forward and called out the rules in a loud, officious voice.

There was nothing complicated about this game of death. Each man was to stand still in the open and, on command, fire as the other fired on him. They would take one shot, and it would be done. That is, unless neither was seriously wounded nor felt his honor restored. In that case, the seconds would reload the weapons and they would start again.

Richard offered Thomas his pistol and, with his back to Geoffery and his friends, spoke softly. "Don't worry, lad. I saw his face. He's so scared, he couldn't hit you if you were standing on his boots. Just aim for the center of his body and squeeze the trigger." Thomas tried to keep his hand from shaking as he reached for the gun.

Richard winked reassuringly and walked away. Thomas saw now that all the officials, friends, and witnesses had moved safely clear of the rivals, and a fresh wave of fear washed over him.

"Gentlemen," said the mediator, "this is the last chance either of you have to settle this dispute without violence. Can't we come to some amiable solution?" Thomas felt the gawkers begin to fidget, afraid of being cheated out of the promised spectacle of bloodshed. The mediator turned to Geoffrey.

"Mr. Harrington?"

Geoffrey, now pale and perspiring, hesitated. Thomas held his breath and prayed, but Geoffrey finally said, "Let's be on with it!"

"Mr. Mackay?" Thomas couldn't force any words from his throat. He felt total despair. With effort, he jutted out his chin and gave one decisive nod.

"Very well, then. Gentlemen, cock your pistols!" Thomas struggled with the large iron hammer. It clicked.

"Raise and aim!" He raised the pistol and tried desperately to steady the barrel, pointing at Geoffrey's chest. His gut knotted in terror.

"Fire!"

A crack echoed off both sides of the meadow. Thomas lost sight of Geoffrey as the gun's retort jerked his arm upward. But before he could pull it down, he felt a vicious kick. His body spun, and his face plunged into the wet grass. Instinctively, he doubled up and grasped his knee. Someone cried out; maybe it was Geoffrey. No, it was him. Pain raged up his leg.

Soon, there were feet all around him. Hands were on him, trying to straighten his leg; he heard someone say something about him losing it. Thomas was in agony. Then, a pair of strong hands took his face and turned it upward. He opened his eyes and saw Richard's face close to his.

"You did it, lad!" Richard said, beaming. "You killed Geoffrey Harrington. You may have lost your leg, but you have your honor."

This story is fictitious, but it typifies hundreds of cases that occurred in Europe and America before the 20th century. Also, it illustrates a perception of honor prevalent in that period and still accepted by many people today.

Men through the ages have taken drastic measures to preserve their honor. In this instance, Mackay killed Harrington and was himself crippled for life. Despite his injury, this was quite a coup for Mackay, for not only did he survive the encounter, but tales of his exploit would be told and retold in his hometown for years. Most importantly, he successfully defended his honor... or did he?

Honor is central to warriorship. It's a concept common to all warrior groups, regardless of the cultures in which they formed. Whether you call it *Bushido*, The Code of Chivalry, or something different, all fighting men and women aspire to ethical codes guiding the manner in which they practice the profession of arms and how they live their lives.

Given the moral nature of these codes, they are compatible with most religions and are often mistaken for doctrines of religious origin. However, warrior honor is not based on religion. Warriors aren't honorable because they fear a wrathful god. Warriors are honorable because it's a practical requirement of their profession. They are honorable because it's the most powerful way to live. Most of all, warriors are honorable because to be otherwise is cowardly!

Honor is essential among professional warriors. When hundreds or thousands of lives are at stake, superiors must know their subordinates are absolutely reliable. They must be able to trust those under their command to report information accurately, no matter how bad the news is. They must have their unfailing loyalty. Leaders must know their warriors will march into battle on command and die if necessary to defend their comrades, their groups, their societies, and their ideals.*

The non-warrior elements of society also must rely on the honor of warriors, for warriors can be the most dangerous people in the world. As a group, they are the fittest and the best trained fighters in any society, and they wield most of the weapons, including those most sophisticated and destructive. Warriors without honor quickly become tyrants, as some third-world countries today demonstrate.

*Loyalty works from the bottom up. Although leaders and followers often espouse lofty ideals, in the heat of battle, warriors will always fight hardest to defend their comrades and most immediate organizational elements. The most effective leaders recognize this fact.

Whether you are a military member or not, personal honor is just as important. Studying the martial arts makes you stronger than your non-warrior peers, and you're much more capable of injuring those around you. Without the moral compass that honor provides, citizen-warriors can be dangerous indeed. Only honor separates the warriors from the thugs.

This chapter will teach you the foundations of warrior honor. You'll learn to weigh the basic tenets of honor to distinguish between issues of honor and those of face. This chapter won't make you an honorable person; only you can do that. But once you understand the foundations of honor, you'll easily see the most honorable course of action in any situation. The rest is up to you.

In the West, men have dueled in the name of honor. Dueling was common among feudal Asian warriors as well, but they rarely attempted to rationalize it with honor.

THE BASIC TENETS OF HONOR

For Bushido, *the three qualities of Loyalty, Right Conduct, and Bravery are essential. We speak of the loyal warrior, the righteous warrior, and the valiant warrior, and it is he who is endowed with all three of these virtues who is a warrior of the highest class.*

From *Budo Shoshinshu*, by
Daidoji Yuzan (17th Century)
(Sadler, 1988, p. 33)

Honor is a term many people use but few understand. For most, the word still conjures up scenes of duels or military exploits, but people are hard pressed to explain exactly what role honor plays in these adventures. In other words, they can usually describe situations in which someone did or didn't act honorably, but they can't quite say why what that person did was or wasn't honorable.

Many people equate honor to honesty; if you tell the truth and pay your debts you're honorable. Others link honor to their reputations. If they are respected in their communities or peer groups, they feel their honor is intact. Marr that image, and they believe their honor has been damaged. Sometimes these folks wear honor on their sleeves as a badge of courage. "I am a man of honor. Cross me and I'll make you pay for it!" is a common theme among them. Unfortunately, while some of these issues do relate to honor, others have nothing to do with it at all.

Indeed, truth, self-restraint, loyalty, and the other virtues are honorable. But practicing one or more of these ideals doesn't necessarily ensure one is a man or woman of honor—at least not in the warrior model. To recognize and practice warrior honor, one must understand it. Warrior honor is founded on three basic tenets:

- Obligation.
- Justice.
- Courage.

OBLIGATION

It is forbidden that one should, acting disrespectful of The Way of Heaven, attach little importance to the duties of his master and be overly attentive to his own business.

From *The Regulations of Imagawa Ryoshun*,
by Imagawa Sadayo (1325-1420)
(Wilson, 1982, p. 60)

Obligation is the root of all warrior honor, and meeting one's obligations is the principle part of what makes a warrior honorable. I'm not talking about financial obligations alone. Nor am I referring specifically to obligations to perform duties assigned by one's boss or superiors, although both of these examples certainly apply. I'm talking about all the obligations inherent to human society.

As John Donne wrote, "No man is an island, entire of itself; every man is a piece of the continent, a part of the main." Life is a social contract. We all rely on others, no matter how independent we would like to think we are. And when someone helps us, provides a service, or does us a favor, we acquire a social and moral obligation to repay that person. That is duty.

Most people are reasonably mindful about repaying favors, but warriors are particularly circumspect about recognizing and fulfilling their obligations. And among warrior societies, none are more diligent than the Japanese.

In Japanese, a word closely associated with honor is *giri*. *Giri* translates literally as "right reason." Generally speaking, it means duty, but it really means much more. *Giri* can best be defined as a moral obligation to fulfill one's duty. Its role in society involves a basic social system of debt and repayment.

Giri works like this: whenever someone does something for you, you assume an obligation to repay him. You carry this obligation as a burden until you relieve yourself of it by repaying the individual in a manner commensurate with what he did for you. The Japanese would say you carry his *on*. Fulfilling that obligation is *giri*.

It has different names in different cultures, but *giri* plays a crucial role in every warrior society. Capable leaders train, support, and look after their subordinates. In return, dutiful followers are obligated to obey, protect, and sacrifice for their superiors. Honorable warriors look out for one another. Each covers his comrade's back and, in return, knows his back is covered if his compatriot is honorable. All are honor-bound to defend their lords, chieftains, generals, or nations that provide them shelter, employment, and stability.

Giri is the glue that binds warrior societies together. But obligation without justice is hollow and meaningless. In fact, without justice, *giri* can be twisted into something ugly and dishonorable.

JUSTICE

> *Here we discern the most cogent precept in the code of the samurai. Nothing is more loathsome to him than underhand dealings and crooked undertakings.*
>
> From *Bushido: The Soul of Japan*, by Inazo Nitobe, 1899

Justice lies at the heart of honor, for no obligation fulfilled is honorable if the act of fulfilling it creates an injustice. I could wax philosophical here and ask what justice is or how one recognizes it, but that would belabor this very basic principle and reduce its impact. Justice is simply knowing the difference between right and wrong and doing right.

In *Budo Shoshinshu*, Yuzan defines three degrees of doing right. He illustrates his point with a parable about a man who dies during a journey. Before leaving, the dead man had trusted one hundred *ryo* of gold with his neighbor for safe keeping. No one else knew of this transaction, so the neighbor is left with the dilemma of whether or not to act honorably. Of course, taking the money is the dishonorable option, but Yuzan proposes there are varying levels of honor, depending on why the friend returns it.

The first and most honorable course of action is to return the gold to the dead man's family without ever considering theft. A second alternative would be to covet the money briefly, but then be overtaken with shame and return it. The third possibility is to consider keeping the money but decide against it for fear of being discovered by family, friends, or servants. All three situations result in the same outcome: fulfillment of *giri* and remaining honorable. However, each case reflects a different degree of moral conscience and, therefore, a different level of honor the individual has attained.

Actually, this example illustrates very well the three levels of character growth everyone passes through as his sense of honor develops. Early in life, we begin learning the difference between right and wrong by enjoying the positive results of doing right and experiencing the negative consequences of doing wrong. Parents, teachers, and even peers are quick to reward or punish us for our actions, based on their sense of justice. We come to weigh our prospective actions against the possible outcomes and choose those in which the results are positive or at least not so negative as to be unacceptable. As we grow and come to understand the difference between right and wrong, we develop a conscience or sense of shame. This leads us to weigh alternatives and avoid wrong actions even when they could go undiscovered; we choose to do right even when we see no outward negative consequence of doing wrong. Finally, honor becomes a habit and we find ourselves not even considering wrong alternatives.

On the other hand, some people never develop a sense of honor. I won't go into sociological causes, but whatever the reasons, they just don't develop a moral conscience. They go through life constrained only by the negative results they perceive for their actions; if they think they can get away with an evil deed, they do it with no remorse. These people are all the more dangerous if their judgment is faulty and they can't connect the inevitably self-destructive consequences with their heinous deeds. Fortunately for us all, people of this ilk are relatively few.

Actually, most of us are neither pillars of virtue nor moral derelicts; we're someplace in between. We struggle through each day, moving from situation to situation, weighing our alternatives, trying to do right. Unfortunately, many problems don't have clear-cut right or wrong solutions. Too often, obligations conflict, and we find ourselves forced to default on one to meet another.

The famous Confederate general, Robert E. Lee, faced the greatest moral dilemma of his life just before the outbreak of the American Civil War. Already recognized as one of the most talented officers in the U.S. Army, the War Department asked him to

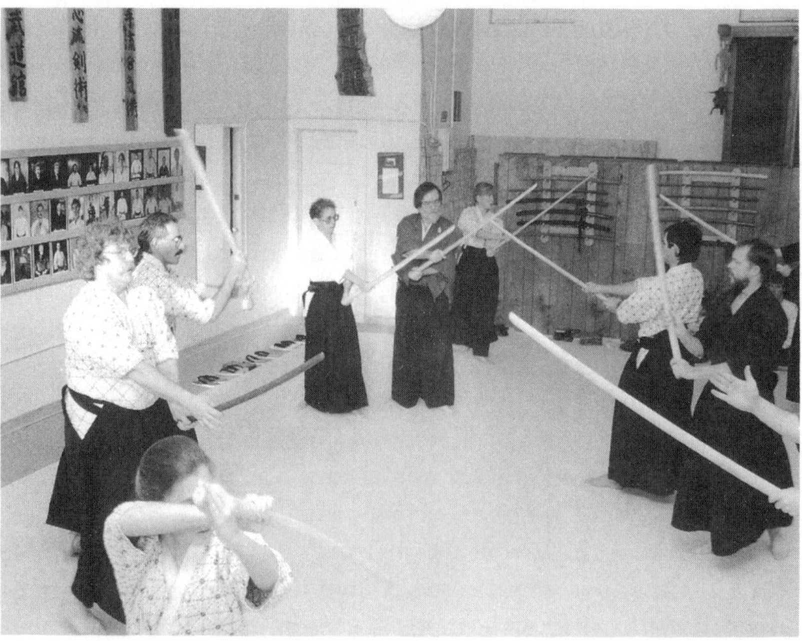

For Bushido, the three qualities of loyalty, right conduct, and bravery are essential.

take command of the U.S. Army of the Potomac. Meanwhile, the Confederate government wanted him to lead the Army of Virginia. Lee was a man of honor, and he didn't take his duty lightly. As a professional army officer, he was sworn to defend the United States of America. But as a Virginian, he was obligated to defend his family, friends, and homeland.

Now, more than a hundred years later, it's easy for us to say Lee made the wrong choice. But it was a gut-wrenching decision for him, and he decided on the basis of honor. No one has ever questioned that—not today, not in 1865. Robert E. Lee was so respected by friend and foe alike, that when he surrendered to Union General Ulysses S. Grant at Appomattox, Virginia, Grant refused to accept his sword. Grant knew he stood before the greatest, most honorable warrior of his day.

Although most of us will never have to decide which side to fight on during a war, conflicts of obligation are common for warriors. So it's imperative that we hone our sense of justice to guide us through life honorably. In each situation, we must weigh the alternatives on the scales of honor and choose which is most right. Above all, we should avoid becoming obligated to dishonorable people.

Obligation without justice can be dangerous and destructive. It's a common plight in the *yakuza*, Japan's crime organization comparable to Sicily's mafia. Like the mafia, the *yakuza* controls vice operations, including narcotics, gambling, and prostitution, and often uses strong-arm tactics and murder to maintain discipline.

The *yakuza* is centuries old. They enforce an archaic code of conduct patterned after that of the *samurai*. Members are considered soldiers, and the code is fashioned around a rigid adherence to *giri*. Rank-and-file members are obligated to obey, support, and protect their leaders who, in turn, take care of them much as military leaders look after their troops. All of this sounds fine and honorable until you remember the very purpose of the organization—to raise money through crime.

Notice I was careful not to call the *yakuza* system a code of honor. There is no justice in crime, and compelling people to incriminate themselves through their own sense of obligation is manipulation at its worst. Therefore, before you step into a situation that may obligate you to someone, consider whether or not that individual is honorable. If he isn't, avoid accepting his help. Otherwise, you may find yourself facing the moral dilemma of being asked to dishonor yourself to meet your debt.

Remember, to be honorable you must always examine your obligations for justice. But simply recognizing your just obligations isn't enough; you must also have the courage to carry them out.

COURAGE

To see what is right and not to do it is to want of courage.

Confucius

Courage is the virtue most often associated with warriorship. Both the profession of arms and a calling to The Martial *Way* demand it. Courage is an honorable quality; warriors are justly obligated to risk their lives fighting at their leaders' command. But the courage needed to live a life of honor is often different from the daring expected of warriors in battle.

Moral courage is the fortitude it takes to do what is right, no matter what the personal cost. While not as dramatic as physical bravery, it's the kind of courage most often called upon in every warrior's life.

We all face situations in which we see the right course of action, but taking it puts us in jeopardy. Perhaps when you were a child you had to own up to having broken your neighbor's window, or maybe you had to face your father after your high school prank ran amiss and damaged someone's property.

As adults we face similar situations, and our personal honor depends on whether we have the courage to face them responsibly. Have you ever had to explain to your boss why your sales quota, production schedule, or some other measure of performance was substandard? Did you face the challenge with truth and valor? How about that car you backed into in the parking lot? Did you find the owner and offer to make restitution? You may feel these issues are insignificant, but how you handle the small conflicts in life says a lot about your sense of honor.

Moral courage is a crucial requirement of warrior honor. When things go wrong in war, it's vital that leaders at all levels admit their mistakes and report circumstances to their superiors accurately. Given the correct information, leaders can alter strategies and change plans to salvage the situation, but handed information altered to whitewash incompetence, then more mistakes are made and lives lost. The Vietnam War provided classic examples of how misinformation within the chain of command results in combat ineffectiveness.

There's one more point to understand about courage: having it doesn't mean you don't feel fear. Fear is a natural human emotion, and honorable people experience it just as dishonorable people do.* What determines your level of courage is how you handle fear. Warriors face it, get control of themselves, and do what must be done; cowards run.

HONOR AND FACE

As you see, honor means recognizing your obligations, then having the courage to do what is right. So where does reputation fit in, and how do you go about defending your honor? To con-

*Imperiled warriors learn to block fear by entering *mushin* (see Chapter 5), but that is only a temporary remedy. Once your rational thought process returns, so does the fear.

sider these questions, let's look again at the story that opened this chapter.

In summary, Thomas Mackay and Geoffery Harrington had a public confrontation in which Harrington did something to embarrass Makay. Publicly humiliated, Mackay felt his honor was damaged, and the only way he could restore it was by forcing Harrington to apologize or by defeating him in a duel. So, according to custom, Mackay challenged Harrington and killed him.

As was usually the case, neither of these men really wanted to fight. They were compelled—compelled by convention and by their peers. Had the confrontation occurred in private, they probably wouldn't have considered risking their lives over it. But since their egos had collided in public, each felt honor-bound to get satisfaction. To withdraw would have implied cowardice and resulted in the perception of dishonor.

But was this confrontation really an issue of honor? Well, let's examine it against the basic tenets. We'll start with courage: dueling as these men did, certainly took courage. Standing still, only yards from a man shooting at you, is a terrifying experience. Both men were scared, and rightfully so. Yet both kept their fear under control and did what they felt had to be done. However you feel about them, you can't deny they were courageous.

What about justice? Well, Mackay believed his response to the humiliation Harrington had dealt him was just. After all, he was defending his honor, wasn't he?

I know what you're thinking—how can you determine whether Mackay's response served justice when I haven't told you what Harrington did to embarrass him? But does it really matter? Is there anything Harrington could have said or done that would have prevented Mackay from meeting a just obligation? Of course not. And since nothing Harrington could have done would have diminished Mackay's honor, how could there have been any justice in Mackay's killing him or putting his own life at risk? Regardless of what offense Harrington committed, neither man had justification for fighting to the death.

Finally, there's the question of obligation. As you recall, it's the very root of honor. So what obligation did Mackay have to fight? If you asked him, he'd probably tell you he was obligated to defend his reputation, his family name. No doubt, killing Harrington as he did enhanced his reputation in the community, given the social conventions of the day. But since his honor really wasn't at stake, the case for an obligation to kill is pretty weak. You see, like most duels over "honor," this really wasn't an issue of honor at all. It was an issue of face.

Fighting for honor was once a fairly common theme in many cultures, and it still is in some. But once examined, fights for honor almost always turn out to be fights to save face.

Face refers to one's reputation in the community or circle in which the individual must live or work. It is, in essence, prestige. In some cultures, face is very important. Citizens of certain Asian countries place great value in face when measuring a man's worth. Likewise, Middle Easterners and Latins consider face crucially important. Face is even more important in most warrior societies. Men and women of power tend to have great egos, and where ego is involved, pride in one's reputation is an inevitable by-product.

Face is closely tied to ego and often results in senseless fighting. Even so, face isn't necessarily bad, nor is it always wrong to fight for it. Leaders at all levels must command face. The moment a warrior loses the respect of his troops, effective command becomes impossible. Teachers must have face with students, parents with children, and police officers in the local community. In fact, all people in authority must have face with their subordinates to exert their leadership effectively.

With that in mind, you should always consider the role face plays in any conflict. When you find yourself in confrontation, there is usually more than one road to resolution. Of course, your goal is to get your way. You want to end the conflict as quickly as possible, getting the results you want. But too often, feeling the sting of being challenged, you decide you want more than what you originally set out for. You decide you want to teach your opponent a lesson. In essence, you want to take some face.

That is a very dangerous move if you're confronting a warrior. True warriors value honor above all. Nonetheless, they are still among the most dangerous people in society, and they'll usually defend their face fiercely. If you want to end the conflict without escalation, it's usually wise to protect your opponent's face. I'm not telling you to back down or sacrifice your own face. Get your way, but find some small compromise that will save face for your opponent. Perhaps you can admit some small error on your part. Maybe he'll want to claim he misunderstood the issue early on, even though you know he didn't. Give him ground. Unless you want a fight and know you can win, let him have his face. After all, one day you may need this warrior as an ally.

Yes, face is an important facet of warriorship, and no doubt, you'll fight for it from time to time. Perhaps you'll be justified, but even if you are, don't think you are defending your honor. You're not. Face can be taken from you, so it's something you can fight to keep. On the other hand, honor depends solely on your commitment to meet your just obligations. Since only you can do that, no one can take honor from you.

You can have all the face in the world and still lose your honor. Conversely, you can remain honorable no matter what the world thinks of you. Forced to choose between these two conditions, the superior warrior will pick the latter.

DEVELOP YOUR OWN SENSE OF HONOR

With the basic tenets in hand, you understand The *Way* of honor and can separate issues of honor from those of face. But just understanding what honor is all about isn't enough; you must learn to apply The *Way* in your life.

Don't be discouraged if you've been dishonorable in the past; we all have. No living warrior is a saint. We've all failed in our obligations or turned our faces from justice at one time or another. But the past is behind us, it's a memory, it no longer exists. All we can do now is live as honorably as we can today. Each of us must cultivate and nurture our own sense of honor. We must practice the principles of obligation, justice, and courage until they become second nature.

To develop you own sense of honor, consciously examine each of your social interactions for how the tenets of honor pertain. Use this 3-step process to make honor a way of life:

1. DETERMINE YOUR OBLIGATION.

Every time you interact with someone, take a moment to examine the situation for obligation. Is that person doing something for you? If so, are you paying for his service in some way? Perhaps he's your friend and doesn't expect anything from you in return. Well, that doesn't relieve you of the *giri* to return his kindness. You carry his *on*. The fact that he expects nothing in return binds you all the more!

2. WEIGH THE SITUATION FOR JUSTICE.

Look for the right and wrong in every situation. Whenever you feel you've obligated yourself to someone, examine that circumstance for justice. What is the right thing to do? Usually, you'll see the right action is to fulfill *giri* and pay your debt. However, blind obligation is self destructive.

Watch how your associates conduct their affairs, and avoid obligating yourself to dishonorable people. If you always watch people with an eye for justice, you'll usually know who the dishonorable ones are. Treat them courteously and deal with them as your duties demand, but keep them at arm's length and never turn your back. Most of all, never accept anything from them that would bind you. Carrying the *on* of a dishonorable man is a dangerous burden.

You can almost always see the right and wrong in any situation, but sometimes just obligations conflict. All too often, warriors end up carrying more obligations than they can meet. Worse yet, they find themselves, as General Lee did, obligated to conflicting causes. Obligations to your job may interfere with commitments to your family. Obligations to your employer may conflict with obligations to your community or society at large. In these cases it's especially important to step back and weigh the situation for justice. What is the right thing to do?

In any case, don't whine and don't procrastinate. Like Lee, choose the most just course of action and do it without looking back. That takes courage.

Kenjutsu may be the most direct art for forging courage, and wooden swords can be just as deadly as live blades.

3. TAKE COURAGE AND ACT.

The final step in developing honor is the easiest to explain but the hardest to apply. Too often, people see where their obligation lies and know the right thing to do, but they are afraid to do it. That is not the warrior's *Way*.

Warriorship is a profession of courage, a calling to valor—not just on the battlefield but in all of life's conflicts. So steel your nerve and march forward. Far better to fail in an honorable endeavor than to succeed in a cowardly one. That is the *Way* of honor. That is the *Way* of the warrior.

POINTS TO REMEMBER: THE FOUNDATIONS OF HONOR

- Honor is central to warriorship. It's common to all warrior groups, regardless of the cultures in which they formed. Although its moral values are compatible with most religions, codes of warrior honor sprang from necessity, not from any religious doctrine.
- Truth, self-restraint, loyalty, and the other virtues are honorable. But practicing one or more of these ideals doesn't necessarily ensure one is a man or woman of honor—at least not in the warrior model. Honor is founded on three basic tenets: obligation, justice, and courage.
- Obligation is the root of all warrior honor, and meeting one's obligations is the principle part of what makes a warrior honorable. Obligation is best explained in the Japanese concept of *giri*, or "right reason." When someone does something for you, you carry that person's *on*, or burden. Relieving yourself of that burden through repayment is *giri*.
- Justice lies at the heart of honor, for no obligation fulfilled is honorable if the act of fulfilling it creates an injustice. Justice is simply knowing the difference between right and wrong and doing right.

■ Courage is the virtue most often associated with warriorship. Both the profession of arms and a calling to The Martial *Way* demand it. Moral courage is the fortitude it takes to do what is right, no matter what the personal cost. While not as dramatic as physical bravery, it's the kind of courage most often called upon in every warrior's life.

■ Once examined, fights for honor almost always turn out to be fights to save face. Face refers to one's reputation in the community or circle in which the individual must live or work. It is important in all warrior societies. You may fight for face, and maybe you'll be justified. But even if you are, don't think you are defending your honor. You're not.

■ To develop your own sense of honor, consciously examine your social interactions for how the tenets of honor pertain. In each: determine your obligation, weigh the situation for justice, then take courage and act.

Chapter 7

HONOR IN ACTION

The wise man, after learning something new, is afraid to learn anything more until he has put his first lesson into practice.

TZU LU

How many times have we seen men and women who clearly know the difference between right and wrong, stray nonetheless? Often the most talented, educated, and successful members of our society—those whom we count on to lead most nobly—fail most abysmally in their obligations.

Follow the news and you'll see presidents who fix elections and senators who peddle influence to line their own pockets. Judges are arrested in drug stings. Corporate officers bribe the government for lucrative contracts, then pad their profits by selling shoddy parts at inflated prices. Even religious leaders fling mud at one another before being caught wallowing in moral turpitude, all the while professing to lead us to salvation.

Of course, warriors aren't immune to the temptations of dishonor. Generals and admirals have been party to all kinds of conspiracies, from smuggling arms to seizing power from those they are sworn to serve and defend. We find police officials, high and low, in league with the foulest of criminals. And vice isn't the province of the powerful alone; corruption finds its way into all levels of service, military and civil, when those attending to the public trust do not first attend to their own honor.

So what do we do to make the world a better and more honorable place? Shall we mount a holy crusade to expose and vilify those around us who are less ethical, less moral than we? Shall we crucify our peers any time we discover a hint of dishonesty or conflict of interest? Well maybe we should in some cases, but we need to examine the circumstances before acting rashly.

As warriors, we have a moral obligation to attend to the cause of honor. We have a responsibility to see that justice is served in any area in which our duty leads us. But right and wrong are not so black and white as the supposed moral paragons would have us believe. And the call of honor does not entitle us to meddle in areas in which we have no business, responsibility, or direct knowledge.

Our society is addicted to the scent of scandal, and most people eagerly assume the worst when a questionable situation begins to surface. Too often they leap to attack others they think have violated some point of law or morality, without knowing the facts. Of course, when we have direct knowledge of injustice, we have a responsibility to speak out, to right any wrong within our sphere of control. But blindly condemning someone in our own court of opinion isn't justice, it's defamation.

Jesus once faced scribes and pharisees who wanted him to condemn a woman they caught in adultery. He said, "let he among you who is without sin be the first to cast a stone at her." Indeed, as more and more of life passes behind me, I find myself growing ever less eager to throw stones at others. There are professionals in our society who carry the responsibilities to investigate, charge, judge, and sentence. I gladly leave the burdens of condemnation to them.

But once again we're left with the question of what we can do to make society more honorable. Well, just as charity begins at home, so does honor.

We must attend to our own honor first. If we all do our best to meet our obligations—if we find the courage to see that justice is served in all our dealings—then not only will our own small spheres of influence be cleaner, but others around us may be inspired by our example. So the challenge we all must face is how to put our honor to work.

PUTTING HONOR TO WORK

As a warrior, you are growing stronger, more educated, and more powerful than most of your non-warrior associates. But these treasures don't come without a price. Strength breeds power, and as an emergent leader you assume the responsibility to lead ethically, to apply your power justly and benevolently. You must put your personal honor to work for the good of society.

In the last chapter you learned to recognize issues of honor and separate them from challenges of face. Now it's time to take up your responsibilities and act. But to apply honor to situations in your own life, you must understand how it factors in the following key issues:

- Truthfulness
- Courtesy
- Restraint
- Loyalty
- Service

TRUTHFULNESS

In the absence of any positive commandment against bearing false witness, lying was not condemned as sin, but simply denounced as weakness, and, as such, highly dishonorable.

From *Bushido: The Soul of Japan*
(Nitobe, 1899, pp. 70-71)

Honesty is the virtue most often associated with honor. Even non-warriors, those who don't really understand the foundations of honor, sense a dishonest man is a dishonorable one, though they may not be able to explain exactly why.

Truthfulness is rooted in the foundations of honor, most notably, obligation. We are obliged to be truthful. Others place their trust in our words, and that trust obligates us to be truthful with them. Furthermore, when others act on our word, the information we've offered must be correct. Otherwise, calamity may befall those who've put their trust in us, and that would be an injustice.

Truthfulness is a crucially important virtue for warriors. When lives depend on the accuracy of strategic and tactical information, leaders can't tolerate even the slightest suspicion that the warrior reporting a situation may be lying to cover his own mistakes or to protect his own interests. But the strongest element binding truthfulness to honor is courage.

"Even when you are quietly seated, not the roughest ruffian can dare make onset on your person."

The *samurai* were quick to realize that honesty requires, above all, courage. Bravery was a central theme guiding these warriors, and they intuitively understood that lying wasn't so much an act of immorality as it was one of cowardice.

When people lie, it's usually out of fear—fear of the consequences of others knowing the truth. A man lies to his boss because he's afraid of his superior's reaction to discovering his failure to meet a deadline or to fulfill some other responsibility. He lies to the IRS because he's afraid of how much money the government will take from him. He even lies to his wife because he's afraid of how she would react if she knew he really didn't have to work late but chose to have a drink with the boys instead of coming home to supper.

All of these lies, big and small, are acts of cowardice and are dishonorable. Therefore, truthfulness is clearly an issue of honor, as is courtesy.

COURTESY

The end of all etiquette is to so cultivate your mind that even when you are quietly seated, not the roughest ruffian can dare make onset on your person.

An anonymous adage from the Ogasawara school of classical Japanese etiquette (Nitobe, 1899, p. 54)

Isn't it interesting how when certain members of our society reach high station, they seem to think it's perfectly all right to treat people in lesser positions rudely? I see it every day—businessmen abusing waiters, doctors and lawyers condescending to store clerks as if they were idiots—and I know first hand how it feels.

I grew up in a blue-colar suburb of Detroit. My father made it clear to me from as early as I can remember that I would go to college; I was to work with my mind instead of my hands as he did. But Dad made it just as clear that he didn't have the money to give me a free ride, and with my mediocre high school grades, there was no scholarship available. I soon discovered what working for a living while going to school was all about.

Over the next several years I worked all kinds of menial jobs, from manning a dormitory switchboard to flipping burgers. I don't think a day went by during this period that someone didn't treat me as if I was a dullard or beneath their social standing.

One day while working as a gas station attendant, I waited on a sports car full of well dressed college girls. They giggled and whispered as I pumped their gas and cleaned the windshield. When I counted out change for the driver's fifty, she turned to her girlfriends and said, "Oh, so he can count."

Even after I had finished several years of college, less educated people for whom I worked still treated me as if I was dull. You see, the fact they had financial power over me seemed to give them the prerogative to assume they were socially and personally superior, just as the businessmen, doctors, and lawyers I mentioned above seemed to believe. Of course, now I have some degree of education and status, so it's my turn to lord over those who serve me, right? Wrong!

Throughout history, warriors have risen to the top castes of nearly every culture. Historians often attribute this phenomenon to the fact that since warriors bear the arms of society, non-warriors can't effectively challenge their claims to power. While that may be true, the fact remains that warriors, by the very nature of their calling, tend to make themselves physically, mentally, and spiritually superior to the rest of society. As a result, even in egalitarian cultures, they tend to rise to the top, just as cream floats to the top of milk.

The personal superiority and upward mobility of warriorship brings with them an obligation: warriors are compelled to be courteous to their subordinates and non-warrior lessers as a matter of honor. It's too easy for a powerful man or woman to abuse those less capable. A true warrior would no more demean a non-warrior to demonstrate his power than a grown man would slap a child just to demonstrate his strength. Either action would be grotesquely dishonorable.

Nowhere is the honor of warrior courtesy more graphically demonstrated than in the classical martial arts. Spend time in any traditional school and you'll quickly observe that the most humble, patient, and courteous members are those most senior. Courtesy, like any other aspect of martial training, is a discipline that demands daily practice to master. It's an advanced art, a key element of warrior training. And like other martial disciplines, practicing courtesy strengthens the mind and spirit, contributing with the other elements of training to eventually produce *zanshin*.

Indeed, even when quietly seated, the master of courtesy needn't worry about being accosted by even the roughest ruffian.

RESTRAINT

> *The power we learn is awesome, and it carries with it an awesome responsibility which cannot be taken lightly. Remember, if you harm someone, you will have to answer for it—and live with what you have done.*
>
> Taekwondo Master Richard Chun
> (1982, p. 20)

As men and women of power are expected to treat people in lesser positions courteously, warriors have a solemn obligation to restrain themselves from tyrannizing and assaulting weaker members of society.

Historians and fiction writers have made a great deal of the *samurai* privilege of *kirisute gomen*, or "killing and going away."

That was the legal right each warrior had to kill a disrespectful commoner on the spot. This privilege, acknowledged for centuries, was codified in Article XLV in the laws of *Shogun* Tokugawa Ieyasu, which read:

> *The* bushi *(warriors) are the masters of the four classes. Agriculturists, artisans, and merchants may not behave in a rude manner towards* bushi. *The term for a rude man is "other-than-expected fellow;" and a* bushi *is not to be interfered with in cutting down a fellow who has behaved to him in a manner other than is expected (Draeger, 1969, p.84).*

Indeed, *samurai* had the legal right to summarily execute disrespectful members of the lower classes, but in fact, they rarely exercised it. *Bushido,** their rigid code of ethics, taught them that benevolence and self control were virtuous elements of honor. Indeed, it was the *samurai* warrior's sense of restraint and honor that protected the commoners of feudal Japan.

Today, warriors are still dangerous people. We are stronger and faster than our docile, sedentary peers, and we still handle most of society's weapons. But most importantly, warriors are trained to be violent; we're hardened to the pain and emotional trauma of fighting.

Faced with a physical attack, most men and nearly all women, crumble in shock. But it's different for a warrior. Once a confrontation turns physical, the warrior's, body, mind, and spirit fuse into an unthinking, unfeeling weapon. At this point, there are no considerations of honor, no thought of consequences. In this

*Some historians assert that *Bushido* (*Way* of the Warrior), was an ethical concept manufactured by rulers of the Tokugawa Shogunate (1600-1868) to keep their warriors under control. Others point to the book, *Bushido: The Soul of Japan*, written by Nitobe in 1899, and charge he created the concept to romanticize the *samurai* era. The fact is, warrior ethics evolved in Japan many centuries before either of these examples and was first known as *kyuba no michi* (way of the bow and horse) during the reign of *Shogun* Yoritomo Minamoto in the late twelfth century.

mode, the warrior will only think of destroying his enemy. So it's vitally important he doesn't cross this threshold unless he's physically threatened. Restraint is still a crucial component of honor.

LOYALTY

Be loyal to your king.
Be obedient to your parents.
Be honorable to your friends.
Never retreat in battle.
Make a just kill.

Hwarang Warrior's Code of Conduct
Korea, c. 6th century
(Choi, 1972, p. 17)

Loyalty is one of the strongest expressions of *giri*. It grows from an obligation to repay a great service—specifically, an extended, personal sacrifice someone makes for you. Filial duty is a central theme in all warrior societies. Men and women of honor learn to recognize whenever they carry someone's *on*, and who can deny the great burden of debt we owe our parents?

All of our parents could have lived more comfortably had they not provided for us. They fed and clothed us and saw that we were educated. But most importantly, they instilled in us whatever ambition and ethical foundations we carry as adults. Those are priceless gifts.

Too often children today forget the sacrifices their parents made for them. This breakdown in the cycle of obligation and filial loyalty is a central factor in the erosion of the family and society at large.

Recently, I saw a teenage boy confront his father in public. "Leave me alone, old man," he said, "I don't owe you anything." It took all the restraint I could muster to keep from walking over and tossing that young ingrate into a nearby fountain. But some families are in worse straits.

Years ago, I knew a family in which the grown sons lived at home and physically abused their parents. In and out of prison, these young men took what they wanted from the household and provided no support. You might conclude that since they obviously had no moral character, the parents were to blame, having failed to provide them any foundation. Perhaps that was true, and if so, the parents failed in their obligations. But everyone is responsible for his own conduct, and these sons were reprehensible. Indeed, dishonor breeds dishonor. The only consolation in this sad example is that this was not a warrior family.

Loyalty is the most respected virtue among warriors. Men and women of honor are loyal to their parents, their superiors, and

Warriors are dangerous people. Therefore, restraint is a crucial component of honor.

their country. Being disloyal can be one of the darkest stains on a warrior's honor.

I once worked for an Air Force colonel who was the classical warrior leader. He demanded the best from his people, expecting them to excel in dedication and performance.

Other officers in the headquarters where we worked feared and avoided this powerful and influential taskmaster, and it was no secret they were glad they didn't have to work for him. He was a hard man, driving his subordinates mercilessly and rarely giving praise. Even his physical appearance was imposing; he stood more than six feet tall, weighed over 200 pounds, and shaved his head. What's more, he had an explosive temper and a stare that could pierce armor plate.

But the other officers didn't realize that this colonel was actually one of the best men they could ever hope to work for. Sure, he was abrasive and demanding, but he was also loyal and protective. He took care of the people who worked hard for him, always pushing them before the commander for recognition and awards. And despite his hard exterior, he was forgiving too.

I made a lot of mistakes while learning the ins and outs of military staff work. The colonel didn't miss a single flaw, and he never hesitated to express his dissatisfaction to me. He'd rant and yell; sometimes he was so angry I thought he was close to a stroke. But I soon learned that despite his explosive episodes, he was solidly behind my career. He took extra pains to write me the best performance reports, and he was always first to champion my causes before the brass. Yes, the colonel was loyal to his staff, and there was no sin he wouldn't forgive—none save one.

During the period I worked for the colonel, there was a gifted young lieutenant who served with us on his staff. This young lady had a natural talent for cutting to the heart of any murky issue. She was an excellent writer and a spellbinding speaker. The woman seemed blessed for future leadership, and we all knew the colonel was carefully guiding her career in that direction. Unfortunately, she didn't understand the importance of loyalty.

One day she and the colonel disagreed on how to approach a particularly delicate project. In traditional fashion, the colonel listened patiently as she explained her proposal, then firmly said, "Lieutenant, I understand your position, but I disagree. Since I'm the boss, we'll do it my way." The lieutenant sullenly agreed to use the colonel's approach, but secretly, she had other plans.

Later that afternoon the lieutenant met with staffers from another agency. Despite the colonel's orders, she started them on the project according to her original plan. Even worse (and quite foolishly), she casually mentioned the colonel's concerns and ridiculed them. Unfortunately for her, one of the senior staffers from the other agency had more integrity than she did, and he notified the colonel of what she was up to.

Bad news travels fast in any organization, and by the next morning we all knew the lieutenant was in trouble. The colonel called her in, and we all braced for the verbal barrage we had grown so accustomed to hearing through his closed door. But the office was unusually silent.

After a while the lieutenant came out, flushed and teary eyed. There had been no yelling, no incriminations. After having her verify what he had been told, the colonel simply fired her from his staff. The lieutenant was quietly reassigned to an unimportant job, working for a major in a directorate led by an uninfluential colonel about to retire. Her career ground to a halt, and the last time I talked to her she was considering leaving the Air Force.

In most respects, the lieutenant had been an outstanding officer. She had all the gifts necessary for rapid advancement, and she had the luck to find herself working for a powerful boss who recognized her talents. But like a heroine in a Greek play, this bright young lady had a tragic flaw; she was disloyal.

Our colonel was a good leader, and he forgave mistakes stemming from inexperience. But like the classical warrior he was, he refused to tolerate disloyalty because it reflected not on her ability—he could have corrected that—but on her character. The talented young lieutenant lacked a sense of honor.

Loyalty is an unconditional requirement in any warrior society. Past cultures considered treachery so serious a crime that entire families were punished, fearing the character flaw might be a genetic trait. When *samurai* were caught in betrayal, they and their whole families were ordered to commit *seppuku*, ritual suicide. In Europe, traitorous knights were executed, their lands confiscated, and their descendants banned from any claims of heraldry or nobility. Treacherous American Indian warriors were killed, and all their possessions were taken and distributed amongst the rest of the tribe, leaving their families to perish from hunger or exposure. Given this heritage, it's no surprise that traditional martial artists still consider loyalty a crucial ingredient of warrior honor.

We live in a cash-and-carry society. We buy goods and services, and once we've paid the vendor, we feel no further obligation to him. But martial training is different. Yes, you pay fees to support the training hall, but your traditional instructor is not selling a service. He's giving you part of his life.

Qualified instructors devote many years to mastering their craft. They spend countless hours in training halls, usually following days spent at full-time occupations. They pay for their expertise with sweat, blood, and even broken bones. In fact, a classical warrior is probably the most highly trained professional in our society. So how do you think your monthly pittance of dues can pay for his wisdom? It can't. You see, the money you provide doesn't pay for your training, it only supports your instructor and the school, making it possible for him to offer you his art.

The martial arts teacher-student relationship is one of ever-growing *giri*. The instructor gives the student more than he can ever hope to repay. Subsequently, the student assumes an incredible *on*, and the only way he can bear this burden is through his unwavering obedience, respect, and loyalty.

So if you're looking for classical warrior training, you must be very selective when joining a training hall. If the instructor is qualified and you are honorable, you're making a life-long commitment. In essence, you're entering a service.

SERVICE

The long, gray line has never failed us. Were you to do so, a million ghosts in olive drab, in brown khaki, in blue and gray, would rise from their white crosses, thundering those magic words: Duty, honor, country.

From Douglas MacArthur's address to cadets at the U.S. Military Academy at West Point, May 12, 1962

Throughout this chapter I've emphasized that warriors are superior people, and these blessings of superiority bring with them certain costs. Nothing in life is free. Any gift, free as it may seem, always brings with it an *on*, a burden to repay. And the burden warriors bear for their gifts of superiority is the *giri* to serve society.

It's no coincidence that the various branches of the armed forces are referred to as "military services," for service is the ultimate obligation of warriorship. Actually, warriors serve in many professional capacities; soldiers, seamen, police, boarder and security guards, and even spies are warriors in traditional and honorable forms of service. As such, they study and practice martial skills, and they are all bound by the tenets of honor.

But what if you're not engaged in some traditional form of warrior service? What if you're employed as a cobbler, merchant, or construction worker—does that relieve you of the obligation to serve? Absolutely not. If you study, practice, and live the martial *Way*, your *giri* is too great to walk away. You owe your parents, friends, coworkers and superiors. You owe your community and your country. And of course, you owe the other students in your training hall and your instructor.

There are many ways to serve. Some warriors serve their communities in volunteer efforts and charities. Others are politically active, sensing a need to guide their districts in better directions. Of course, instructors and senior students teach, fulfilling their *giri* by guiding others in the ways of warriorship. If nothing else, you can serve society in your occupation by providing the very best product or service possible. After all, the pursuit of excellence is the essence of the martial *Way*.

Yes, if you are a warrior and not just a martial artist, you'll find ways to fulfill your *giri*.

HONOR IN THE FOG OF LIFE

Now that you understand how important these issues of honor are, let me remind you that honor is not black and white. In every situation, the warrior must determine the most honorable course of action by weighing the three keystones: obligation, justice, and courage. There are no static, prescribed commandments binding him. What may be honorable in one instance, would be unthinkable in another.

Truthfulness isn't always honorable. If armed bandits heard your father had come into some money and came to your house hoping to rob him, you wouldn't tell them you expected him home shortly. Likewise, prisoners of war often lie to their interrogators to conceal information from the enemy. Of course, a moralist may insist you could avoid lying simply by refusing to answer, but that isn't always possible. Both of these examples show us cases in which warriors may not be able to remain silent but have greater obligations than to be truthful.

Courtesy and restraint are honorable virtues in a peaceful society, but place the warrior in his native environment, the field of battle, and these disciplines contradict his very purpose. Once a warrior faces his enemy, his survival often rests with his ability to completely unleash his viciousness. And though courtesy to the enemy is honorable in some circumstances, rudeness is usually more appropriate. Even loyalty and service are dishonorable in some rare cases.

Not all leaders or even martial arts instructors deserve your loyalty. Over the years I've seen every kind of martial arts scam—brown belts claiming qualifications to teach, charismatic instructors leading cults and communes, even schools that sell lifetime contracts, then brutalize students to drive them out to make room for others. Even technically competent masters can be dishonorable.

A few years ago a friend of mine, let's call him Jim, was under a great deal of stress as a result of problems in his relationship with his instructor, a widely recognized master. Jim was one of the master's key black belts. He was both skillful and knowledgeable, testifying to the quality of training he had received. Like his fellow black belts, Jim was well aware of the value of his training, and he felt a tremendous obligation to his teacher. Unfortunately, the master didn't feel obligated to respect his students.

As Jim ascended the ranks of his organization, he became more involved in administering its operations. As he did, he learned of many personal and financial improprieties the master routinely engaged in.

The master ran several related businesses, and he often used organizational money to fund travel for his other enterprises and even for personal travel. He compelled students to work for him in the other businesses without pay, promising them preferential consideration at testing. In fact, this man exploited his students in every imaginable way and even cheated them in financial transactions.

Jim was torn in conflict. He knew his master was one of the best teachers in the country, and he felt a tremendous burden of debt for the high-quality training he had received. But he was constantly ashamed of the man's unethical behavior. To his embarrassment, he often found himself making excuses to his own students when they saw the blatant misconduct of the master. Yet year after year, Jim remained loyal.

As a kind of personal confessor, I listened to Jim's private anguish for several years. He was in a terrible position, indebted to a man without honor. As a result, the situation was taking its toll on his emotional health.

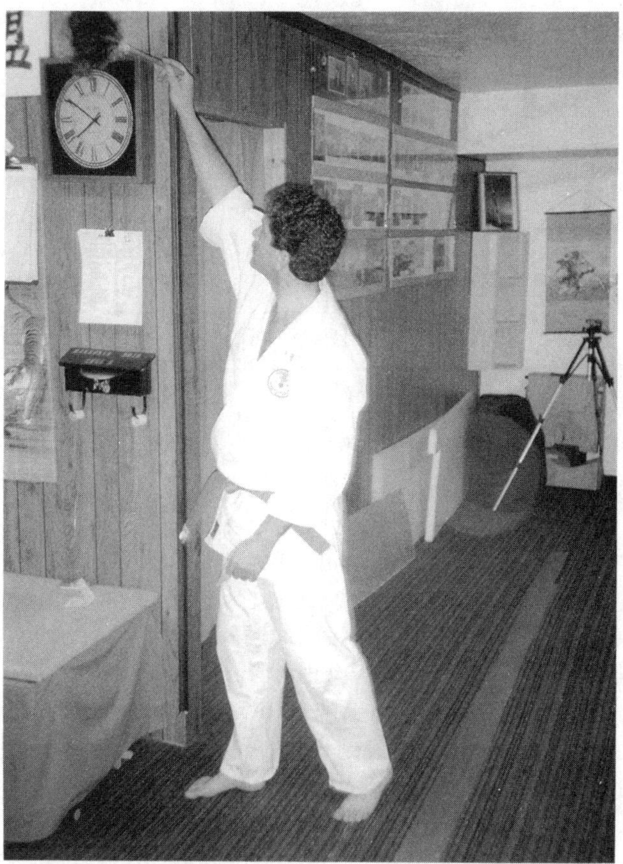

Service takes many forms. Outside the *dojo*, this man is a prominent physician.

Finally, I could stand it no longer. I sat Jim down and explained that *giri* is a reciprocal obligation, a two-way street. Although he indeed carried the master's *on* for his training, the master carried his *on* for his unwavering loyalty. In making Jim a party to his dishonesty, the man had violated his trust and soiled their relationship. I believed that canceled any remaining obligation Jim had.

I urged Jim to leave that master's organization; he had to train somewhere else. I encouraged him to be courteous and respectful but firm. Jim's future, his self esteem, and even his health depended on him making a clean break.

Jim followed my advice. Today, he's working under another master, a man of honor and integrity. The black belts in his new training hall admire his skill and tell him he's lucky to have had such capable training. But he tells them they are the lucky ones. You see, Jim now carries a new *on*, a debt to the master who took him in. But Jim is happy now; he's obligated to a man of honor.

POINTS TO REMEMBER: HONOR IN ACTION

▪ Corruption finds its way into all levels of service, military and civil, when those attending to the public trust do not first attend to their own honor.

▪ We have a responsibility to see that justice is served in any area in which our duty leads us. But we must attend to our own honor first. If we all do our best to meet our obligations—if we find the courage to see that justice is served in all our dealings—then not only will our own small spheres of influence be cleaner, but others around us may be inspired by our example.

▪ As an emergent leader you assume the responsibility to lead ethically, to apply your power justly and benevolently. You must put your personal honor to work for the good of society.

▪ Truthfulness is rooted in the foundations of honor, most notably, obligation. But the strongest element binding truthfulness to honor is courage. All lies, big and small, are acts of cowardice and dishonorable.

■ The personal superiority and upward mobility of warriorship brings with them an obligation: warriors are compelled to be courteous to their subordinates and non-warrior inferiors as a matter of honor.

■ Warriors are dangerous people. Therefore, they have a solemn obligation to restrain themselves from tyrannizing and assaulting weaker members of society.

■ Loyalty is one of the strongest expressions of *giri.* It grows from an obligation to repay a great service—specifically, an extended, personal sacrifice someone makes for you. No one makes a greater sacrifice for you than your parents.

■ Loyalty is one of the strongest expressions of *giri* and the most respected virtue among warriors. Men and women of honor are loyal to their parents, their superiors, and their country. Being disloyal can be one of the darkest stains on a warrior's honor.

■ The martial arts teacher-student relationship is one of ever-growing *giri.* The instructor gives the student more than he can ever hope to repay. Subsequently, the student assumes an incredible *on*, and the only way he can bear this burden is through his unwavering obedience, respect, and loyalty.

■ The burden warriors bear for their gifts of superiority is the *giri* to serve society. There are many ways to serve. If you are a warrior and not just a martial artist, you'll find ways to fulfill your *giri.*

■ Honor isn't always black and white. There are sometimes greater obligations than to be truthful, courteous, and restrained. Even loyalty and service can be dishonorable if misapplied.

■ Not all instructors deserve loyalty. *Giri* is a reciprocal obligation, a two-way street. Although you carry your instructor's *on* for the training he provides, he carries your *on* for your unwavering loyalty. When an instructor dishonors himself and his students, that cancels their obligation to him.

Chapter 8

REVENGE AND SUICIDE: PERVERSIONS OF HONOR

We, the ronin *serving Asano Takumi no Kami, this night will break into the mansion of Kira Kotzuke no Suke to avenge our master. Please be assured that we are neither robbers nor ruffians and no harm will befall the neighboring property.*

PLACARD THE 47 *RONIN* POSTED THE NIGHT THEY AVENGED THE DEATH OF THEIR LORD (Allyn, 1970, p. 223)

A rite often associated with warriorship is the practice of taking revenge. It's a popular theme. Hundreds of books have been written and movies made celebrating underdogs who endure the cruelest of treatment only to rise up and destroy their evil oppressors.

In most of these stories, the hero is strong and noble but confronted with forces no ordinary champion could resist. He faces an evil king or an ambitious general. Honest cowboys lose their ranches to wicked cattle barons, and heroic women face all sorts of torment from powerful adversaries who take their families, property, reputations, chastity, and even force them into marriage.

The revenge plot is more popular than ever in modern drama. Today's heros face a new assortment of villains, from crime lords and crooked politicians to the system itself.

Yes, noble suffering followed by long-awaited revenge is a favorite topic in the drama of many cultures. It's not surprising. We all like to see heros take their vengeance on the wicked. We empathize. We've all felt the frustration of losing something important to someone more powerful than us, and we've all fantasized getting revenge. So we identify with those gallant heros of fiction who, after suffering so bravely, bring down the foes we can't seem to conquer in real life. We love to see the honest hero come back from defeat to crush the enemy and regain his property, reputation, and... *honor.*

Nor is it surprising that the revenge theme is so often linked with warriorship. Warriors aspire to honor, so they're often more honest, courageous, faithful—in essence, more noble—than their non-warrior peers. Add to this the superior abilities warriors command, and you can see why they so frequently find themselves in conflict with the forces of evil, both in drama and in real life.

But warrior tales often take the idea a step further than do stories of revenge carried out among commoners. Often, warriors are faced with adversaries they can't beat or situations in which they can't survive. So the next logical step, at least in the minds of some romantics, is for the warrior to make the ultimate sacrifice. He takes his own life for glory and for the sake of his noble cause.

In real life, warriors most often sacrifice themselves only when doing so would save their comrades or bring them victory. We've all heard tales of heroic soldiers falling on grenades. We've also studied naval battles in which captains sacrifice their own crippled ships ramming the enemy and air battles in which pilots crash their damaged planes in last-ditch efforts to destroy important targets. But there is another kind of sacrifice warriors are known for, one more futile, yet more striking in its audacity.

Warriors have fought to the death and even killed themselves knowing full well that doing so wouldn't bring them victory or save their colleagues. Examples of this extreme self sacrifice are seen in all cultures. In 480 B.C., 300 Spartans sacrificed themselves fighting a Persian army of many thousands at a mountain pass called Thermopylae. Likewise, in 72 and 73 A.D. a small army of Jewish Zealots withstood a siege by a 15,000-man Roman army at Masada for two years. When it finally turned out there would be no victory or escape, the remaining 960 men, women, and children took their own lives to avoid capture.

This martial fanaticism isn't unknown to American history. In 1836, a handful of Texans held the Alamo, a small Spanish mission in present day San Antonio, against a Mexican army of more than 4,000. After nearly ten days of siege, when a Mexican attack by storm seemed imminent, the 180 defenders voted unanimously to fight to the death rather than surrender.

The sacrifices these warriors made were unquestionably honorable. And we've all heard other stories about warriors and nonwarriors alike who carry out revenge or commit suicide. But let's not be too quick assume everyone carrying out acts such as these do so in honor. Indeed, revenge can be honorable, but more often it's self serving. Suicide may be noble, but more times than not, it's the act of a coward.

In this chapter you'll learn to recognize circumstances in which revenge and suicide are honorable and those in which they are not. Then you'll have the insight to weigh the cases of revenge and suicide you hear about for their basis in honor. More importantly, you'll have a weathervane to objectively ponder your own motives at times when you may be tempted to act rashly. You'll know whether your impulses are honorable or merely perversions of honor.

Remember, a noble warrior weighs his plans for their basis in honor. The pretender acts first, then justifies himself afterward.

THE FORTY-SEVEN FAITHFUL *RONIN*

Eastern history provides many examples of warriors carrying out revenge and suicide for noble causes. None, however, is more celebrated or better illustrates one ideal of warrior honor than the true story of the 47 faithful *ronin* of Ako. The story provides a classic example of how *giri*, loyalty, revenge, and suicide factor into the Japanese cultural interpretation of warrior honor.

The episode involves a chain of events that began in Edo (now Tokyo) during the Tokugawa Shogunate. The year was 1701, a hundred years after Tokugawa Ieyasu had unified the country under his sword. His descendant, Tokugawa Tsunayoshi, now ruled the islands and ensured loyalty of the *daimyo* (warlords) by the institution of *sankin kotai*, or "alternate attendance." This law required all *daimyo* to maintain residences for their families in Edo and to spend every other year in the feudal capital themselves. That way, the weak and paranoid *bakufu* administrators could ensure loyalty of the still rugged, rural *daimyo* by holding their families hostage.

Asano Takumi no Kami was one such *daimyo*. Lord of the rural province of Ako, Asano was still a warrior in the truest sense. Unfortunately, he was young and impetuous, and his crude, martial manner didn't set well with the genteel sycophants who cluttered the *shogun*'s court. When one of them insulted him, Asano drew his sword and attacked.

Asano only managed to wound his enemy, Kira Kotzuke no Suke, but it was enough to cost him his life, for drawing a sword at court was a capital offense. For his lack of restraint, the *shogun* ordered Lord Asano to commit *seppuku*, ritual disembowelment. Asano was an obedient vassal, and he ended his life later that day.

This suddenly left Asano's retainers, the *samurai* of Ako, with two problems. First, they were without their master and unemployed. This was a bad situation, for under Tokugawa rule Japan had been at peace for most of the hundred years prior, and *ronin* (masterless *samurai*) had little chance of finding work. But more seriously, since their master had been condemned for breaking the *shogun*'s law, all his retainers were honor-bound to follow him in *seppuku*. Most of them were ready to do this, for they were men of honor. But when they learned of how their lord had been duped into his fate by his enemy, Lord Kira, they knew they couldn't end their lives before taking care of business.

All *samurai* were trained in the Confucian principle, "a man should not live under the same heaven with the murderer of his leader-lord-father." Of course, *seppuku* would have taken them out from under the same heaven as Kira, but the *ronin* of Ako saw their *giri* in this situation as something more than merely to join their master in death. They concluded they had a solemn duty to avenge the death of their lord.

This would be no easy mission. All of Edo suspected the *ronin* would attempt some sort of attack, and Kira was under the *shogun*'s protection. The *bakufu* had spies everywhere. Kira, a rich man with powerful friends, had a large security force as well. So meeting in secret, the men of Ako decided to play out a ruse until they convinced the eyes and ears of Edo they weren't a threat and attention on them tapered off.

For the next two years, the 47 *ronin* of Ako went their separate ways. To the loathing amazement of Edo society, the men didn't attempt any revenge or even honor their fallen master in *seppuku*. They walked in disgrace, many taking up various non-warrior occupations. Some even left their families and became womanizers and drunks. In the eyes of the *shogun*, the other *samurai*, and even the commoners of Edo, these men had no honor and no face.

It was all an act.

By 1703 attention had shifted away from the degenerate *ronin* from Ako. So late one December night, the 47 faithful gathered one last time, then departed in a snowstorm for Kira's mansion.

They caught the compound completely unprepared. In a surprise assault followed by a short skirmish, they killed Lord Kira and everyone in his household. Then, they took Kira's head, washed it in a nearby well, and placed it as an offering on Lord Asano's grave.

That morning the 47 faithful *ronin* of Ako surrendered to *bakufu* authorities. Following fretful discussions with his councilors, the *shogun* sentenced them to death but ruled that they would be permitted to perform *seppuku* and die as warriors rather than face execution as common criminals. Within days all 47 joined their lord and entered the annals of history as Japanese national heros.

REVENGE AND THE SCALES OF HONOR

> *"What is the most beautiful thing on earth?" said Osiris to Horus. The reply was, "To avenge a parent's wrongs,"—to which a Japanese would have added, "and a master's."*
>
> From *Bushido: The Soul of Japan*
> (Nitobe, 1899, p. 126)

The story of the 47 *ronin* is a classic account of warrior revenge, and it's a rousing good tale. It has all the elements of good drama: a romantic setting, noble heros in conflict with a despicable villain, and a period of growing tension followed by an explosive climax. More importantly, the story clearly describes a martial society in decay and contrasts it with examples of warriorship at its finest.

But most significantly, the story of the 47 *ronin* provides a sterling example of warrior honor in its purest form. These men saw through the fog of law and recognized justice. They courageously fulfilled their obligations, knowing full well their actions would lead to their own destruction. Finally, these *samurai* bore no illusions about the difference between honor and face. They publicly humiliated themselves for two years hoping to get that one chance to fulfill their *giri*. These were truly men of honor.

But what of revenge today? Perhaps you've been wronged and you're wondering if avenging the injustice you've suffered would be honorable. Well, let's examine revenge in light of the foundations of honor—obligation, justice, and courage. Then, you can weigh your own case on the scales of honor.

Let's start from the bottom and look at revenge from the viewpoint of courage. Taking revenge on someone usually requires courage. Besides the probable risks involved in carrying out the act itself, you may be inviting criminal or civil penalties or even reprisals from your enemies, depending, of course, on the nature and severity of your vengeance.

But too often in today's world, those who set out for revenge do so secretly. They try to find some way to harm their enemies

In a surprise assault, the 47 faithful *ronin* of Ako killed Lord Kira and everyone in his household.

without the authorities or even the targets of their vengeance being able to confirm the source of the attack. They may vandalize property or damage their enemys' credit. I've even seen people order merchandise or magazines in their enemy's name in childish attempts to cause harm. These are the acts of cowards.

So hear this, warrior: unless you have the courage to face your enemy and act against him in the open, your revenge is fearful and dishonorable! Assuming you have this courage, let's look at your vengeance in terms of justice.

You'll insist, of course, that since your enemy wronged you, justice is on your side. Well, that's not necessarily so. Are you sure you're an objective arbiter of justice? What would your enemy say if I asked him or her whether or not you have a just cause for vengeance?

Our society provides us with both criminal and civil courts. They have the mandate to determine justice in conflicts between citizens or with the state. Of course, many conflicts don't fall within the jurisdiction of the legal system, and even when they do, there is no guarantee that justice will prevail. Consider the plight of the *ronin* of Ako—justice was clearly on their side, but the law not only protected their enemy, it actually brought about the destruction of their master. Nonetheless, you have a social obligation to seek remedy through administrative, legal, or other formal means before you resort to personal revenge.

One more point about justice: the old standard "an eye for an eye" means more than just a declaration of vengeance. It implies the avenger should do no more harm than was done in the offense for which he seeks restitution. Too often, I see people respond to some minor offense by vowing to destroy the perpetrator. Blowing your enemy's legs off for a petty grievance is a crime deserving its own retribution.

However, the main factor for weighing the honor in revenge is obligation. What obligates you to avenge a personal grievance? Nothing. All the warrior codes I've reviewed are consistent on this point. Revenge is only honorable when carried out to fulfill an obligation to someone else. In fact, Nitobe went so far as to say:

> *Though Lao-Tse taught to recompense injury with kindness, the voice of Confucius was very much louder, which taught that injury must be recompensed with justice;—and yet revenge was justified only when it was undertaken in behalf of our superiors and benefactors. One's own wrongs, including injuries done to wife and children, were to be borne and forgiven. A samurai could therefore fully sympathize with Hannibal's oath to avenge his country's wrongs, but he scorns James Hamilton for wearing in his girdle a handful of earth from his wife's grave, as an eternal incentive to avenge her wrongs on the Regent Murray (1899, pp. 80-81).*

While I agree with Nitobe in principle, I find his position a bit extreme for this day and age. Remember, his discussions of obligation and honor referred to interpretations from Japan's feudal era, a time when a wife and children were considered little more than a man's possessions. In this age of social equality, men and women are obligated to protect their families at least as much as their employers or other benefactors. I would feel completely justified in avenging injury to my wife or children. Indeed, it would be my *giri*.

But you must not miss this point: revenge is only honorable when carried out to fulfill an obligation to someone else. Otherwise, it's self serving. The 47 *ronin* didn't act because Kira's treachery put them out of work or put them in disgrace. They acted because, according to the mores of their society, they were obligated to protect their lord in life and avenge him in death. What made these men so honorable was that, failing in the first obligation, they willingly sacrificed their lives to fulfill the second.

Afterward, they all committed suicide. So now let's explore the issues of honor surrounding that act.

SUICIDE: COURAGE OR COWARDICE?

It is a brave act of valor to condemn death, but where life is more terrible than death, it is then the truest valor to dare to live.

Sir Thomas Browne (1605-1682)

The last obligation the 47 *ronin* fulfilled for Lord Asano was to follow him in death. Today, it's hard for us to understand how anyone would expect his followers to commit suicide simply because he did. It's even harder to fathom the degree of commitment these men must have felt to their lord and to a system that would obligate them to kill themselves. But we can't judge them by modern standards of social morality. To understand the *giri* of these 47 and others like them, we must see them through the lens of their own feudal society.

No one can deny this act demanded great courage, for *seppuku* is one of the most painful forms of death imaginable. But you might ask what justice this final act served. For that matter, where were the scales of justice when Asano was ordered to disembowel himself?

Once again, you must consider this episode in light of the mores of feudal Japan. As a *daimyo*, Asano was a sworn vassal to the *shogun*. He knew the laws of the Edo court, and he knew the penalty for breaking the *shogun*'s law. Although he realized he'd been duped, he also understood and accepted his obligation.

As I already explained, on learning of their lord's fate, Asano's retainers understood their obligation immediately. They were prepared to end their lives as expected, but when they learned of Kira's role, they realized their *giri* was more complicated.

But the fact they fulfilled their duty to avenge their lord didn't absolve them from the obligation to follow him in death. Nor did it reduce the gravity of what they had done; they too had broken the *shogun*'s law. Therefore, they were obligated to die on that count as well. It was only because they had conducted themselves so honorably in avenging their lord that the *shogun* was compelled to let them die nobly instead of executing them as criminals.

But how does all this relate to issues of suicide today?

Well, first, we must realize that with very few exceptions, no one in our society is obligated to kill themselves. Of course, I opened this chapter with accounts of warriors from history who chose to fulfill obligations to their nations or cultural groups by dying in futile battles. We will always see some warriors in those straits as long as man engages in war, but fortunately, most of us will never experience it.

Warriors sometimes end up as prisoners holding information that must be kept from the enemy at all costs. In these situations, they also may find themselves used as pawns against their superiors or their nations. Some courageous warriors have died to keep from being used in this manner, but once again, these cases are very rare. The fact is, it's extremely unlikely any of us will ever personally encounter a case in which a warrior or anyone else is obligated to kill himself.

As for courage, suicide is almost always the act of a coward. Unlike the 47 *ronin*, men and women who decide to end their lives today look for the easiest way out. Neither a bottle of sleeping pills nor a bullet in the head is an act of bravery. Even hanging one's self, agonizing as it may be, is usually used as a quick escape. So it's difficult to claim any honor in most cases of suicide today.

When it comes right down to it, suicide, like revenge, is never honorable except when done to fulfill an obligation to someone else. Men and women who take their lives in honor usually don't want to die; they abhor death, and they aren't looking for an escape. These people only kill themselves when doing so is the only route left to achieving an honorable objective, the only road left to victory. They die in service.

STANDARDS FOR PLANNING REVENGE AND SUICIDE

Throughout this chapter, I've given you ample information to determine when revenge and suicide are honorable and when they are perversions of honor. We've reviewed both issues from a historical perspective, mainly by examining the case of the 47 *ronin*, then we applied key factors we observed there to situations modern warriors could face.

But when I introduced this book, I emphasized it wouldn't be a collection of anecdotes or a monologue on philosophy, but instead, a step-by-step manual for applying the principles of warriorship. Therefore, I'm obligated to do more than just sermonize on these issues. I'm compelled to offer you guidelines for evaluating the merits of any plots of revenge or suicide you may be contemplating.

Revenge is a time-honored practice among warriors. But no one, not even the most rigid traditionalist, respects someone who carries out vengeance for dishonorable ends. To weigh your plans and motives for their basis in honor, take the following steps:

1. DETERMINE WHO YOUR REVENGE WILL SERVE.

Who did the target injure? Are you acting to fulfill an obligation to someone else, or are you merely serving your own selfish ends? If your vengeance won't fulfill an obligation, stop right now.

2. RECONFIRM YOUR OBLIGATION.

What obligates you to the person you believe you are serving, and what is the strength of that obligation? Is there an undeniable bond, such as filial duty to a parent, or are you exaggerating a relationship with an acquaintance to rationalize moving against someone you want to harm?

3. EXAMINE YOUR MOTIVES FOR JUSTICE.

Does whatever injury the target caused really warrant reprisal? If so, is what you intend to do an appropriate level of response?

4. EXPLORE CONVENTIONAL ALTERNATIVES TO PERSONAL REVENGE.

Do you have recourse in the civil or criminal courts? Can you take some kind of administrative action? You have a social obligation to

Seppuku, ritual disembowelment, is one of the most agonizing forms of suicide imaginable.

use whatever impartial arbiters are available to litigate your case before you personally act against your enemy.

5. FINALLY, REVIEW YOUR PLAN FOR VALOR.

Do you have the courage to face your enemy in revenge, or are you planning to snipe at him anonymously. Of course, classical strategy endorses secret planning and surprise attack, even ambush, but when all is said and done you should have the courage to own up to what you did. Your enemy, if no one else, must understand that you caused his loss and it's the direct consequence of his misdeed.

If situations that make revenge honorable are rare, then those justifying suicide are even more uncommon. Since you are reading this book right now, I dare say you aren't in such dire circumstances that would make taking your own life honorable. Nonetheless, I offer these guidelines for you to consider and apply later, should you be so unfortunate as to need them:

1. DETERMINE HOW YOUR DEATH WILL FULFILL AN OBLIGATION.

Will it serve your nation, your superiors, or protect your family, or will it simply remove you from an unpleasant situation?

2. PONDER YOUR PREDICAMENT FOR ALTERNATIVES.

Is their any way for you to fulfill your obligation or complete your mission without dying? Remember, living makes it possible for you to serve another day; your benefactors will need you then too.

3. ONCE AGAIN, EXAMINE THIS FINAL OPTION FOR VALOR.

Are you really acting courageously, or are you running from life? If you really are honorable... if there really is no other way to fulfill your obligation without embracing death... then life should appear all the more sweet. If, on the other hand, death seems to be offering a source of comfort, you'd better re-examine your motives.

In either case, revenge or suicide, you must isolate your emotions. Frustration and anger can cloud your judgment regarding the propriety of revenge. Pain and deprivation can make death seem more appealing. You must review your options objectively. Only then can you avoid perversions of honor.

POINTS TO REMEMBER: REVENGE AND SUICIDE: PERVERSIONS OF HONOR

- Revenge and suicide are themes often associated with warriorship. While revenge can be honorable, more often it's self serving. Suicide may be noble, but more times than not, it's the act of a coward.
- Taking revenge on someone requires courage. But too often in today's world, those who set out for revenge try to find some way to harm their enemies without them being able to confirm the source of the attack. Unless you have the courage to face your enemy and act against him in the open, your revenge is fearful and dishonorable!
- Before you seek revenge, ensure you have just cause. You also have a social obligation to seek remedy through administrative, legal, or other formal means before you resort to personal

revenge. Finally, if you embark on a course of revenge, you should do no more harm than was done in the offense for which you seek restitution.

■ Most importantly, revenge is only honorable when carried out to fulfill an obligation to someone else. Otherwise, it's self serving.

■ With very few exceptions, no one in our society is obligated to kill themselves. As long as man engages in war, there will always be some warriors forced to fulfill obligations to their nations or cultural groups by taking their own lives, but fortunately, most of us will never find ourselves in those straits.

■ When used as a means of escape, suicide is almost always the act of a coward. Therefore suicide, like revenge, is never honorable except when done to fulfill an obligation to someone else.

■ Honorable men and women only kill themselves when doing so is the only route left to achieve an honorable objective, the only road left to victory. They die in service.

PART III

THE *WAY* OF LIVING

Chapter 9

WARRIOR FITNESS

> *The taekwondoist must try to bring each effort to the point at which the kick is so fast it cannot be followed by the human eye. After several years of 50 to 100 kicks a day with each foot, the taekwondoist will be surprised to find that his kicks are indeed becoming very fast. He will get there only by relentless practice. It will be worth it.*
>
> CHUNG DO KWAN MASTER SON DUK SUNG (1983, p. 117)

Back in the late 1970s, martial arts was a topic of renewed attention and sometimes, hot debate. By then, we had seen several seasons of David Carradine pummeling cowboys in the popular television series, *Kung Fu*, and neighborhood bars hummed with arguments over whether martial arts could ever make any scrawny Chinese monk a match for a beefy American construction worker. In my circle of friends, this argument always seemed to drift along, and often it evolved into a quarrel about whether martial artists, particularly karate men, could beat professional boxers.

Being a brash, young black belt, I had very strong opinions on that issue, and I never hesitated to air them. "Of course karate men can beat boxers," I'd argue. "How could a boxer stand a chance? He only has two weapons—he'd never get close enough to punch us. We learn to use both our hands and feet, not to mention the knees and elbows he'd meet if he ever did get inside. Besides, boxers are trained to fight according to very restrictive rules; we aren't." I had a hundred arguments, none of which ever really convinced my drinking buddies. But soon, all the arguments were settled.

Apparently, this was a controversy that interested a lot of people beyond our neighborhood, because I soon heard that *ABC's Wide World of Sports* was about to air an exhibition match to settle the question once and for all. I was delighted. Now those guys would see what I was trying to tell them.

That Sunday afternoon we gathered in a buddy's living room in front of the television, where my friends had mustered enough beer and snacks to last out a minor siege. We tuned in just in time to see the fighters introduced and a replay of a short interview with the karate man, done a while earlier.

"I'm ready," he said. "I've been training hard, and I'm in shape. Yea, I'm ready for this fight."

But looking at him, standing bare-chested in *gi* trousers, I didn't feel so confident. He was a big man, and he looked pretty strong. But he had a noticeable layer of fat on his large frame, and his gut looked as if he'd just polished off our first six-pack. In fact, put a beer in his hand and he could have passed for one of my sedentary pals sitting there beside me.

As the camera came back to the introductions, I saw the opponent standing over in his corner—muscular, lean, and defined. He was an unknown boxer with a mediocre record but a professional nonetheless. Our karate man was introduced as a competitor on the point-tournement circuit, but I didn't recognize his name or face. I'd have rather had Chuck Norris or Bill Wallace champion my cause, but since the boxer was also an unknown, I decided this was a fair enough test.

The bell rang, and the two fighters danced out to the center of the ring. They circled warily for a few moments, each unsure of what to expect from the other. They exchanged a couple of probing jabs and the karate man poked out a reluctant kick or two. Then it happened: the karate man snapped up a solid round kick, planting his instep squarely on the side of the boxer's head. The boxer stumbled momentarily, and the camera caught the look of shock that flashed across his face.

"See?" I said, lurching to the edge of my seat. "That's what I told you would..."

But before I could launch into the lecture I had all prepared, the boxer recovered his composure and was wading straight into the karate man. Several quick punches, and the black belt went down. My buddies hooted wildly as I sat in shock whispering, "Get up. Get up!" But he didn't get up.

During the next several minutes, I sat silently as ABC gave us the replay again and again, showing us the knockout from every angle. I watched the shock waves ripple through the big man's fleshy body as he hit the canvass in slow motion. Then, I got up to leave.

"Hey, where are you going?" said my host, jolted from his victory celebration. "We've got a lot of beer and munchies to get through here."

"Yeah," another said. "I think they're going to women's volleyball next. If not, there's gotta be a game on another channel. Come on, man. Don't take this so seriously."

But I did take it seriously.

"Thanks guys, but I think I'll go to the gym."

THE GREAT SHAM OF MODERN MARTIAL ARTS

That afternoon, I realized that what many non-martial artists think about us is true—for all the hoopla about training and techniques, most martial artists can't really fight. The training they get isn't necessarily poor, nor the techniques they learn, ineffective. But most martial artists just aren't trained or conditioned to be fighters.

There are several reasons our karate man did so poorly against the boxer, and I covered some of them in part 1 of this book.* But his most glaring deficiency was his lack of appreciation for the level of physical conditioning he needed to fight a professional athlete or, for that matter, even a competent street fighter.

However, we shouldn't judge the man harshly, because what happened to him wasn't his fault. This karate man, who found himself embarrassed on nationwide television, was the victim of the great sham of modern martial arts. That is the myth that if you give the 90-pound weakling some training in the seemingly magical fighting systems from Asia, he can go out and beat up the 200-pound bully who once kicked sand in his face.

Ever since the late forties when martial arts began flooding into the West, we've been told that judo and karate "experts," no matter how small or frail, needn't worry about attacks from thugs and robbers. Women and children can fend off mashers and drunken assailants—size and strength won't matter once you have the deadly secrets of the martial arts.

Of course our karate man was no 90-pound weakling. He looked more like the proverbial 200-pound bully. Nonetheless, in terms of physical conditioning, he was a featherweight compared to any professional fighter and any serious warrior. But he thought he was in good enough shape. He believed, like most martial artists, that his techniques would carry him through... that his Asian secrets would be the great leveler that would cancel any disadvantage he might have in physical conditioning. Well, he was wrong.

Most of the stories you've heard about timid, little martial artists beating up big street fighters are exaggerated. Of course, as in any myth, there is an element of truth to that idea. With *proper*

---

*I doubt this man trained as warriors train, as I encouraged in Chapter 3. And what little I saw of him in the short fight showed poor tactical preparation, one of the topics of Chapter 4.

training and conditioning small men, women, and even children can indeed better defend themselves against dangerous assailants. But don't ever let anyone tell you that size and strength don't matter. They do.

There are stories you can believe. Those are the stories about members of elite military forces, such as Green Berets or Navy SEALs, who get into bar fights and stack their attackers like cord wood. These guys are well trained martial artists, but they have no illusions about technique making up for fitness. They know the stronger, faster, more agile, and more durable they are, the better their odds of survival in combat. So they condition themselves relentlessly. You see, despite what I just said, and despite the fact that they practice martial arts, they aren't really martial artists. They're warriors, and they understand the need for warrior fitness. So should you.

This chapter will teach you about warrior fitness. It will describe the qualities of fitness and teach you how to acquire them. You'll learn about body types and different kinds of muscle tissue, and you'll discover how to develop the three components of conditioning. Finally, you'll learn a few basics about good nutrition and how to control your weight. Once you understand what proper conditioning entails, you'll be one step farther from being a martial artist and one step closer to warriorship.

THE QUALITIES OF WARRIOR FITNESS

The sporting world has many fine athletes playing a wide range of games. To reach world-class level in any of these contests, competitors have to achieve a degree of conditioning far beyond what most ordinary men and women can even imagine. And champions of the various sports are the most highly conditioned athletes in the world. But the definitions of what physical fitness is differs dramatically from game to game.

A football player, for instance, trains for power, ruggedness, and quick acceleration, but he lacks the stamina of a distance runner or the grace and fine motor skills of a tennis player. Basketball players have remarkable jumping ability and hand-eye coordination, but they don't have the strength or agility that gymnasts command. I could go on, but the point is, athletes train to develop specific physical capabilities, determined by the demands of their chosen sports.

Warriorship too requires development of a precise set of physical qualities. Therefore, before you can set out to get yourself into condition, you must identify exactly what warrior fitness is. Of course, the kind of conditioning required differs somewhat from one martial art to the next and between different body types as well. I'll address that later. But for now, accept the fact that generally, warriorship demands development of the following five interrelated, physical attributes: power, speed, endurance, agility, and coordination.

The amount of force you can direct against a target is determined by your size, strength, and speed.

1. POWER.

Power is an essential ingredient in any form of combat. This is most evident, of course, in hard styles that rely on forceful movements, but it's important in soft styles as well, despite what some people claim.

But notice, I didn't say strength. I specifically chose the word "power," and I'm using it the way a hard stylist would define it—that is, in terms of the ability to exert force, of which strength is only one component.

You see, the ability to strike with force isn't determined by strength alone. It actually depends on how much mass you have and how quickly you can accelerate that mass into a target. The amount of mass you can employ in any movement is determined by your body weight and, if you're planted, how strongly you can lever between the ground or some other solid foundation and the target. How quickly you can move that mass against the target is a function of your strength and flexibility.

If all this sounds confusing, just remember: the amount of power you can generate is determined by your size, strength, and speed. Of course, there isn't too much you can do about your size. So you'll want to follow a conditioning program that will develop your strength and speed.

2. SPEED.

Speed is an essential quality, and every good fighter can be extremely fast when he or she needs to be. But the need for speed goes much farther than tactical applications such as maneuver or evasion. As I said above, speed is a key component of power. Since the ability to exert force is determined by how fast you can move mass, you can make up for having less mass than your opponent by having more speed. In other words, a well-conditioned, small fighter can hit just as hard as a slow-moving giant (or even harder) with twice the strength and mass.

Conditioning for speed involves building strength and flexibility and learning to relax the antagonistic muscles, those counterproductive to motion in the direction desired, during performance of any technique.* Flexibility and relaxation are extremely important, because you want the least resistance possible to slow down the desired action. But strength is also important, specifically the development of "fast-twitch" muscle fibers. I'll explain that shortly.

3. STAMINA.

Stamina is an important requirement in most sporting events, and it's an essential quality in warriorship as well. Although most real fights last only a few seconds, you have to know you can last out the long ones if necessary. Furthermore, serious warriors often study field skills and a host of other disciplines, all of which demand stamina. In fact, nearly all the physical training warriors undergo, in and out of the training hall, requires stamina.

Stamina training concentrates on two functions: aerobic conditioning and muscular endurance. Building muscular endurance involves conditioning the muscles, specifically the "slow-twitch" fibers, to perform without fail for long periods of time. Once again, relaxation is important, as is breath control, but I covered those topics in Chapter 5 so I won't belabor them here. In this chapter, I'll teach you how to train your muscles for endurance and build your aerobic capacity.

4. AGILITY.

Agility is the ability to move quickly and easily. An agile fighter starts and stops quickly and changes direction with grace and ease.

*I explained how important relaxation is and how to develop it in Chapter 5.

It's an enviable quality, one essential for effective technical execution and tactical maneuver.

Developing agility is a matter of cultivating the proper balance of strength, flexibility, and relaxation. Your body has to be flexible and relaxed to move quickly, especially in respect to sudden acceleration and maneuver, but what many people don't realize is that strength is an essential ingredient as well. If you don't believe me, then just watch how clumsy an out-of-shape fighter is or even a conditioned warrior once he's tired. Agility is the product of nimble, relaxed, power.

5. COORDINATION.

Coordination is the single most important physical quality required in warriorship. It's simply the ability to perform required movements smoothly, powerfully, and gracefully. Well, it may be simple to say, but perfect coordination is that elusive quality we all envy and pursue throughout our warrior careers. A warrior's level of coordination is the measure of his skill, and one's command of coordination is a mark of technical mastery.

In essence, coordination is technical agility, and it requires development of all the previously mentioned components of fitness. The warrior must be strong, flexible, and relaxed to achieve the necessary speed and agility, and he must have the stamina to maintain them. So to achieve a high degree of coordination, you must develop all the qualities of fitness. But more than that, you must train your body to perform your given art. You must develop the neuromuscular pathways to perform the complex techniques demanded of you. That is to say, you must teach your muscles precisely how to move.

Therefore, the single best conditioning program for any given activity is the activity itself, and that includes conditioning your body to perform martial arts. The best way for a hard stylist to acquire speed and power in his punches is to practice punches relentlessly. The best way for a judo player to develop the muscular endurance required for long, hard *randori* is to *randori* long and hard, day in, day out. A taekwondo stylist can achieve better leg conditioning doing a few hundred kicks each day than he can by doing any number of other leg exercises. The bottom line is this: those long hours you spend in the training hall in hard, serious practice will be your most productive act toward achieving warrior fitness.

But just practicing your martial art won't get you to your full fitness potential. You see, not all martial arts lead to balanced physical conditioning. Some help you develop great strength while doing little for your flexibility. Others focus on supple grace but neglect to develop the strength and endurance that would help make you effective in a real fight. And even if your art does offer a balanced program, you've probably discovered that no matter how hard you train, some aspect of your physical conditioning always seems to lag behind.

The answer to this dilemma is supplemental physical training. There are specific exercise programs that can help you build your strength, stamina, and flexibility. They won't replace your martial arts training; they'll complement and enhance it. Properly tailored supplemental training will improve your general health and fitness while providing your techniques a source of strength and agility that non-warrior martial artists rarely manage to tap.

Yes, there is more every warrior needs to know about conditioning and fitness than just to practice hard every day. But before you can embark on an effective supplemental training program, you have to know what kind of training your body needs. You need to understand the roles different body types and different kinds of muscle fiber play in your potential capabilities. Then you'll realize why you always seem to progress quickly in some areas but lag behind in others. Given this knowledge, you can tailor your own conditioning program to best achieve your potential. So let's take a moment to discuss...

BODY TYPES AND MUSCLE PHYSIOLOGY

Around 1940, a psychologist named William H. Sheldon conducted a study attempting to correlate behavioral traits to certain body types. While the conclusions he offered in his 1942 book, *The Varieties of Temperament*, and several later publications, have fallen in disfavor in most behavioral science circles, his system of body type classification, or "somatic typing," has become a helpful tool for planning physical conditioning programs.

Sheldon identified three main somatic types: *endomorph*, *ectomorph*, and *mesomorph*. Endomorphs are people whose bodies tend to be round and soft, and they always seem to be overweight. Ectomorphs, on the other hand, have long, angular bodies. They tend to be tall and skinny, with slender, even fragile bones. Mesomorphs are what we all long to be. These people are medium build, muscular, and well defined. They are strong, agile, and tend to be natural athletes.

Building on Sheldon's work, physiologists have observed other characteristics common to the three somatic types. Not only are endomorphs typically soft and overweight, but they tend to lack strength and endurance as well. Ectomorphic people usually aren't very strong either, but they're often blessed with great endurance. What strength they do possess is usually concentrated in their lower bodies. A mesomorph's strength, on the other hand, is usually well balanced between his upper and lower body, but it tends to be of the short-burst variety, rather than of the endurance type.

Actually, very few people fit cleanly into one of these classifications. More often, an individual will tend towards one somatic type but exhibit traits of one or more of the others. I, for instance, am ectomorphic; I'm tall and lean with very slender bones. But I lack the endurance of the classic ectomorph and instead have the upper body strength more common to mesomorphs. You may have some other combination of physical traits. Perhaps you have an endomorphic body with the strength of a mesomorph. Or, if you're lucky, you're a mesomorph with ectomorphic endurance. Whatever the combination, the important thing to understand is the better you know your natural attributes, the better you can tailor your own conditioning program to capitalize on your strengths and reduce your weaknesses. But before we begin planning fitness routines, you need to know a little bit about muscle physiology.

Not all muscles are the same. Of course, there are voluntary muscles, such as the skeletal muscles that move us about, and there are involuntary muscles, such as those controlling digestive functions. But even among skeletal muscles, fibers differ from one part of your body to another and from one person to the next.

All our skeletal muscles are made up of some combination of "fast-twitch" and "slow-twitch" fibers (Fox, 1979, p. 98). Fast-twitch muscle fibers respond quickly to command, and they exert greater strength in contraction than do slow-twitch fibers. When exercised regularly, they grow in cross-sectional area—said more simply, they get bigger—and as they do, they get even stronger and quicker. The drawback of fast-twitch muscle fibers is they tire quickly. They lack endurance.

Slow-twitch fibers respond more slowly to command. They lack the strength that fast-twitch fibers possess, and they don't get much stronger or larger with exercise. However, the advantage slow-twitch fibers do have is great endurance. Although they don't respond as quickly or powerfully, slow-twitch muscle fibers keep on performing long after fast-twitch fibers have been exhausted.

The various muscles throughout our bodies are made up of differing combinations of fast- and slow-twitch fibers. For instance, many men have high concentrations of fast-twitch fibers in their upper arms and thighs, and these muscles grow larger and stronger with exercise. But we all have slow-twitch fibers in our jaw muscles. That's good; we need the ability to chew for long periods without tiring. We don't need quick-responding muscles there, and we certainly don't want our facial muscles to grow large with exercise.*

If you compare muscular composition between different people, you'll find differing combinations of fast- and slow-twitch muscle fibers. Look at Arnold Schwarzenegger. It's immediately apparent that his muscles have very high percentages of fast-twitch fiber. But examine the typical marathon runner and you see the classic traits of small, high-endurance, slow-twitch muscles.

These comparisons directly apply to somatic typing. Schwarzenegger is an arch-typical mesomorph. Successful distance runners are invariably ectomorphs. You may not want to hear this, but our strength and endurance potentials are, to a considerable extent, predetermined. We have only limited control.

Although it's been debated, most physiologists now agree that the ratio of fast- and slow-twitch muscle fibers each of us carries is genetically predetermined. Furthermore, fast-twitch fibers respond very little to endurance training, and slow-twitch fibers don't get much stronger or larger no matter how much strength training you put them through (McArdle, Katch and Katch, 1986, p. 388). That means, if you're a classic mesomorph, you have little chance of becoming a champion distance runner no matter how hard you work at it. And try as we might, ectomorphs like me will never look like Arnold Schwarzenegger. But there is hope, particularly for warriors.

Some physiologists believe they've identified a third kind of muscle fiber which they call "fast-twitch, fatigue-resistant." These fibers grow in strength (though not in size) like their fast-twitch cousins, but like slow-twitch fibers, they don't tire nearly as quickly. What's encouraging about this type of muscle is it responds to both kinds of fitness training: strength and endurance. (Vander, Sherman, and Luciano, 1980, pp. 237-240)

*You may have heard about the great force our jaws exert in biting, but this strength is due more to mechanical leverage than muscular strength.

This kind of muscle tissue seems ideal for warriors since we're more interested in these two elements of performance than we are in looking pretty. Either way, we shouldn't worry too much about what somatic type or which muscle fibers we possess; what we are is what we are. Each of us has some combination of the three types of fiber. If our muscles are composed of predominantly one kind, we should train to take advantage of those strengths, but we also want to ensure the other fibers are conditioned to their

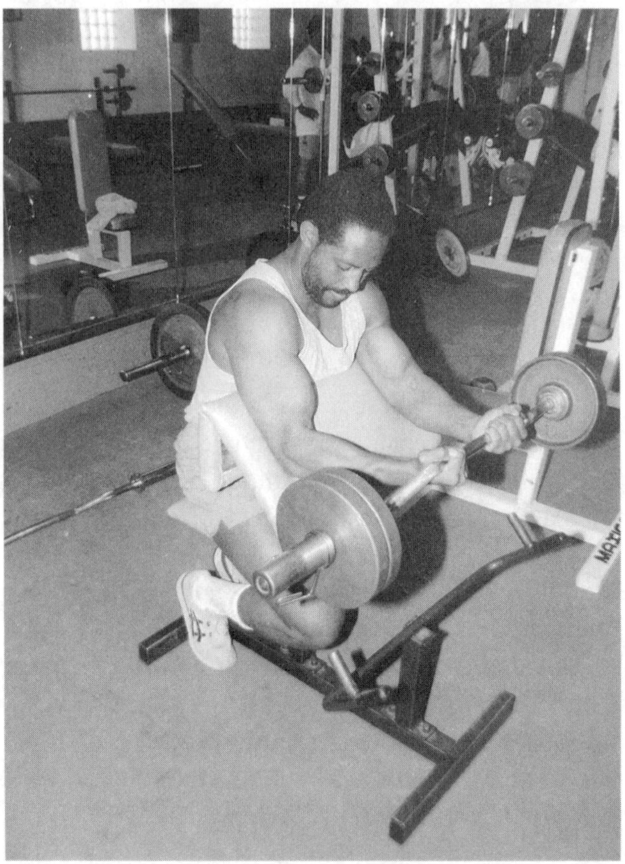

Weight training is one of the most effective ways to develop muscular strength and endurance.

maximum, so we can enjoy as much of the other qualities of fitness as we can. Warriors always train for balance.

There's one more area I want to address before we move on to specific conditioning programs: the endomorph. Descriptions of these round, soft individuals, lacking both strength and stamina, make them sound hopeless, at least in terms of warriorship. Sheldon went on to associate "visceral" behavioral traits to them; he said their lives revolve around comfort, pleasure, and satisfying their physical desires—particularly, regarding food.

But one of the reasons Sheldon's conclusions were questioned, is that some experts weren't convinced he established the correct cause and effect relationship in his observations. He believed endomorphic tendencies are genetically predetermined, and these folks exhibit their lazy, self-indulgent behaviors as a result of their endomorphism. I'm more inclined to believe the behavioral patterns were learned first, and the endomorphic body type resulted as an effect of those lazy habits. Our muscular physiology may be genetically predetermined, and some people may be more prone to obesity than others, but take an endomorph and teach him fitness-oriented behaviors and he may discover he's really and ectomorph or even a mesomorph.

With the proper mind-set and disciplined training, anyone can become a warrior.

THE THREE PILLARS OF FITNESS

If you scan back through the five qualities of fitness, you'll notice there are some components common among them; they all require some combination of muscular strength and endurance, aerobic capacity, and flexibility. In fact, every aspect of fitness involves one or more of these three physical traits. As I explained, traditional martial arts training is good, and that should be the backbone of your fitness program. But to reach your peak potential in warrior fitness, you need something more.

In order to condition yourself most efficiently, you need to understand your own body—know its strengths and weaknesses—then tailor a supplemental conditioning program focused in the three key areas. You want specific physical conditioning routines to shore up the weak points while making the most of your natural strengths. This training is done in addition to your regular martial arts practice.

To condition the three pillars of fitness, you need to:

- Train for muscular strength and endurance.
- Condition for aerobic capacity.
- Develop flexibility.

TRAIN FOR MUSCULAR STRENGTH AND ENDURANCE

Miyagi thrust his hand into a bunch of bamboos and pulled out one from the center. He struck his hand into a slab of meat and tore off chunks. He put white chalk on the bottoms of his feet, jumped up, and kicked the ceiling—leaving his footprints on the ceiling for all to see. Spectators hit him with long staffs with no effect. With his fingers, he tore off the bark of a tree and with his big toe, he punctured a hole in a kerosene can.

Account of a demonstration in 1928 by karate master Miyagi Chojun, as reported by Okinawan Journalist, Tokuda Anshu (Kim, 1982, p. 32).

Strength is an important goal in all fitness programs. Whether you are male or female, a hard stylist or soft, you need to train for strength. And the most effective method of building strength is progressive resistance—in other words, weight training.

Ever since Charles Atlas made it famous in the 1930's, weight training has been the foremost method among athletes for building muscle mass and strength. Of course, times have changed since 1930; science has gotten involved, and we know a great deal more about how to tailor routines for specific goals than Atlas did. Nonetheless, old Charles certainly was on the right track. His discoveries were key stepping stones to the modern methods of athletic strength training.

I'm not going to spend a lot of time talking about specific exercises, and I'm certainly not going to teach you lifting form or technique. There are lots of other books devoted to those purposes. Instead, I'm going to give you some basic principles for developing your strength and muscular endurance, and I'll show you how to integrate strength training into your warrior lifestyle.

The first thing to understand is that strength training isn't a half hour in front of the television with Jack LaLane—it's hard, grueling work. You drive the muscles to the point of failure, rupturing cells. Therefore, you don't work any given muscle group two days in a row. You need at least one day of rest between workouts.

Second, always train for balance. Many men only train their upper bodies because they think broad chests and shoulders look good. Serious bodybuilders call these guys "bar bodies," because the only reason they train is to impress women. Well, scrawny legs don't look good, and even if they did, warriors don't train for looks. We train for combat effectiveness. Strength in the *tanden* and below is vitally important. Train all parts of your body evenly unless you have a particular part that lags behind in strength. In that case, work it harder.

With those points out of the way, let's talk about training for strength. Your fast-twitch muscle fibers will respond best if you do each of your exercises with as much weight as you can handle for 3 to 5 sets of 6 to 10 repetitions. Push yourself hard. Your muscles should literally fail on the last repetition of each set. Of course, that means for saftey's sake, you must never train alone, and you need a training partner to spot you if you use free weight.

Training your slow-twitch fibers for endurance calls for a different approach. Here, you use less weight and exhaust each muscle group with sets of 10 to 20 repetitions. Once again, drive your muscles to failure as often as you can.

But how do you tailor a strength program, given the fact that, like most people, you probably have a mix of fast- and slow-twitch muscle fibers? Well, I handle it this way: since I'm mainly ectomorphic, I constantly need to work on strength training. So I do most of my sets with high weight and low repetitions. But since, unlike many ectomorphs, I tend to suffer from a shortage of endurance, I make sure I do at least one set at the end of each exercise with low weight and high repetitions. This final "burnout set" serves to work my slow-twitch muscle fibers, keeping my endurance up to an acceptable level.

You need to analyze your own strength training requirements and tailor a program appropriate to your personal needs. With proper training, you'll have ample strength and muscular endurance to carry you through martial arts training and live combat.

But stamina isn't a matter of muscular endurance alone. Aerobic conditioning also plays a key role.

CONDITION FOR AEROBIC CAPACITY

Most beginning athletes are unwilling to drive themselves hard enough. They should punish themselves and then rest adequately, only to increase the output of effort after the rest. Long hours of work made up of many short, high-speed efforts interspersed with periods of milder activity seem to be the best endurance-training procedure.

Bruce Lee from *Tao of Jeet Kune Do*
(1975, p. 46)

Aerobic capacity is one of the most neglected areas of martial arts conditioning. Most students develop their strength and flexibility, and many condition their muscles for endurance, but too few condition their cardiovascular systems for long, arduous performance. That's what aerobic conditioning is all about.

The word "aerobic" literally means to live in oxygen. It was coined by Dr. Kenneth Cooper, a physician at the United States Air Force Academy in the 1960's. Dr. Cooper conducted a study among Academy students in which he discovered that daily, aerobic exercise strengthened their hearts and lungs, improved their circulation, reduced their body-fat percentages, lowered their blood pressure, and improved their overall health. Most importantly for warriors, Dr. Cooper determined that aerobic condi-

For most hard stylists, *kata* is a superb method of interval training.

tioning dramatically increases an individual's capacity for prolonged, vigorous, physical activity. And this quality is equally important for athletic performance or personal combat.

Coupled with muscular endurance, aerobic capacity gives a warrior the Herculean stamina that sets him apart from the two-night-a-week martial artist. But what does aerobic conditioning entail?

Aerobic conditioning involves performing an exercise that raises your heart rate to a specified level for a period long enough to produce a "training effect." The period of time required varies with what heart rate you maintain. Cooper stipulated that if the exercise is vigorous enough to achieve a sustained heart rate of 150 beats per minute or more, the training effect begins about five minutes after the exercise starts. But if the sustained heart rate is less than 150 beats per minute, the exercise must be continued considerably longer (1968, p. 23).

A good rule of thumb for aerobic training is to do moderately vigorous exercise—forcing you to breath deeply but not to gasp—for at least 20 minutes without stopping. A typical routine might involve elevating your heart rate to 120 beats per minute (achievable with slow jogging) and maintaining that level for 30 minutes. Of course, as your fitness improves, your body becomes more resilient, and you need to increase the intensity of exercise, the length of time you do it, or both to continue achieving the training effect.

To condition yourself most efficiently, you need to train aerobically at least four times a week. Many martial artists, particularly hard stylists, manage that through regular martial arts practice. Classes that emphasize vigorous, nonstop activity can be very aerobic. But not all students attend class four times a week, and many arts just aren't physically intense enough to achieve the aerobic training effect. These students need to supplement their martial training with other exercises.

Many exercises are aerobic when done nonstop for periods long enough to produce the training effect. Running is the most effective, but swimming and cycling are common substitutes for those who can't run due to physical problems or because they simply don't like to. Even brisk walking can be aerobic, but with an exercise with such a low level of intensity, the period of nonstop performance must be considerably longer (60 minutes or more) to get the desired training effect.

Aerobic conditioning can do wonders for your health, and it will improve your personal fitness. But the steady, plodding approach most runners use won't give you the combat endurance you want. In fact, it may even erode your speed and agility. Let me tell you what happened to me.

I became a true believer in aerobic conditioning in 1978, while at the Air Force Officer Training School. Following graduation, I continued my running program, getting increasingly more ambitious as I became ever more aerobically fit. In less than a year, I was running an hour a day, sometimes covering seven miles or more. I thought certainly this would give me the stamina I sought for fighting. Wrong!

The more I ran, the more my fighting suffered. I lost all my burst speed, the ability to spring at the opponent to take advantage of a sudden opening. Furthermore, I lost the ability to jump; it seemed my feet were anchored to the floor. But most frustrating, for all the work I was putting in, I didn't seem to have any more fighting stamina than before I started running. I tired just as quickly as I ever did. I discovered what track and field athletes have known for decades: the steady, plodding pace of distance running produces a steady, plodding athlete.

I was extraordinarily healthy. I was physically fit. My cardiovascular system was in prime condition, and my slow-twitch muscle fibers were fully developed. But my fast-twitch fibers had completely atrophied. Since sparring requires strength and sudden bursts of speed, trying to force that from my muscles simply tired them out. They just couldn't react quickly or strongly. I had conditioned myself for the wrong activity, one very different from fighting.

Aerobic conditioning is a key part of stamina, and it's the single most important aspect of fitness in terms of general health and wellbeing. But stamina for fighting requires more than a well-developed cardiovascular system. It requires muscles conditioned for both endurance and speed. The fast-twitch muscle fibers must be developed, but not just by using the slow, powerful movements of weight training. They must be trained to react with sudden, explosive force. This kind of conditioning can only be achieved through interval training.

Interval training involves mixing your steady aerobic training routine with sessions of repeated, short, gut-busting sprints. Ideally, you begin this phase of training once you've achieved a basic, aerobic foundation—usually after about three months of running 30 minutes a day, four days a week. At that point, replace every other slow-running day with a 30-minute, wind-sprint session.

Start each session with five to ten minutes of slow running until you're warm and loose. Then, as you jog along, pick a target 40 to 50 yards ahead and break into a sprint, trying to reach that point as fast as you can. Don't stop, once you get there; you don't want your heart rate to fall out of the training zone. Just slow down to a gentle jog and continue on until you've recovered enough wind to sprint again. Every sprint should be all out, as hard as you can run.* Try to do 15 sprints during each 30-minute session. I guarantee it will be a while before you succeed.

Interval training needn't be confined to running; it can be applied to swimming, cycling, or virtually any method of aerobic conditioning. Simply drive yourself as hard as you can for short intervals, followed by recovery periods of easier aerobic work. In fact, one of the best interval training methods available for some hard stylists is *kata*!

*Interval training is an advanced approach, and it puts a good deal of stress on your muscles and joints. So don't start it until you're already in good condition, and always remember to warm up thoroughly before your first sprint.

Systems that employ powerful, high-speed *kata* provide their students an ideal vehicle for interval training. Interspersed with slower patterns and done for periods of 30 minutes or more, these forms provide wind-sprint exercises that work well as interval training tools. What's more, you have the advantage of using the activity you are training for as the conditioning program for that activity. You not only get the benefits of stamina training, but you condition your muscle fibers and the nerves directing them for the very movements they will be called to perform in combat. Now that's an offer you can't refuse.

Oh, there's one other benefit to using *kata* as your method of interval training: it helps you develop flexibility.

DEVELOP FLEXIBILITY

*The recommendation that you keep your body supple like that of an infant in order to counteract the rigidity and stiffness of the aging process is a very old one which ancient Japanese masters of martial arts often stressed to their disciples. This advice may be traced all the way back to ancient Chinese classics such as the Taoist texts, and having found its way into the manuals of martial strategy, soon became the foundation for that famous principle of nonresistance or fusion (*wa*) which according to a predominant school of thought in this area underlies the principles of suppleness (*ju*) and harmony (*ai*).*

From *Aikido and the Dynamic Sphere*
(Westbrook and Ratti, 1970, p. 114)

Flexibility is an essential quality for warriors; it's a must in all martial arts. Rigidity makes it hard or impossible to execute your techniques quickly. And in some arts, advanced techniques can't be done at all without a great deal of suppleness.

No doubt, your instructor begins each class with a series of stretching exercises as part of his warmup routine. Indeed, stretching is an important element of physical warm up, but don't confuse stretching to develop flexibility with warm up; they're two different things.

Warm up is the process of increasing blood circulation to your muscles and extremities. In involves energizing your body with a fresh burst of adrenaline, putting it in an active state, ready for sudden, intense, physical exertion. The purpose of warm up is to reduce the chance of injury from physical strain, and suppleness is important, since rigidity leads to injury. Therefore, stretching is a key part of the warm up process, but only a part. Gentle stretching should be done near the end of your warmup routine, after the muscles are already warm and invigorated. Stretching cold muscles can lead to the very injuries you're trying to avoid.

As I said, the stretching you do during warm up isn't intended to develop your flexibility. It's only meant to loosen you up—to take advantage of whatever flexibility you already have in order to prevent injuries during the practice to come. Stretching to develop flexibility is done *after* your regular training session.

Stretching is an important aspect of training for all martial artists and virtually all athletes. If you don't stretch for flexibility, not only will you not become more supple, you'll actually become less as your body grows stronger from the exercise.

You see, your muscles are strung from bone to bone, each pair acting as a lever with the joint between them as a hinge. Flexibility is largely a function of the lengths of the muscles pulling those levers. As each muscle fiber grows stronger and thicker from training, it tends to grow shorter as well. That's because, whenever you put your muscles through an extended, vigorous workout, they become fatigued and cells are damaged. Your body's natural defensive reaction is to shorten the muscles for healing and to resist further physical activity during the healing process. In other words, you get stiff. If you simply relax and let nature take its course, your muscles heal stronger than they were before the work, but they also remain a bit shorter. Therefore, the more you work your muscles, the less flexibility you'll have unless you make a conscious effort to counteract the shortening process by stretching them out.

So the key time to stretch for flexibility is immediately after a hard workout, before the muscles cool down. In fact, you actually want the muscles to cool down and enter their recovery mode while in the stretched state, if possible. Sports training experts call this "warm-down" stretching.

Correct stretching is a very deliberate process. The casual swinging and bouncing you see many students doing is counterproductive and dangerous. To stretch properly, move slowly into the stretch position and bear down until you feel the first hint of discomfort. Hold that position for five to ten seconds, then press just a bit farther and hold there for at least 30 seconds.

The reason you do each stretch in two phases is because your muscles will first react defensively to being stretched out—they will tighten and resist. But with gentle persistence, they'll relax and stretch to their full length. That's where you want to hold them with gentle pressure for as long as you can comfortably stand it. Bouncing only stimulates the muscle's tightening reflex, so always move slowly and smoothly.

Throughout each stretch, concentrate on relaxing your muscles completely. You'll feel them flex defensively against the stretch. Teach them to respond to your mental commands to relax. This aspect of the exercise not only promotes effective stretching, it also helps train your body to relax at other times.

Stretch the muscles around all the major joints in your body, and always stretch both agonistic and antagonistic muscles for each direction of movement. In other words, after you stretch the *femoral biceps* on the backs of your thighs, put just as much effort into stretching the *quadriceps* on the fronts.

If you choose to stretch without the benefit of a workout to warm up your muscles, go through your full routine twice. Do it extra-slowly the first time, and don't stretch hard. By the time you get through the first cycle, you'll be warm enough to stretch more seriously the second time through. A full stretching routine should take 30 minutes or longer.

Stretching should be the final phase of all your workouts, in and out of the training hall. Never run, cycle, or do any other aerobic exercise without following it with a thorough series of warm-down stretches. And never, under any circumstances, neglect stretching while weight training.

Lifting weights damages more muscle tissue than any other form of exercise. So it's imperative that you stretch extensively following every workout. In fact, I'm so concerned about losing flexibility in my legs, I do selective stretches between every set on days when I work my lower body. You may want to as well.

NUTRITION AND WEIGHT CONTROL

It's a typical outgrowth. As students advance in the arts, getting stronger and ever more attuned to their bodies, sooner or later they begin to get self-conscious about nutrition.

"What should I be eating?" they ask. "Maybe I should become a vegetarian like the Chinese monks." I used to respond by daring them to eat raw fish like the *samurai*. But now, with the growing popularity of sushi bars, the yuppie students are only too willing to take me up on it. Actually, even with all the fads going around, I'm still an old fashioned advocate of eating a sensible, balanced diet.

It's appalling the number of useless food supplements there are on the market. Body builders, ever desperate to grow, are particularly susceptible to marketing gimmicks promising to make them giants in record time. The shelves of health food stores are lined with protein powders and "carbo-explosive" concentrates guaranteed to give you "he-man" muscles. I guarantee these products too—guarantee they'll fatten their manufacturers' profits by slimming your wallet. All the while, the real problem isn't that we Westerners are malnourished, it's that we are overfed.

In 1983, a clinical nutritionist, Dr. Robert Haas, explained the issue quite convincingly in his book, *Eat to Win: The Sports Nutrition Bible*. According to Haas, many American athletes stuff themselves with protein and vitamin supplements, hoping to improve their physical development and athletic performance. But they really should be eating less, not more—less protein, and especially, less fat!

The typical Western diet has several times more protein and saturated fat than most people need. Constant, daily consumption of these excess nutrients leads to obesity, heart disease, and a host of other physical maladies. Even protein, long believed to be the lifeblood of muscular growth is useless, even harmful, if taken in excess.

Protein is essential for building and repairing your body. But most people only need 40-80 grams of it a day, one-fourth to one-fifth of what the typical American consumes. The rest is metabolized into fats and sugars and stored in your body for later use as energy. But protein makes a very poor energy fuel. It's metabolism creates toxic by-products, and their disposal strains your liver and kidneys, leaches out essential minerals and electrolytes, and dehydrates you (Haas, 1983, p.19). The result is sluggishness, decreased stamina, and overall poor physical performance.

Fats are an equally poor source of fuel for athletes and warriors. Most foods high in fat are also high in cholesterol, and the process of metabolizing saturated fats actually creates cholesterol within your body. Furthermore, most people use little or none of the fat they consume for energy.

Breaking fat down for energy is a slow process. Although each gram of fat carries twice the energy that a gram of protein or carbohydrate holds, your body has difficulty metabolizing it. So you can't get to the energy stored in fat molecules, even those floating free in your bloodstream, when you need quick bursts for fighting or other forms of short, intense, physical performance. As a result, most of the fat you eat ends up stored in cells around your organs and muscles and deposited, along with the cholesterol, as deadly plaque on the walls of your arteries.

The ideal energy foods are the complex carbohydrates. These are the substance of fruits, vegetables, and grains. Unlike fats, these nutrients metabolize directly into glycogen, the kind of sugar stored in your muscles for immediate energy. And unlike proteins, carbohydrates metabolize and burn cleanly; they produce little or no toxic by-products to degrade your performance or harm your body.

Notice that although your body burns sugar, I'm not recommending you eat it. Table sugar is a simple carbohydrate, and it does contain energy. But eating sugar jolts your body and triggers a sudden insulin surge, counteracting any positive effect you may hope to gain. Sure, you feel energized momentarily—that's the effect a sugar rush has on your brain—but within minutes the insulin takes effect leaving you physically and emotionally depressed. So despite the belief that a candy bar eaten ten minutes before the big match will give you a burst of energy, eating sugar will degrade your performance, not help it.

I recommend you eat a balanced diet, high in complex carbohydrates, low in protein, and with almost no fat. That means eating mainly fruits, vegetables, and grains, a little lean meat, and avoiding most dairy products, nuts, oils, and other sources of fat. This regimen will keep you healthy and make you lean as well.

Doctors will tell you that losing weight is a simple matter of arithmetic—burn more calories than you eat. While that's true, anyone with a weight problem knows it's easier said than done. But if you follow these nutritional guidelines, losing weight and keeping it off will be easier than you could ever imagine.

You see, while every gram of protein or carbohydrate has four calories, a gram of fat provides eight. Add the fact that fat molecules are more difficult to metabolize into energy—they are more often stored than burned—and you can see why people who love their fried foods and cream pies tend to have weight problems. However, if you cut fats out of your diet, it's literally hard to eat enough food to become or stay obese.

But nutrition is only half the equation of weight control; the other half is exercise. Of course, the more you exercise, the more calories you burn. But like most other things in life, there is a single best way to exercise to lose weight. That single best way can be summed up in one word: aerobics!

Aerobic exercise is, beyond a doubt, the best way to lose weight. You burn more calories in 30 minutes of aerobic work than you could ever burn in two hours of weight training. And the source of calories burned is even more important.

When your body performs an *anaerobic* exercise, such as weight training or sprinting, it burns glycogen for energy. First, it uses the glycogen in your muscles, then it takes it from your blood. When it runs out of glycogen, you're out of gas—you simply can't go on. Athletes call this "hitting the wall." But when you do a mild to moderate aerobic exercise, your body has time to begin metabolizing the fat molecules in your bloodstream before the glycogen burns out. After the first 15 or 20 minutes, you're burning calories directly from the very substance you want to eradicate—the fat about to be stored in your body.

So avoid putting fat into your body, and burn out the little amount that gets there. You can't help but get slim and stay trim. Concentrate your diet on complex carbohydrates, and avoid excess protein. These are the tenets of good nutrition and weight control. But how well does all this work? Well, let me tell you.

In 1988 I decided to try a high carbohydrate diet following the results of a routine medical examination. Although already quite fit,* the exam turned up a blood pressure of 130 over 90. That didn't surprise me; I'd had marginally high blood pressure since my early 20s. But noting my family history of cardiovascular problems, the doctor became concerned and gave me a stern lecture.

*During this period I was working out three times a day, five days a week: an hour of karate at 6:00 A.M., running or weight training at noon, and an hour or more of jujutsu every evening.

Feeling a bit indignant, I went home and immediately cut out all fried foods, dairy products, and most meats. I began living on fruits, vegetables, cans of tuna packed in water, and bread... lots of bread.

The first noticeable result was that I lost six pounds in a week. But even more dramatically, the doctor checked my blood pressure the following week and was startled to find it at 100 over 60, a drop of 30 points! This was no fluke. Over the next several months, he checked my pressure weekly—the same reading each time.

Over the years since, I've drifted from that Spartan menu to a more liberal diet. I still avoid fats wherever possible, but I eat a fair amount of meat. With regular exercise and a sensible, balanced

Stretch before training to avoid injuries and after training to develop flexibility.

diet, I manage to enjoy eating while staying lean and fit and keeping my blood pressure stable at a healthy 110 over 70. Balance. That's the secret of nutrition and weight control. And that's the essence of warrior fitness.

One final word: physical conditioning is long, hard work, and extended periods without noticeable results can lead to frustration. In these situations, some athletes resort to anabolic steroids, blood packing, or some other shortcut to give them an edge. Don't do it! Warriorship is a life style in which you aim to strengthen your spirit as well as your body. Drugs and other shortcuts are emotional crutches. Using them destroys your will and shows your weakness of spirit. That is not The Martial *Way*.

POINTS TO REMEMBER: WARRIOR FITNESS

- Generally, warriorship demands development of the following five interrelated, physical attributes: power, speed, endurance, agility, and coordination.
- The single best conditioning program for any given activity is the activity itself. But just practicing your martial art won't get you to your full fitness potential. You need to enhance your martial arts practice with supplemental training.
- Somatic typing is a helpful tool for planning physical conditioning programs. Basic knowledge of muscle physiology will help you tailor your training to condition yourself more efficiently.
- The five qualities of fitness all require some combination of muscular strength and endurance, aerobic capacity, and flexibility.
- The most effective method of building strength and muscular endurance is weight training. Push yourself hard; the muscles should literally fail at the end of each set.
- Do aerobic exercise at least four times a week. But the steady, plodding approach most runners use won't give you the combat endurance you want. For Herculean stamina, alternate regular aerobic workouts with interval training.

■ Stretching is an important facet of training for all martial artists. The key time to stretch for flexibility is immediately after a hard workout, before the muscles cool down.

■ Eat a balanced diet, high in complex carbohydrates, low in protein, and with almost no fat. The best way to lose weight is to avoid fats and exercise aerobically. If you avoid putting fat into your body and burn out the little amount that gets there, you can't help but get slim and stay trim.

Chapter 10

RELIGION AND MYSTICISM

The Way of the warrior does not include other ways, such as Confucianism, Buddhism, certain traditions, artistic accomplishments, and dancing...

MUSASHI FROM *A BOOK OF FIVE RINGS*

The most discouraging seminar I ever attended took place back East, in 1984. The flyer promised a "unique, total, martial arts experience, uniting mind, body, and spirit." I was intrigued, and since it was to be taught by a high-ranking master, it seemed an ideal way to spend a weekend. So, I gathered up a group of students and went.

The seminar took place at a family campground and began on a Saturday morning. The first session started with a uniform inspection and followed with a moderate workout on basic fundamentals. This consumed the morning, and following lunch, we were told the afternoon would be filled by a lecture, so we gathered in the camp auditorium. So far, this wasn't a very dynamic seminar. Still, I was eager to hear what the master had to say—that is, until he announced his topic, "Christ and the Martial Arts."

Several of my students turned to me with a look of shock as the master opened his bible and began reading scripture. I stared at the floor in embarrassment. During the break an hour later, we discussed leaving. Nowhere in the flyer or in my previous conversations with the master had anything been said about this being a religious retreat. But we'd driven a hundred miles and paid a considerable, nonrefundable fee to be there. Maybe, the man would get this out of his system and give us what the flyer promised, a weekend of martial arts training.

We were wrong. The afternoon dragged into evening, during which the master brought in a guest speaker, a local minister. Of course, the next morning was Sunday, so the first half of the day would be filled with a worship service. You see, the master was also an ordained minister.

My students and I were livid. It wasn't that we objected to the man expressing his religious convictions. In fact, several of us were Christians and shared his beliefs. But we had come for a weekend of martial arts instruction, not bible school. My students wanted to know why they were being subjected to this? In fact, one was so indignant that he asked the master himself.

The master said the martial arts have always been linked to religion. In Asia, warriors practiced martial arts as part of their "heathen faiths." One couldn't be separated from another. But since he was Christian instead of Buddhist or Taoist, he felt it was completely appropriate to practice and teach his religion as a part of his martial art. In fact, he believed the martial arts were ideal vehicles to bring people to Christ, *even if they didn't know they were coming to a religious retreat.*

That's poppycock, of course. It's unethical to draw people under false pretenses, no matter how noble your cause. The ends don't justify the means. But there was another flaw in this master's argument, one stemming from his misconception about the relationship of the martial arts to religion. Despite what he believed, the true martial arts have nothing to do with religion. They are methods of warfare, not worship!

But is it any wonder that Westerners so often associate Asian religions and mystical practices with the martial arts? After all, most of them got their first impression of Eastern fighting systems from television shows and movies depicting monks meditating in darkened temples between sessions of walking across rice paper runners or snatching pebbles from the hands of priests. In fact, ask most any American student where the martial arts first began, and he'll probably tell you they started in a temple in China.

Many Westerners, particularly fundamentalist Christians, shy away from studying the Asian martial arts because they believe doing so would draw them into practicing Eastern religions. The bowing makes them uneasy enough, but the temple-like decor and the smell of incense burning in some training halls sends them literally running for the door. But the martial arts are not religions, and observing tradition by taking part in ceremonial customs is not practicing religious rites—at least, not in most cases.

In this chapter, I'll explain the relationships martial arts do and don't have with religion. We'll begin by comparing Eastern and Western religious thought. Then I'll outline four major Eastern doctrines and explain how they relate to the martial arts. We'll look at Eastern mysticism, and I'll show you some things to recognize and avoid. Finally, I'll explain how past warriors in Asian and European cultures oriented their methods of warfare to their religious beliefs, and I'll give you some guidelines to help you reconcile your martial arts training with your own religious convictions.

EASTERN VERSUS WESTERN RELIGIOUS THOUGHT

As a warrior and practitioner of the Asian martial arts, it's important for you to reach a basic understanding of the key Eastern religions and philosophical doctrines, if only from an academic perspective. But Asians perceive and practice religion in ways far different than Westerners do. So before you can understand how Eastern religious thought relates to the martial arts, you first need to understand how it differs from the Western concept of religion.

First, most Eastern religions began as philosophies, not methods of worship. In most cases, they were never originally intended to be used to praise deities, nor did they address reaching a heavenly reward. Even today, doctrines such as Confucianism are mainly philosophical and only secondarily, theological.

In fact, nearly all the Eastern religions have strong philosophical foundations. Even Zen, the meditative sect of Buddhism, can be approached from a purely philosophical perspective. Many people, Westerners included, enter Zen monasteries to master the curriculum and find enlightenment, without ever converting to Buddhism or even being asked to.

The second thing to understand is that where Western religious doctrines are exclusive, Eastern religious and philosophical thought is inclusive. Westerners believe they can only practice one faith, follow only one path to salvation. That means a Roman Catholic cannot worship in a Jewish Temple, nor could a Lutheran join the Greek Orthodox Church and remain Lutheran. Most Asians, on the other hand, don't believe any one doctrine holds a monopoly on truth. Subsequently, a Japanese might very well be married in a Buddhist Temple one day and take part in a Shinto ritual the next. He wouldn't feel any moral conflict in that behavior, nor would the clergy of either faith object.

Indeed, Eastern religious thought is woven deeply into the fabric of Asian culture, and you will never truly understand the martial arts until you have a fundamental grasp of it. But it's important for you to understand: not only are the martial arts not religions, but the Eastern religious doctrines themselves need not be treated as religions in order to study and apply their principles. So don't be afraid. You're not exposing yourself to demonic possession by reading the *Tao te Ching*. Nor are you committing heresy by participating in the Shinto-based formalities so often performed in Japanese-style *dojo*.

Furthermore, no one expects you to swallow any one of these philosophies in total. There are useful points of view in each, vitally important for warriors, so take what you can use and discard the rest. That's the accepted method in Asia and the pragmatic approach of The Martial *Way*.

THE PRINCIPLE ASIAN RELIGIOUS DOCTRINES

There are three main Eastern doctrines that shaped the development of the martial arts and contributed significantly to The Martial *Way*. For centuries, China was the cultural center of Asia, so it should be no surprise that two of these philosophies, Confucianism and Taoism, originated there. The third, Buddhism, began in India but entered and spread across the Far East through China. During that process the doctrine evolved, becoming distinctively Chinese as well.

None of these philosophies developed in a vacuum; each was influenced by the cultural beliefs current during their rise. And as each new doctrine came about, it incorporated popular elements of the previous philosophies. This being the case, I'll discuss them in chronological order—the order in which they developed in history—and I'll show how each succeeding doctrine borrowed from and built on its predecessors.

By now, you've probably realized that in my introduction I said I'd tell you about four religions, and so far I've only mentioned three. Well, once I've discussed the three major doctrines, I'll address the Japanese faith, Shinto. Being uniquely Japanese, it had relatively little impact on Asian society at large. But it influenced development of the Japanese martial culture and still plays a key role in the customs observed in Japanese-style training halls. So, it bears discussing.

Let's begin with an overview of the teachings of the father of Chinese philosophy, Confucius.

CONFUCIANISM: THE *WAY* OF THE SAGES

The superior man has a dignified ease without pride. The common man has pride without dignified ease.

Confucius

Confucius was born in Shantung province, China, in 551 B.C. His real name was Chung Ni Chu, and he was the self-educated son of a poor family. But Confucius had a powerful mind, and he saw beyond the confines of his humble surroundings. Like Greece's Plato and Aristotle, he developed a cosmology which defined ethical morality, particularly regarding the role of the family and the state. And like those Western thinkers, the people around him quickly recognized his exceptional intellect. He never had a large patronage during his lifetime, but K'ung Fu Tzu (Master K'ung),* as his disciple's called him, had a devoted following, and he founded his own school of philosophy.

Confucius' doctrine focused on man's role in society. He emphasized the importance of loyalty to the state, filial duty to parents, and veneration of ancestors to maintain the social order. His teachings were legalistic, insisting that every creature and every object has an appointed place in the order of nature and should behave as his station requires.

Another tenet of Master K'ung's philosophy concerned the role of the "superior man." Since Confucius had to struggle to educate himself, he placed great value on knowledge and learning. He asserted that educated men were superior and should be entrusted to lead society. Subsequently, many of his proverbs are devoted to describing the qualities of the superior man.

Confucius taught his doctrine as a philosophy, not a religion. His teachings dealt exclusively with man and society. He never

*The name "Confucius" is a Westernization of K'ung Fu Chu.

claimed to be anything but an ordinary man and never asked to be worshiped. In fact, he rejected all forms of supernaturalism and remained a skeptic right up to his death in 479 B.C..

In the centuries following his death, Confucianism became fashionable throughout China. But as it spread among the populace, the focus of its teachings began to change, and people of limited intellect began to regard Master K'ung as a saint. Where earlier followers studied the logic inherent in his doctrine, later devotees, superstitious and unable to grasp the essence of its tenets, began conducting rituals and sacrifices in his name. As Confucian lore evolved, it incorporated a host of major and minor deities, usually borrowed from local nature cults then popular in China.

Bowing, particularly the kneeling version used in Japanese *dojo*, often frightens Judeo-Christian Westerners. But bowing in martial arts is not a religious rite.

This shift towards religious dogma was endorsed by the state. With its legalistic nature, emphasizing loyalty and obedience, Confucianism had become a favored doctrine among the nobility and the civil bureaucracy. It helped them bridle the masses and maintain the political status quo. But the intellectual flavor of Confucius' teachings made them hard for the common man to grasp. So by replacing thought with ritual, the doctrine became more acceptable to the general populace.

By A.D. 59, Confucianism was China's official state religion emphasizing good moral behavior, everyone keeping to his own station, and the performance of rituals. Sacrifice played a key role in Confucian ritual, and the Emperor led the nation in four main sacrifices a year: to heaven, earth, the royal ancestors, and the gods of soil and grain. In turn, chief government officials in each district conducted sacrifices to subordinate deities, and heads of families were expected to hold sacrifices on behalf of their ancestors (Cavendish, 1980, p.89).

This was all a far cry from Confucius' original teachings. Where he was interested exclusively in man's role in society, later adherents focused their attention on man's relationship with the powers of nature. Where Confucius abhorred supernaturalism and exalted the superior man, superstitious commoners perverted his doctrine to justify empty rituals, and the "superior men" who led the nation used that perverted doctrine to manipulate the masses.

Even so, Confucianism is first and foremost a philosophy, and its principles have had a profound influence on Asian civilization. As China's political and economic influence spread, so did her culture and with it, the precepts of Master K'ung. As a result, Confucian ethics are the backbone of nearly all legal systems in Asian nations and the foundation of all Eastern military codes of honor. An example of this is the *Hwarang-Do*, the ethical code developed by warriors in the Korean kingdom of Silla.*

*Today, a modern Korean combative system is taught under the name hwarang-do. Do not confuse this with the *Hwarang-Do* of Silla, which was not, itself, a martial art but an ethical code similar to Japan's *Bushido*.

Silla's exposure to Confucianism began in A.D. 634 when Queen Songdok developed relations with the T'ang government and subsequently, sent students to China to study methods of warfare. When the students returned, they founded a military-religious school for selected young noblemen. This academy matured under the guidance of King Chinhung and reached its zenith in the 8th century. It's curriculum focused on Confucian ethics and the military principles of the Chinese strategist, Sun Tzu. The ethical training in *Hwarang-Do* centered on five moral precepts: loyalty, filial piety, trustworthiness, valor, and justice. And since the Silla government also had contacts with the Japanese, some historians believe *Hwarang-Do* may be a source from which *Bushido* eventually evolved (Draeger, 1969, p.72).

Whether or not the roots of *Bushido* reach into Korea, Confucianism is the source of all Asian codes of honor, and you can see Master K'ung's precepts at work in every traditional training hall. The loyalty and respect your art teaches you to hold for your instructor, parents, and country are tenets of Confucian origin. And the master would be proud if he could see you dutifully holding your appointed place, as you obediently submit to your school's codified ranking system.

Yes, whether you are Christian, Jewish, Islamic, or agnostic, you practice Confucianism every time you take part in traditional martial arts training. And if you're a warrior, you're Confucian outside the training hall as well—not in the religious sense but in the philosophical one.

TAOISM: IN PURSUIT OF THE ONE TRUE *WAY*

He who devotes himself to learning seeks from day to day to increase his knowledge. He who devotes himself to knowing his true nature seeks from day to day to diminish his doing.

Lao Tzu

Lao Tzu (Old Master) was the father of Taoism. Some historians place his birth around 600 B.C., making him an older contemporary of Confucius, but more recent scholars believe he was born in the 4th century and that he wrote his *Tao te Ching* about 300 B.C.. In any event, all agree that Taoism developed and grew as a counter-movement to Confucianism.

Although Confucianism, the doctrine of loyalty and obedience, was the preferred religion of state, its lofty intellectualism was lost on the common man. The state tried to overcome these limitations by nurturing a cult around the memory of Confucius, and with some success, but the mystic tenets of Taoism quickly became the first love of the Chinese people.

The word "*tao*" literally means "way," and Taoism is built around a concept of the "*Way*," a single principle which lies behind surface appearances, a unity of which all phenomena are part.

The philosophy of Taoism seeks to recognize and harmonize with the *Tao* in all things. The *Tao* is nature, and according to Taoists, the only appropriate attitude to nature is noninterference. Lao Tzu taught, "Do nothing and there is nothing that will not be done." This is both a passive philosophy and a statement of power, for Taoism teaches that by becoming one with the *Tao* you become one with nature, thereby discovering and enjoying all her forces.

Water provides an example of this principle. Water is passive. It never strives or seeks to be something it isn't. It always settles to its own level, according to nature. You can strive against water, resist it with force, and for a time you may think you've succeeded. But in the end, water will always have its way. That is the *Tao*.

This dualism of doing by not doing is pervasive in Taoism. And appropriately, the Taoists eventually adopted an older principle, the theory of *yin* and *yang*, as part of their own doctrine. This duality of opposites is an ancient Asian concept first written about by the Chinese philosopher, Tsuo Yen, in the 4th century B.C. *Yin* represents all the soft, dark, yielding, or female characteristics of the universe and *yang* the hard, strong, male attributes of existence. According to Taoism, everything in creation passes through endless cycles of *yin* and *yang*, and wisdom consists of being in harmony with these rhythms of nature. The opposing forces of *yin* and *yang* are reconciled and transcended in the *Tao*.

Of course, this is all very mystical and therefore, very appealing to the simple Chinese commoner when compared to the legalistic, intellectual tone of Confucianism. But Taoist philosophy is not a religion. There is no concept of a supreme being, no concern with an afterlife, and therefore, no incentive to worship. Taoism simply addresses man's role in harmonizing with untouched nature. Its mystical overtones leads to metaphysical theories, but its emphasis on observing natural cycles points adherents toward the physical sciences as well (Feibleman, 1976, p.146).

But once again, place a philosophy in the hands of the superstitious and they'll build a cult around it. So by the 2nd century A.D., Taoism had become a popular religion with rituals and sacrifices conducted in thousands of temples across China. Like religious Confucianism, Taoism incorporated many local folk deities formerly worshiped in other sects. But with Taoism's mystical orientation, it also took a strong bent towards alchemy, astrology, spiritual divination, and other magical practices. Some sects, apparently influenced by Tantric rites from India, even incorporated orgiastic sex in their rituals.

So despite all the efforts of the Chinese government to promote Confucianism as the official state dogma, Taoism was clearly the religion of choice among common people. Conceding that, the state began making official sacrifices to Lao Tzu in A.D. 165. But philosophical Taoism survived and like Confucianism, spread throughout Asia with the advance of Chinese culture.

Today, Taoism is still a strong current in Eastern thought. We can see references to the *Tao* in writings from every corner of Asia. And nowhere is this philosophy more strongly expressed than in the martial arts.

Taoism is the very basis for most of the soft, yielding arts. Harmonizing with nature and doing by not doing are the central tenets for arts ranging from tai chi to aikido. And whether you call it *yin* and *yang*, *um* and *yang* (Korean), or *in* and *yo* (Japanese), the duality of opposites is a central principle in virtually every martial system, hard or soft. But Taoism finds its boldest expression in the various martial ways.

Asian combative systems with names ending in "*Do*," such as judo, taekwondo, karate-do, etcetera, are not martial arts in the traditional sense. Although some of these systems are effective methods of combat, learning to fight is always a secondary aim to developing moral character. The word "*do*" means "way" in

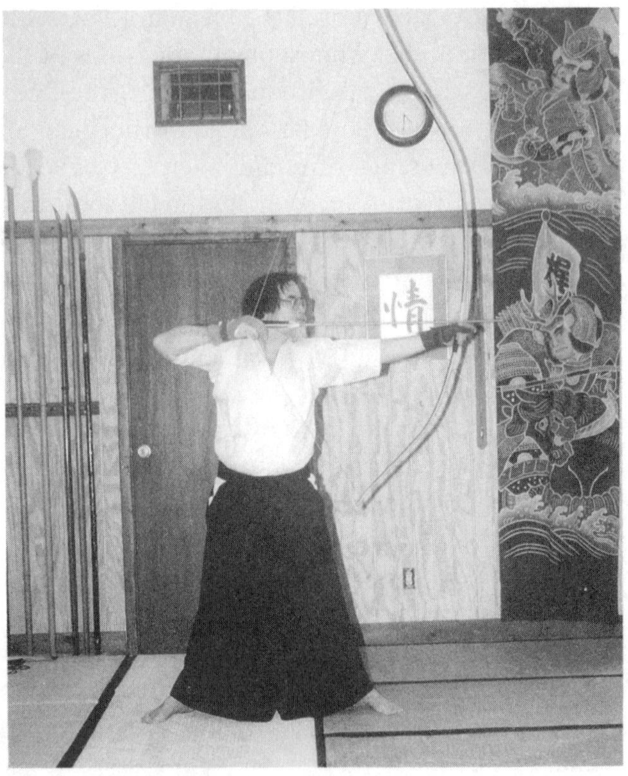

Kyudo, like all Japanese classical *budo*, is a deeply spiritual discipline, but it's not a religion.

Japanese and Korean and would be translated to "*tao*" in Chinese. These martial *ways* are actually modern systems founded by masters of older fighting arts who believed their ways would be ideal vehicles for guiding students towards self-perfection. Therefore, they are literally physical expressions of philosophical Taoism.

So if you study one or more of the various combative systems whose names end in "*Do*," you are practicing Taoism, whether you realize it or not. Of course, you're not reciting magical incantations or offering sacrifices to Lao Tzu; those would be the superstitious expressions of religious Taoism. But your acceptance of a martial way as your way of life makes you a Taoist, nonetheless. And all the more so, if you are a warrior.

Taoism teaches there is one single, unchanging principle behind all things. Recognizing and harmonizing with this one, true *Way* is the secret of wisdom and the source of all the powers of nature. So how can there be so many different martial ways, each believing they have the *Way*? The answer is simple, and I mentioned it toward the end of chapter 1 of this book: all systems are artificial. They are the limited contrivances of man and therefore, reflect his efforts to strive against the *Tao*.

Don't misunderstand me; I'm not attacking the martial ways. Most of these systems are very good. They provide valuable training, and the *Tao* can be seen moving in them as it can be seen in all things. But exponents of the martial ways often insist their way is best, theirs is the only way to follow. That is absurd, and if you allow them to limit you to any one of these artificial, man-made systems, you'll put your mind and your spirit in a box. From there, you cannot see the *Tao*. As Musashi said:

> *The* Way *of the warrior does not include other ways, such as Confucianism, Buddhism, certain traditions, artistic accomplishments, and dancing. But even though these are not part of the Way, if you know the Way broadly, you will see it in everything.*

Remember, there is one true martial *Way*. That is the *Tao*.

BUDDHISM: FOLLOWING THE EIGHTFOLD PATH

Now this, monks, is the noble truth of the way that leads to the cessation of pain: this is the noble Eightfold Way, namely, right views, right intention, right speech, right action, right livelihood, right effort, right mindfulness, right concentration.

From the Pali Sermon
Gautama, the Buddha

Buddhism began in India in the 6th century B.C. as an outgrowth of an ancient form of orthodox Hinduism called Brahmanism. The Brahmanist doctrine held that before a soul could enter *Nirvana* (eternal bliss*), it had to undergo extensive refinement and perfection. This process occurred through multiple incarnations, during which the individual achieved ever higher levels of moral excellence. Eventually, after thousands of rebirths, the soul was sanctified and granted access to *Nirvana*.

The Brahmanist religion, like Hinduism later, worshiped a pantheon of gods. It was a ritualistic faith holding offerings and sacrifice as the means by which the soul was gradually cleansed. Buddhism was born when a young prince, Siddhartha Gautama, found spiritual enlightenment and escape from the cycle of rebirth while meditating under a fig tree.

Gautama grew up a wealthy Brahman,** and he enjoyed all the sensual pleasures wealth could provide. But as he indulged in his luxury, he began to see the vanity of physical gratification. He saw the old, the sick, and the poor, and he realized that all wealth and worldly pleasures are transitory. In the end, there is only suf-

*Unlike Christian concepts of Heaven or Paradise, *Nirvana* is envisioned as a state of unconscious peace, a release from the pain of existence and the cycle of rebirth.
**Brahman is the highest of the social and religious classes in India, occupied by the wealthy nobility and members of the Hindu priesthood.

fering. So at 29 years of age, Gautama left his wealth and comfort and entered the world as a beggar to find answers to life's misery.

According to Buddhist lore, Gautama wandered across India searching for a key to release from the pain of life. Death was no answer, because that would only lead to rebirth and further anguish. For a while he studied philosophy under a guru, but he found no answers there. Next, he joined a group of ascetic monks and for five years, subjected himself to severe fasting and every kind of self deprivation imaginable.

Finally, the turning point came one day when, due to his weakened state, he fainted and fell into a stream. The cold water revived him, and he realized that although he had followed the ascetic's life to an extreme, he still hadn't found what he was looking for. So he picked himself up, ate at a local tavern, then sat down beneath a fig tree, determined to meditate until he found enlightenment.

After meditating for 49 days, Gautama was enlightened. During his meditation he had a vision in which he saw that man is bound to the endless cycle of rebirth and pain because of desire. All suffering is the result of unfulfilled desires. Gautama himself had craved salvation. In his fervor, he had pursued it through knowledge and ascetism, still it had eluded him. But when he ceased to desire, he found enlightenment and therefore, salvation.

Enlightenment attained, the 35-year-old Gautama arose and began to preach. He spent the rest of his 80-year life teaching disciples his four sacred truths: First, life is pain. Second, you must still the craving for life, which is fed by perceptions and feelings. Third, the cessation of pain, resulting from the cessation of craving, brings man into *Nirvana*, to end the cycle of rebirth. And finally, the way to achieve *Nirvana* consists of following the Eightfold *Way*, the prescribed methods of meditation designed to subdue the self and curb the craving for life.

At this point, let me emphasize the radical nature of Gautama's doctrine. He had grown up a Brahmanist in a superstitious, polytheistic society. But Buddhism, as Gautama taught it, was a dramatic break from Indian tradition. It wasn't a religion; it was a philosophical program of training, a system of discipline and mystical self development.

Gautama did not believe in the gods. He was atheist or, at most, agnostic. Subsequently, nowhere in his doctrine did he prescribe any form of ritual or worship. He believed man must achieve his own salvation rather than relying on gods for help or support. Oddly, Gautama didn't even believe in the existence of the soul. He said people live in a state of *anatman* (nonsoulness), and what we call the soul is actually a combination of five physical aggregates: the body, feelings, understanding, will, and consciousness (Hopfe, 1976, p.129). So once again, we have an Asian doctrine that began as something very different than religion.

During Gautama's lifetime, Buddhism had no temples, no scriptures, and no rituals. But all that changed following his death. Almost immediately, his followers began to disagree over the interpretation of his teachings, passed to them orally during his travels. Over the next few centuries, hundreds of Buddhist sects appeared, but most of them can be divided into two opposing camps: *Theravada*, "the tradition of the elders" and *Mahayana*, "the larger vehicle."*

Theravada Buddhism remains closest to Gautama's teachings. Its tenets insist that followers must work out their own salvation without any reliance on gods. Subsequently, Theravada adherents are more likely to shave their heads, don coarse yellow robes, and become monks, just as Gautama's disciples did. However, that lifestyle has never appealed to many people, so Theravada has always been in the minority to the more popular, Mahayana sects.

Mahayana Buddhism developed following several radical changes its adherents made to Gautama's basic doctrine. First, they claimed that Gautama secretly taught many more principles

*Mahayana Buddhists often refer to the Theravada sect as "*Hinayana*," or "the smaller vehicle."

to his closest disciples than he released publicly. Since the Mahayana leaders professed to carry the legacy from those most-favored followers of the Buddha, this opened the door for introducing new doctrinal tenets. Next, the belief developed that Gautama was not a mere man but instead, a compassionate, divine being who came to earth to help mankind. What's more, they stated that Gautama was not the only Buddha. Others must have come before him, after him, and more were yet to come. All these Buddhas, being divine, should be worshiped and adored. Finally, they introduced the concept of the *bodhisattva*, or "enlightened being."

Bodhisattva was a route by which ordinary people could become minor deities. It worked like this: at some point in life, an aspirant could take a vow to become a bodhisattva. Then, living an exemplary life, he or she would earn merit. At death, the individual would not enter *Nirvana*, but remain in some heavenly abode, answering prayers of the living. But in practical application, many more personages became bodhisattvas than just those who chose to. As Buddhism spread, it gradually absorbed many deities from popular local cults, and they often took their places as bodhisattvas. Local heroes and other famous people frequently became bodhisattvas as well, sometimes centuries after their deaths.

Well, that closes the circle. Once again we have a system that was founded as a secular doctrine but transformed into a method of worship by later followers. In Buddhism's case, it sprang from a ritualistic religion, developed separately as a secular mental discipline, then returned to religious dogma several centuries later. And significantly for historians and martial artists, it was Mahayana Buddhism that took root in China and spread so fervently across the rest of Asia.

Historians believe Theravada Buddhism was the first to reach China, sometime early in the 1st century, A.D.. But it was Mahayana Buddhism, arriving later that century, that really caught hold. By then, Mahayana was a mystical, ritual faith with a host of Buddhas and bodhisattvas. The Chinese, mystical and polytheistic by nature, were ripe for this kind of doctrine. This brand of Indian Buddhism seemed very Chinese—so much, in fact, that Taoist intellectuals first dismissed it as nothing more than an inferior version of Taoism.*

Buddhism and Taoism do have striking similarities. In their original forms, both were introspective, mystical doctrines aimed at helping man find his true nature. Each proposed humankind would find its answers by turning inward, rather than by seeking external knowledge. The concept of reincarnation was new to the Chinese, but the Taoists considered Buddhism's enlightenment to simply be another expression of harmonizing with the *Tao*. And Mahayana Buddhism, with its deities and rituals, was nearly a mirror image of religious Taoism.

So the two doctrines merged. It was a marriage made in heaven—or at least, in China. Over time, Buddhism absorbed religious Taoism and adopted many of its Chinese deities as Buddhas and bodhisattvas. New sects, distinctively Chinese, emerged and spread with Chinese culture throughout Asia, arriving in Korea in the 6th century and Japan over the next several centuries. The most significant of these sects, at least in the minds of most martial artists, are the "intuitive" or "meditative" sects.

Though drawn from Mahayana, meditative Buddhism is, in many respects, a return to the original teachings of Gautama. Instead of emphasizing ritual and worship, these groups once again stressed turning inward to find one's own enlightenment through meditation. The meditative sects were called *Dhyana* in India, *Ch'an* in China, and *Zen* in Japan.

Ch'an was founded in the late 5th or early 6th century when the Indian monk, Bodhidharma, went to China to spread Dhyana Buddhism. Much about Bodhidharma is folklore, but according to

*They insisted that Lao Tzu had taken Taoism to "the barbarians" in India and now it was returning to China in a slightly different form (Cavendish, 1980, p.93).

one story, he first arrived in China in 480 A.D. at the Emperor's invitation. There, he taught the Emperor that all the study, worship, and good works he had done at the urging of other Mahayana priests would not bring him enlightenment or salvation. The Eightfold *Way* of meditation was the only answer.

After finishing in Canton, Bodhidharma supposedly withdrew to a cave and meditated for nine years before retiring to the Shaolin Temple in Hunan. There he reputedly taught the exercises which, in time, evolved into those fighting systems that made the Shaolin monks famous throughout China.

This is the first link between Buddhism and the martial arts. And, to some extent, the connection is valid. Martial arts have been taught in thousands of Buddhist temples, and in many, they still are. The concentration and discipline they demand is very

This Buddhist temple stands in the heart of a major American city. Masters teach kendo and karate-do in the temple gymnasium, but training there does not make you a Buddhist.

compatible with meditative Buddhism. But studying martial arts, even in a Buddhist temple, is not practicing the Buddhist faith. In fact, even when the monks themselves practiced fighting, it was for reasons very alien to the peaceful aims of personal enlightenment.

Buddhism has had a turbulent history in many parts of Asia, particularly in China. Evolving as centers of intellectual study and free thought, Buddhist temples and monasteries often became gathering places for those opposed to the political repression so frequent in Chinese society. In some cases, the monasteries provided refuge to political fugitives. But more often, the monks themselves were involved in underground movements, secret societies, and all kinds of political subversion against government authorities. In any event, the crucible of political turmoil was probably the biggest incentive for developing effective systems of combat. To fight the government, they had to know how to fight!

Buddhism's history in Japan was no more placid. Almost from the beginning, most sects became large landowners, and their leaders found themselves involved in political intrigues. These often led to open conflicts between the militant clergy and the local *samurai*. But as time went on, it was the mystically-oriented monasteries in the high mountains, with their *yamabushi* (mountain warriors), that proved the most serious threat to the military authorities.

Even as the military class became continually more organized and consolidated its power in populated areas, the remote Buddhist monasteries recruited an ever increasing number of followers and trained them in the arts of strategy and fighting. By the 11th century, they were a genuine threat to the military government of Japan, and it took more than four hundred years of nearly continuous warfare before the *yamabushi* were finally eliminated as serious contenders for political power. Not until the late 16th century, when Oda Nobunaga systematically razed their temples and slaughtered thousands of priests, did the tide of Buddhist clerical power recede.

Even though the *samurai* and the clergy were often on opposing sides, Buddhism had a significant impact on the martial arts practiced by professional warriors. The monks' fighting ability was impressive, and the *samurai* rarely hesitated to study and adopt what worked in battle. During times of peace, warriors frequently retired to monasteries for rest and spiritual renewal. While there, they often studied strategy and fighting systems under Buddhist masters. And in Buddhism, particularly Zen, the warrior found a strength of will that served him well in times of peace and war.

Zen appeared in Japan in 1215 A.D. after Eisai, a Japanese monk from a Mahayana sect, visited China and found enlightenment studying under a Ch'an master. Returning to Japan, Eisai founded the *Rinzai* sect of Zen, which is based on achieving *satori*, a spontaneous enlightenment, by focusing on a *koen*, a riddle with no logical answer.*

In 1253 a monk named Dogen founded the second major Zen sect, *Soto*. Dogen was a student of Eisai, but he rejected the use of *koen*, preferring simply to meditate in *zazen*. *Zazen* is a discipline in which the student attempts to empty his mind of conscious thought and meditate on no particular idea or goal until he reaches *satori*.

Other Buddhist sects may have played more important roles in the formation of the classical martial arts, but Zen was the discipline most significant to the *samurai* for refining the martial spirit. Zen taught the *samurai* to enter combat in *mushin* (mind-no-mind), free of the distractions of rational thought. And, as martial arts historian Donn Draeger pointed out, it also "taught him to be self-reliant, self-denying, and above all, single-minded to the supreme degree that no attachments whatsoever—emotional, intellectual, or material—would detract him from his professional role of fighting for a dedicated cause." (1969, p. 94)

*Modern Rinzai Zen uses a training system employing a series of *koen*. As the aspirant solves each, he is given another until he completes the program. At that point he is considered enlightened and declared a Zen master.

So Buddhism, particularly the meditative sects, did indeed play an important role in the history of the martial arts. But modern students shouldn't confuse the study of the martial arts with the practice of Buddhism. Some arts originated in temples, and Buddhist developments influenced many others, but the Buddhist clergy's motives for studying and teaching systems of fighting were military and political, not religious. The true martial arts are purely methods of warfare, even when taught in temples and practiced by priests!

SHINTO: THE *WAY* OF THE *KAMI*

This land of the Plentiful Reed Plains and of the Fresh Rice-ears has been entrusted to you as the land to be governed by you. Therefore, you must descend from heaven in accordance with the divine command.

From the Kojiki Myth*

Shinto is a primitive nature religion peculiar to Japan. It's an ancient faith, existing since prehistoric times. For centuries it went without name. Not until the 6th century A.D., when Buddhism first began to filter into Japan, was it named to differentiate it from other religions. Unlike other Eastern faiths, Shinto has no known founder, no sacred scriptures, and deals only with this world, concentrating on the family and national kinship.

Shinto beliefs focus on the veneration of *kami*, or the "superior ones." But the exact nature of *Kami* is difficult to explain. In ancient times, they were generally considered gods, or people with godlike qualities. But even the great 18th century Japanese Shinto scholar, Norinaga Motoori, confessed: "I do not yet understand the meaning of the term *kami*." (Hopfe, 1976, p.193)

*These were the instructions Amaterasu, the sun goddess, gave to Ninigi, first emperor of Japan, according to Japanese mythology (Hopfe, 1976, p.196).

The history of Shinto can be divided into three periods. The first runs from prehistory to the introduction of Buddhism, around A.D. 550. During this era Shinto existed without shrines or temples and was practiced according to oral tradition. The *kami* were considered gods, and a mythology evolved in which the emperor was considered the direct descendent of the sun goddess, sent down to govern the country. This belief persisted until 1946 when Governor General of the U.S. occupation forces, Douglas MacArthur, forced Emperor Hirohito to officially renounce it.

The second period covers the time from the 6th century, when increasing contact with the Chinese and Koreans brought an influx of Buddhist and Confucian ideas to Japanese society, to the end of the Tokugawa Shogunate in 1868. Early in this period, the Japanese began venerating their ancestors as *kami*. This notion may have originated in religious Confucianism, whose ancestor worship was quite compatible with Shinto mythology. The Japanese readily embraced the idea of ancestor *kami*, considering them the embodiment of their families' life spirit and therefore, forever present.

During the course of the second period, Buddhism and Shinto influenced each other substantially. Following Buddhism's example, Shinto became more conventional, making use of a formal clergy and erecting thousands of shrines across the countryside. Buddhism, on the other hand, experienced an onslaught of Shinto mysticism resulting in numerous sects professing odd mixtures of Buddhist and Shinto beliefs. Many of these sects resided in remote mountain regions and were a considerable source of the *yamabushi* problem discussed earlier. But Shinto and Buddhism were never fully compatible; the former was concerned with this world and the latter preoccupied with escaping it. Therefore, Buddhism never completely absorbed Shinto as it had other doctrines, and each remained as a separate expression of Japanese culture.

The third period began in 1868 with the fall of the last Tokugawa *Shogun* and the nominal restoration to power of the emperor, Meiji. Japan, subservient to the technically superior Western powers, was desperately struggling to reach military parity and revive national pride. The Meiji government looked for a point around which to rally national spirit, and they found it in Shinto.

The Constitution of 1889 declared Shinto the state religion, and the government made aggressive reforms, re-emphasizing the emperor's divinity and naming him the de facto head of the faith. But this was a secular doctrine consisting mainly of patriotic rituals conducted at state-supported shrines, each devoted to some local hero or historical event. Religious Shinto coexisted with the state-directed dogma, and ancestor veneration at home shrines continued, but only state shrines and patriotic functions received government funding. This state dogma died with the emperor's repudiation in January, 1946.

Today, the Japanese still venerate the *kami* as spirits, though not quite in the sense that Westerners envision when they hear that term. To the modern Japanese, a *kami* is an attitude, a sense of awe or dread. It's a spirit in a sense similar to when we refer to the "spirit of valor" or an "air of death," but much stronger. The *kami* are still considered divine, but they aren't gods or ghosts. Given that admittedly vague description, understand that the Japanese see *kami* in any number of things: the sea, mountains, trees, rivers and streams, ancestors, even manmade objects such as works of art and weapons—especially the sword.

Shinto has had a significant influence on the Japanese martial arts—not so much in their development but in the way they are perceived and practiced. The Japanese martial arts were developed by professional warriors; therefore, they focus on using and defending against weapons. To the Japanese, weapons carry great *kami*, so handling them is a solemn affair and studying combat is almost divine.

This spirit carries over to the training halls in which Japanese arts are practiced, particularly those places where the *bugei*—the old, classical martial arts—are taught. A Japanese training hall is called a "*dojo*" or "*Way* place," and training there involves much more than learning physical techniques. Studying in a traditional *dojo* involves a spiritual transformation that is more a process of *becoming* than one of learning. *Bugei* master Fredrick Lovrett explained it most eloquently:

> *The goal of a school is to teach a person new things; the goal of a* dojo *is to transform the person into something new. A school teaches how to kill; a* dojo *teaches how to die. The member of a* dojo *does not think about fighting. Neither does he think about not fighting.** *He tries to go beyond this level and comprehend the very essence of conflict (1987, pp. 14-15).*

One feels a very spiritual attitude in a Japanese *dojo*, an attitude of reverence—not in a religious sense but in the air of decorum and the sensation of awe. That attitude is maintained and projected by every member of the *dojo*, and it reflects the solemn mind-set each has about the significance of the art he practices. That is what the Japanese call *kami*.

Each member of a traditional *dojo* carries that spirit, that *kami*, in his heart, but there is a focal point in the *dojo* toward which members express their respect for the *kami* of their art. That is the *kamiza*, or "spirit seat," at the head of the *dojo*. The *kamiza* is usually a shelf on the front wall of the training hall. Often it holds various objects of sentimental value to the *sensei*, and sometimes an old and esteemed weapon is placed there. But in the most traditional *dojo* you'll always find a small *jinza*, a Shinto shrine.

*Note the Taoist flavor of this statement.

Formal classes in traditional *dojo* open and close with ceremonial bowing to the *jinza*. Of course, that always frightens Westerners who are conditioned with religious prohibitions against bowing to idols. But understand, this is not a religious act. *Dojo* members aren't bowing to some ghost or god living in the shrine. Bowing to the *jinza* is a traditional expression of respect—respect to the art and its founder, its traditions, and the *dojo* where it is practiced. The *jinza* merely serves as a focal point toward which members direct their mutual deference.

So the Shinto-based rituals practiced in Japanese *dojo* aren't religious functions. They are demonstrations of respect for the *kami* or "spirit" of the martial art and The Martial *Way*.

MYSTICISM AND THE DANGER OF CULTS

Mysticism is a controversial topic among people who study the martial arts. Some shy away from it, associating the term with magic and the occult. Others run toward it, eagerly searching for the mysterious and ethereal side of everything they study. Indeed, concepts such as *ki* and *zanshin* tend to lead the uninformed to ideas of the supernatural as they look for some secret power to enhance their fighting abilities. But just as the functions of *ki* and *zanshin* aren't mystical, neither does mysticism itself necessarily have anything to do with the occult.

Mysticism is the belief that one can only achieve a direct communion with ultimate reality through intuitive sources rather than by objective learning. There is nothing magical about this idea. In fact, founders of most major religions and philosophies were mystical in that they achieved their spiritual awakening through direct communion with what they perceived to be the ultimate truth. They may have called that truth "God" or "*Tao*" or something else, but the fact remains, they received their insights intuitively, rather than by being taught outside knowledge. They turned their eyes inward.

Taoism and Buddhism are classic examples of mystic philosophies. Both encourage followers to turn their attention inward, to block out the distracting influences of objective knowledge and rational thought, so they can awaken to the ultimate reality within. And since the Asian martial arts are influenced by both of these doctrines, they can indeed have mystic connotations if you are open to them. But you don't have to pursue mysticism if you don't choose to. Just as the martial arts aren't methods of worship, they aren't intended to be pathways to spiritual enlightenment. The true martial arts are methods of warfare.

Some organizations that teach Asian combative systems incorporate mystic doctrines in their training programs. Often, they claim to have secret or forgotten knowledge from the *yamabushi* or from other past warrior societies. Of course, you're free to pursue these avenues if you choose, but understand, you aren't open to intuitive insight as long as you are being spoon-fed someone else's ideas. You're simply learning another external doctrine.

But there is a greater danger in these organizations than being misled. Groups claiming to teach mystic, secret, or occult martial arts knowledge are often little more than thinly disguised cults. Webster defines a cult as a "system of religious beliefs, or its adherents, which are regarded as unorthodox or spurious." Of course, most of the world's major religions and philosophies fit that description when they first appeared. So there isn't necessarily anything wrong with being unorthodox. But the kind of groups I'm referring to are the abusive cults, those involved in controlling their members.

Abusive control groups manipulate their members into accepting their definition of truth and reality. Sometimes they do this through intimidation or physical and emotional abuse, but often their methods are more subtle, and victims don't even realize they are being manipulated. These groups prey on the weak. They appeal to people searching for something or someone to reassure them of their self worth. They always claim their doctrine offers a secret that no one else has, an insight the rest of the world desperately needs but hasn't found.

Since martial arts students often crave learning the "secret of *ki*," the "deadly techniques of the *dim mak*,"* or the "invisible ways of the *ninja*," many are susceptible to control-oriented, cults. Of course, we all want to learn techniques our opponents don't know. But some students, particularly the young and naive, are more easily victimized than others. You can protect yourself from this kind of quackery by watching for the following danger signals:

1. AN IRREFUTABLE, CHARISMATIC LEADER.

Cult groups form around a leader whose words are beyond question. He often claims ranks or titles and a remarkable past that can't be verified. Veterans of the group exhibit the "true believer" attitude, and they speak of the leader in tones of awe. If that sounds like a school you are considering joining, don't!

2. AN UNASSAILABLE DOCTRINE.

Cult-oriented schools always claim theirs is the only way. Their techniques and teaching methods, often abusive, are beyond question. Often, they say they teach the original martial art; the others have gone soft or lost the secret over the years. Nobody else knows what they know. Don't believe them!

3. SLOGANS AND CLICHES.

Do seniors seem to have a canned answer for every question you ask? That's a sure sign they aren't thinking for themselves. They are parroting their leader's dogma. Don't you stop thinking too!

---

*The *dim mak* is supposedly a Chinese system of strikes and touches that disrupt the victim's vital force, injuring organs and causing illness or death sometime later.

4. OUTLANDISH PROMISES.

Control groups tend to focus not on who you are but on what they claim they can make you. They hold out the golden ring of secret techniques, remarkable abilities, and anything else they sense you are craving. If they don't seem to like or respect you now, don't wait around to see if they will later.

5. FOCUS ON RECRUITING AND FUND RAISING.

Traditional instructors dislike talking about money and are embarrassed when they have to ask for dues. Furthermore, classical schools are literally hard to join—they don't advertise* and they discourage prospective students they feel may not have the necessary maturity or discipline to stay with the training.

Cult groups, on the other hand, are always recruiting, always trying to raise money. Often, they find subtle ways to bilk their students, such as charging for individual techniques or *kata* or soliciting kickbacks from other instructors for sending students to their seminars. Once they sense they have their hooks set deeply, they get more brazen in their demands. I know one supposed instructor who told a teenage student, "You don't have the money to test? Then, give me your motorcycle and I'll promote you." The student did as he was told. Don't you be so gullible.

6. PRESSURE TO COMMIT.

"Don't be a wimp! Join now or don't come back." "Sign up for the master's seminar or we don't ever want to see you again." These ultimatums sound extreme, but some groups use exactly that kind of pressure. They often do it when the student is most vulnerable,

*Some place a small block in the *Yellow Pages* listing the name of the school, a phone number, and simply saying, "traditional martial arts," but you'll never see a traditional school with picture ads, impressive claims, or menu-like lists of what their training will do for you.

when he's tired or injured. And the longer you stay, the more demanding they become.

One school I know pressures students into frequent 24-hour "training sessions." They charge for time in the training hall, and before students realize it, they owe hundreds of dollars a month. If students object to this extreme commitment of time and money, they're told they either have to, "fight the master to the death, or leave the school forever!" Never allow yourself to be pressured into making commitments. So, don't join, and don't go back!

MARTIAL ARTS TRAINING. AND RELIGIOUS CONVICTIONS

By now you have made the first step towards a firm grounding in Eastern religious thought, and you can discriminate mysticism from cult-oriented behavior. But what if you still have misgivings about bowing in class or studying an art that originated in a Buddhist temple? Well, let me offer you this four-step approach to reconciling your martial arts training with your religious convictions:

1. REMEMBER, YOU ARE STUDYING METHODS OF WARFARE, NOT WORSHIP.

The martial arts are methods of personal combat; they aren't religious rites. Even those arts that originated in temples were developed for military or paramilitary reasons. Of course, Asian warriors were often religious, just as the European knights were, but the combative systems they practiced were no more parts of their religious systems than is Western fencing a part of Roman Catholicism.

Some modern groups may tell you religion or mysticism is part of the martial arts and to learn their art you must take part in rituals, make offerings, or perform other rites. Of course, you're free to do those things if that's what you are looking for. But those things aren't part of the martial arts, nor are they The Martial *Way*.

2. EVALUATE ASIAN DOCTRINES AS PHILOSOPHIES, NOT RELIGIONS.

Several Asian doctrines did impact the historical evolution of the martial arts. But the three principal schools of religious thought in Asia—Confucianism, Taoism, and Buddhism—all began as philosophies. They only became religions when superstitious followers began associating gods and ritual worship with them. The relevance of these doctrines to the martial arts is philosophical, not religious.

An austere *kamiza* with a traditional *jinza* grace the wall of a classical Japanese *dojo*.

3. ACCEPT THE PHILOSOPHICAL PRINCIPLES THAT WORK FOR YOU; DISCARD THE REST.

Study and understand the philosophical principles behind the Asian schools of thought. You'll find some of them keenly insightful and very helpful in your warriorship. Disregard those that conflict with your religious beliefs, don't help you, or just don't seem to make sense. Don't be afraid that you are practicing some pagan religion; you're not unless you choose to accept and worship the deities associated with the religious versions of these doctrines.

4. PERFORM SCHOOL FORMALITIES AS OBSERVANCES OF TRADITION.

Bowing in Asia isn't a religious act. It corresponds to shaking hands or saluting in Western tradition. So the bowing in martial arts training isn't a religious observance, even when the focal point is a *kamiza* or *jinza*.

Martial arts school formalities are demonstrations of respect and the preservation of tradition. But the amount of ceremony observed from school to school varies widely. So if the elaborate traditions observed in a certain school conflict with your religious beliefs, join a school whose traditions you find more acceptable.

POINTS TO REMEMBER: RELIGION AND MYSTICISM

- Westerners incorrectly associate Asian religions and mystical practices with the martial arts. The true martial arts are methods of warfare, not worship.
- Asians perceive and practice religion in ways far different than Westerners do. Most Eastern religions began as philosophies, not forms of worship. Also, where Western religious doctrines are

exclusive, Eastern religious and philosophical thought is inclusive. No one school holds a monopoly on truth; you can select your philosophical beliefs from several schools.

■ Confucianism is a legalistic philosophy which addresses man's role in society. Confucian ethics are the backbone of nearly all legal systems in Asian nations and the foundation of all Eastern military codes of honor.

■ Buddhism, as Gautama taught it, wasn't a religion; it was a philosophical program of training, a system of discipline and mystical self development. Some martial arts originated in Buddhist temples, and Buddhist developments influenced many others, but the Buddhist clergy's motives for studying and teaching systems of fighting were military and political, not religious.

■ Shinto is a primitive nature religion peculiar to Japan. Shinto beliefs focus on the veneration of *kami*. But the Shinto-based rituals practiced in Japanese *dojo* aren't religious functions. They are demonstrations of respect for the *kami* or "spirit" of the martial art and The Martial *Way*.

■ Mysticism is the belief that one can achieve a direct communion with ultimate reality only through intuitive sources rather than by objective learning. There is nothing magical about this idea. But groups claiming to teach mystic, secret, or occult martial arts knowledge are often little more than thinly disguised cults. Always be wary of abusive control groups.

■ Reconcile your martial arts training with your religious convictions by studying methods of warfare, not worship. Evaluate Asian doctrines as philosophies; accept the principles that work for you, and discard the rest. Perform school formalities as observances of tradition. But if the traditions observed in a school conflict with your religious beliefs, join a school whose traditions you find more acceptable.

Chapter 11

THE WARRIOR STANDS ALONE

The superior man undergoes three changes:
Looked at from a distance, he appears stern.
When approached, he is mild.
When he is heard to speak, his language is firm and decided.

CONFUCIUS

The *dojo* was quiet. The students were lined up along the back, kneeling in *seiza*, their eyes glued to the two *yudansha* who kneeled in the center, facing each other across the span of *tatami*. The antagonists sat perfectly straight and stone still, their unblinking eyes locked on one another in placid concentration. Each wore a plain white *gi* jacket over a pleated, black *hakama*, the traditional baggy pants of the *samurai* and the formal training uniform of classical, Japanese martial artists. Without breaking their gaze, the men placed their hands on the mat in front of them—first left, then right—and slowly bowed to one another. The air was thick with *zanshin*.

Without cue, the lesser of the men sprang smoothly to his feet and deftly strode two paces towards his opponent. Almost simultaneously, the senior flashed into motion, a mirror image of the junior's advance. Those watching inhaled audibly. Each man held a precise, fighting posture. With only a moment's hesitation, the men began slowly, warily, closing the distance between them.

Suddenly, the junior exploded in movement, leaping forward to grab the other man's wrists. His hands found their mark but only for an instant. The senior pivoted in perfect harmony with his opponent's charge and whirled into a blinding *shiho nage*. The junior cartwheeled through the air, legs windmilling high overhead, and slammed thunderously to the *tatami*. Without the slightest loss of momentum, the older warrior expertly cranked his fallen adversary's arm, rolling him face down. Another nimble turn and the arm was locked behind the junior's back. The senior quickly pinned it there with his knee and, his posture statuesque, raised one sword hand above his head and barked a short *kiai* of victory.

But the encounter wasn't over. After but a moment, the victor released his quarry and leaped back into stance, eyes fixed on the still-dangerous adversary. The junior, suddenly freed, rolled nimbly into *hantachi*, a half kneeling posture with hands at the ready, and locked his eyes once more on his opponent. He stood slowly, and the two began moving again, ever widening the range between them. They came at last to the starting points, and each carefully sank into *seiza*, never breaking his gaze or his intense concentration. Finally, after one last pause, they bowed to each other and relaxed.

The onlookers sighed together, and as the tension dissolved, I realized I'd been holding my breath too. It was magnificent. Never before had I seen anything in the martial arts so graceful, yet so awe inspiring as this, the ritualized, formal combat of Yamate Ryu Aikijutsu.

Warriorship is a dignified calling. Its professional elite, whether they are military officers, law enforcers, or members of some other warrior vocation,* move with a somber grace, an air of

*Of course, not all members of warrior professions heed the call of warriorship. In this age, true warriors are scarce even in those fields.

power. They aren't arrogant, but they all live with the dark knowledge that their profession may one day call on them to kill other human beings, and they are quietly confident in their physical, emotional, and technical ability to do so.

Real warriors are amused and a little disgusted with the foolish antics some martial artists exhibit today. These imitation warriors strut around studios and tournament floors in their costumes of many emblems, each trying to out-prance the others. They think the martial arts are sports. As a result, they don't live them, they play them. And oh, how they love to perform. They'll kick apples out of the air, chop vegetables with swords, or do any number of other medicine-show tricks that have nothing to do with the arts of warfare. But warrior dignity still exists in the world of the martial arts; there are men and women who keep it alive.

There are still those who quietly walk into crowded rooms and command attention simply by their presence. These people stand straight and tall, and they project a confidence that only comes from years of disciplined training. They don't join in cliques—more times than not, they stand alone—but they recognize and gravitate towards one another. Only warriors understand other warriors.

Warriors are never the life of the party. They're rarely interested in small talk and speak only when they have something meaningful to say. When they do speak, their voices are steady and resolved—strong but not loud, bold but not arrogant. They shake your hand with a firm grip, and when they meet your eyes, you feel an energy you can't describe. These people practice the arts of death, the ways of killing men. These are the men and women who live The Martial *Way*.

This chapter will teach you how to achieve warrior dignity. You'll discover the social and tactical importance of a commanding posture, and you'll learn how to influence others and encourage their respect. Decorum and physical grace are qualities that set warriors apart from lesser people. I'll teach you to avoid the self-defeating antics of the social clown and strive for *shibumi*, the warrior ideal of personal elegance. Finally, you'll learn how combining these forces with the esoteric skills of warriorship will lead you to personal power.

THE THREE KEYS TO WARRIOR DIGNITY

What makes the warrior elite so different from other people? Everyone can sense there is something about that one man or

The warrior's *Way* is a somber calling. Its disciples practice the arts of death, the ways of killing men.

woman that makes them stand out from a group of more common stock, but what is it? Is it pretense? Does he or she simply move and act in ways that convey dignity, or is it something more? It's more... believe me, warrior. It's more!

Dignity isn't something you can take on and off like a coat. It's a deeply-rooted behavior. It takes time to develop, and it can't be faked. So nothing I tell you today will make you a man or woman of substance tomorrow. But there are definitely several physical and emotional elements, that properly cultivated, will lead to the quality I'm describing. And you can certainly learn to avoid the kinds of behavior that make you look foolish.

There are three fundamental keys to cultivating warrior dignity. To become a man or woman of substance, you must:

- Develop a commanding posture.
- Discover the power of physical grace.
- Cultivate the austere quality of *Shibumi*.

DEVELOP A COMMANDING POSTURE

Sit up straight and lift your rice bowl to your mouth. Only dogs hang their heads in their bowls!

A Japanese Parent's Admonishment

Some say the eyes are windows to the soul. This may be true, but posture is most assuredly the reflection of one's spirit. It tells a story, more eloquently than words ever could, of your strength, your resolve, and your confidence. Posture is an essential element of warrior bearing.

Have you ever seen a man suffering from chronic depression? What is the first thing you notice about him? It isn't whether he's shabbily dressed or poorly groomed, although in his emotional state, he may be inattentive to these things. No, you notice his poor posture. He hangs his head and slouches. His eyes are downcast, and his shoulders are slumped. When seated, he slides his rounded back down in the chair and seems to dissolve into the upholstery. Is this a man who commands your respect? Are you inclined to trust his word or follow his leadership? Of course not!

We all know how important first impressions are. Well, of all the factors involved in a social encounter, posture makes the very first impression. Your posture tells people about your physical condition and your spiritual strength. It speaks of your resolve, your commitment to who you are and what you believe. And whether people will admit it or not, your posture reflects your social station relative to those with whom you are dealing.

Posture is the currency of leadership. It's an unspoken language, a tool of command. When a group of people are talking, all fall silent and turn their attention when the man who stands straightest speaks. It's an unconscious reaction, a Pavlovian response. He's the straightest, so he must be the authority. And believe it or not, regardless of who in the group is greatest in stature, all usually assume the man who stands most erect to be the tallest.

At six feet, I'm a little taller than average, but people often think I'm taller than I really am. Friends and associates frequently remark about being only five-eleven or six feet tall—clearly shorter than me. Recently, I practiced jujutsu with an exceptionally tall student. When I mentioned having to modify some of my techniques slightly because of his height, he looked puzzled and said, "Well, I don't know why you're having a problem. After all, we're the same height." The man was six feet four inches tall!

Posture isn't just a social issue. It's a tactical and technical one as well. Keeping your head up centers your field of vision, and keeping your back straight enables you to pivot quickly and deliver more force with less muscular effort. Posture is a key element of *haragei*; a vertically erect body naturally centers its weight over the *tanden*. Only with proper posture can you command your physical center and the concentric circles that emanate from it.

It isn't hard to learn good posture. If your body is healthy and properly conditioned, standing or sitting straight is easier than slouching. After all, a straight body is balanced over the *tanden*, the center of gravity. It takes less energy to hold it there than it does to hang it forward in a slumped position.

Unfortunately, many people no longer have healthy bodies. By the time most Westerners reach 30, the years of slouching in plush chairs have led to rounded shoulders and curved spines that slump forward. To compensate for this unbalanced position, their bodies also bow at the lower back, jutting their pelvises forward to re-center their *tanden* beneath their upper torsos. As they hold this position day after day, the muscles supporting their necks, backs, and shoulders weaken. Eventually, the spine itself begins to collapse.

As in other things, prevention is more effective than cure. But most people, even those with eroded spines, can improve their posture with effort. The key is constant attention. You have to make good posture a habit, and you start by learning what good posture is.

If you take a sidelong look at a man or woman standing straight, you can easily tell if their posture is correct. Drop an imaginary plumb line through the top of the individual's head. If the subject's posture is right, the line will fall through the ear, down the back of the neck, through the shoulder and hip sockets, and exit the foot just forward of the heel. So, to practice good posture, you simply straighten you body and put those key points in line.

Stand up straight, and pull your slumping shoulders back. To get your head squarely over your shoulders, you'll probably have to consciously rotate your hips slightly, pointing your tailbone back just a bit. You see, after years of sitting with your back bowed, standing straight won't feel natural. You'll actually have to arch your lower spine into a position that feels exaggerated until you get into the habit of good posture. But let me offer you a secret—my little trick for quickly correcting my posture.

Do you remember when you were growing up, how the doctor used to stand you on the scales and measure your height? Remember how you used to stretch your back and neck to get as tall as possible as he lowered the bar down on the top of your head? Well during that moment, you stood in your most perfect posture. So to achieve good posture once again, just pretend you're trying to stretch your body upward to make it as tall as possible. In fact, I even imagine a cable is attached to the crown of my head, and as I walk through my day, it constantly pulls me upward—not enough to pull my feet off the ground but enough to pull me up tall and straight.

Practice these principles as often as possible. Do it while standing, walking, sitting in a chair, or kneeling in *seiza*. All through the day, think of posture. Check yourself in mirrors whenever available. Make it an obsession. When posture becomes a habit, you'll be on the verge of discovering the power of physical grace.

DISCOVER THE POWER OF PHYSICAL GRACE

The mind (i) commands, strength (li) goes along, and internal energy (chi) follows.

Anonymous Chinese Adage
(Minick, 1974, p.99)

The teenage years are hard for most people, but they were particularly unkind to me. I was tall, skinny, and awkward. Being acutely self-conscious of my clumsiness, I was shy and I lacked confidence. So as I walked down the halls of my school, I struggled desperately to effect an air of confidence and coordination.

Every day I concentrated on walking decisively, stepping smoothly and confidently, while swinging my arms at just the right rhythm. But it was no use. The more I concentrated on graceful movement, the more awkward I became. My arms would lose timing with my legs, and I'd stiffen up trying to get everything under control. Before long I looked like a stumbling robot and some of the kids who saw me openly sniggered. Others just stared. You see, I hadn't yet discovered the secret of physical grace.

Some men sneer at the thought of moving gracefully. They associate the idea with feminine qualities, the kind of skill a dancer might seek but nothing with which a manly man should concern himself. But they are wrong. Grace is the product of confidence, strength, coordination, and perfect balance—all qualities to be envied in both sexes. Grace is an outward expression of physical and spiritual power.

The prerequisite for grace is confidence. As I so sadly discovered, graceful movement is impossible when you're plagued with self-consciousness and doubt. Unfortunately, there is nothing I can say that will bring you confidence, and you can't fake it. But if you practice the martial arts faithfully, your confidence will grow with your skill. And if you're living The Martial *Way*, developing confidence in all facets of your life is inevitable; it's just a matter of time.

But don't sit around waiting for confidence to arrive. You see, all of us lack confidence now and then. No matter how advanced we are, there are days on which we don't feel so self assured, situations in which we don't have complete command. In these circumstances, true warriors don't lose their physical grace. On the contrary, these are the times they are strongest. In situations where you lack confidence, you must fill the void with courage.

Physical strength and coordination are also essential assets for moving with grace. The stronger you are, the easier you can maneuver your body, and coordination—the control and balance of muscular tension and relaxation—is the very essence of graceful movement. You'll develop these qualities from the technical training in your martial art and through the physical training principles I explained in Chapter 9. So train hard and be patient. In time, your body will mature and develop a powerful, machinelike precision.

As for balance, I have just one word... *haragei*! This esoteric "belly art" I explained in Chapter 5 is the very core of physical grace. By focusing attention on your *tanden*, relaxing, and keeping your weight underside, you'll lose the self-consciousness that leads to stiff, awkward movement. And this is where proper posture is so important. Standing straight and balancing your upper body over the *tanden* is essential for achieving *haragei*.

But where posture alone is static, physical grace is fluid. So you must learn to maintain your posture and your *haragei* throughout all your movements, in everything you do. That means you must always focus on your *hara*, your center. You don't walk, run, or execute fighting techniques with your arms and legs. You do those things, and all things, with your *hara*. Your arms and legs just come along for the ride.

Always move from the *hara*. As you walk, glide your *hara* forward. Let your arms and legs follow as they will. You see, that was my problem as a teenager. Where I was trying to conquer my awkwardness by commanding and coordinating the movements of my arms and legs, I should have simply ignored them and focused on moving my center. Had I done that, everything else would have fallen into place.

And I would have been the most powerful student in school had I known how to cultivate the austere quality of *shibumi*!

CULTIVATE THE AUSTERE QUALITY OF *SHIBUMI*

One of the best examples I ever saw of military bearing and the dignity of warriorship took place at a formal dinner I attended as an Air Force second lieutenant in 1980. I was new to the officer corps, and I didn't have much experience in military social functions. Nonetheless, this "dining-out" sounded like fun. It offered a chance to dress up and enjoy a little pomp and circumstance. But the day before the event, the major responsible for coordinating the whole affair assigned me to what sounded like a tedious detail.

"Morgan, tomorrow night I want you to serve as aide-de-camp for Colonel Grimes, the base commander." Uh-oh, I thought.

"Okay, but what does an aide-de-camp do?"

"He facilitates... you know... opens doors, gets drinks, that sort of thing. As base commander, Colonel Grimes is attending our dining-out as a matter of protocol, but he doesn't know anyone from our squadron. I want you to make him feel at home. Stand at his shoulder and ease him in and out of various social circles. Introduce him around and make sure he has people to talk to so he doesn't stand there feeling awkward."

Great! The Air Force sure knows how to screw up a good thing. Just when I'm looking forward to an evening of fun and relaxation, I get to baby-sit some stiff-necked, old-fogy colonel. My friends will avoid me like the plague.

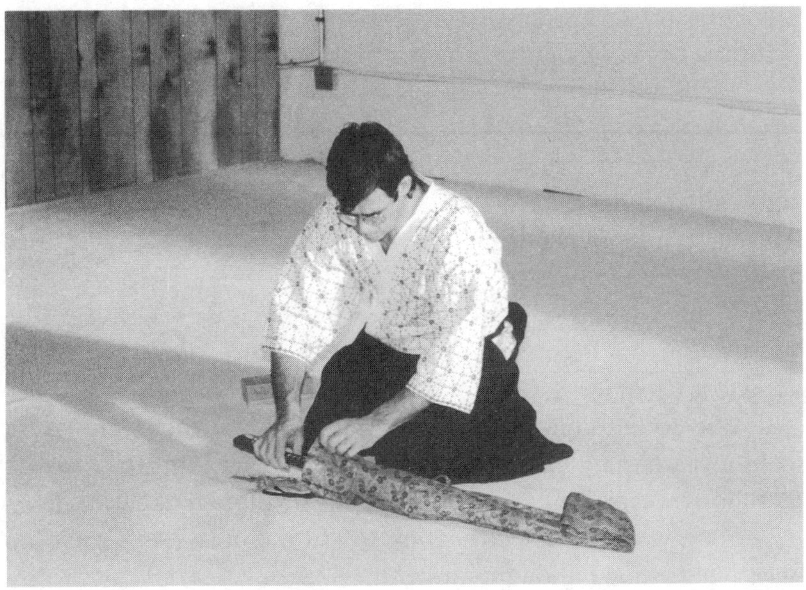

Shibumi is a quality that few Westerners appreciate. This warrior lovingly attends to his prize possession—his sword.

Boy, was I in for a surprise!

The next evening I arrived at the Officer's Club early in the cocktail hour. Stepping into the ballroom, I saw a few officers and their dates milling around with drinks in their hands. There was a cluster of lieutenants at one end, and as I expected, the major was in the middle, issuing last-minute instructions. I wandered on over.

"Okay, Sir. So where's this Colonel Grimes?" I said when the major turned to me.

"He's waiting for you over there." he said, pointing to a tall man looking at a picture on the far wall.

I started across the room, and as I approached, the man turned my way. I nearly stopped midstride. The colonel was an imposing figure—lean with broad chest and shoulders, and he stood straight as a utility pole. His hair was closely cropped, and his face was framed by a jaw of granite. But his gaze was what startled me most. He had firm, deep-set eyes beneath a heavy, scowling brow. I swallowed hard and went on over.

"Good Evening, Sir. I'm Lieutenant Morgan, your aide-de..."

"John Grimes." the man said, breaking into a warm smile and thrusting out his hand. "Looks like you folks are going to have quite a gathering here. I think this is going to be a great evening. Hey, let me get you a drink!" He subtly took my elbow and started us off toward the bar.

What's going on here, I thought. I'm supposed to ease this guy around, but before I can start, he's in control and I feel like his long lost nephew.

We got into line at the bar, and over the next ten minutes the colonel commanded my attention. I'm usually pretty guarded around strangers, but before I realized it, this guy knew where I was from, where I went to school, what I did in the Air Force, and whether or not I thought the Denver Broncos would get to the Superbowl that year. Not that he actually said much, but he asked just the right questions and appeared genuinely interested in what

I had to say. I felt like the most important person in the room, and before I could help myself, I really liked Colonel Grimes.

As we got our drinks and turned from the bar I decided I'd better start introducing the colonel around. But before I could act, Colonel Grimes said, "Hey, there's General West! Come on, I'll introduce you." Off he charged with me tagging behind.

As we approached, the general and a circle of colonels around him all stopped talking and turned to Colonel Grimes. The colonel strode up and greeted General West warmly. Totally at ease, he introduced us both around the circle, then expertly guided the conversation, ensuring everyone took part—even me!

The entire evening followed that pattern. With me in tow, Colonel Grimes moved smoothly and decisively from one social group to the next. He didn't spend much time in any one circle and he never said more than he needed to. As the evening drew on and the liquor flowed, other officers got loud and acted foolishly. But the strength and power Colonel Grimes radiated made him the center of attention everywhere he went. He was the model of composure, the image of confident dignity.

Had I known the colonel's record, I wouldn't have been so surprised. The man was genuinely humble, and rather than brag about his background, he cleverly got others to talk about themselves instead. But during the course of the evening I learned he had been a fighter pilot in Vietnam, with several confirmed kills. Later, he'd served in the Office of the Secretary of Defense. And just before becoming the base commander, he had been the Air Attaché for the U.S. Ambassador to Brazil. I don't know if he ever practiced Asian martial arts, but one thing I do know: Colonel Grimes personified the warrior ideal. He exuded *shibumi*.

Shibumi is a Japanese word describing a highly-prized quality that few Occidentals understand or appreciate. It's a sense of simple elegance, an aura of quiet perfection. *Shibumi* has nothing to do with the flashy, decorative beauty admired in the West but refers instead to a clean, restrained sense of distinction, refinement, and taste. *Shibumi* is austere. It never appears busy or embellished. The smooth curve of a Japanese sword is *shibumi*, but a gold-plated, pearl-handled pistol is merely garish.

You can see *shibumi* in every facet of Asian culture. It's reflected in the simplicity of Japanese art and in the modest decor of Asian homes. But nowhere is *shibumi* more strongly reflected than in the traditional martial arts. There, it flavors everything from the stark, Spartan atmosphere of the training hall to the clean, efficient nature of classical technique.

It's hard to find *shibumi* in modern combative systems. Today's martial artists are flashy and impressive, but they aren't elegant. Jumping, spinning kicks and flurries of chops and punches are athletic, but a single, perfectly-executed, killing blow is exquisite in its efficiency. Today's tournament competitors wear colored costumes and make billboards of themselves with their emblems and monograms. Modern "masters" vie with one another for ever-wider, multi-striped belts. Meanwhile, the traditional stylist outshines them all in a plain, unadorned uniform bound by a simple, ragged belt. That is *shibumi*.

Warriors pursue *shibumi* in and out of the training hall. They strive to find that essence of quality, that simple elegance, in everything they do. To seek *shibumi* is to strive for perfection. But cultivating it isn't a matter of adding something to your life; it isn't a question of doing anything more. Indeed, it's just the opposite. Developing your sense of *shibumi* is a slow, deliberate process of carving away. You pare away everything in your technique, your conduct, and your manner that is imperfect or superfluous. What is left is simple, elegant, and dignified. What is left is *shibumi*.

THE SECRET OF PERSONAL POWER

There is an old story often told in traditional training halls about a confrontation between a master of the Japanese tea ceremony and a *ronin*, a rogue *samurai*. It seems the *ronin* was passing through the village and while in the crowded square, turned abruptly, banging his scabbard against the tea master's hip.

"You banged my sword," the *ronin* said coldly. "That is a grave insult, and I will kill you for it."

The tea master knew immediately the *ronin* really meant to kill him, and he was gripped with fear. "I meant you no insult, Noble Sir. Please excuse my clumsiness and let me live. As you can see, I'm not a warrior and I have no sword."

The *ronin* could smell the man's fear, and it excited him.

"Then get a sword and meet me on the road tomorrow at noon. There, I'll let you die like a man. But if you don't show up, I'll find you wherever you are and cut you down like a dog." He turned his back on the stunned tea master and walked away.

The tea master was beside himself with fear. What can I do, he thought. I'm a dead man. Then he remembered hearing that another *ronin*, a famous master swordsman, was also in the village. Perhaps he will help me, he thought. So he sought out the swordsman and told him his story. He explained that he had money to pay for his services and offered to hire him for protection.

"I don't hire to commoners," the swordsman said coolly. "Use your money to buy a sword and fight your own battles."

"Then, will you teach me swordsmanship? I can pay you handsomely."

"I don't teach martial arts to commoners either. Besides, what do you think you can learn in a day?" the swordsman said.

"What have I to lose?"

Indeed, thought the swordsman. Even though the man was a commoner, the *samurai* realized he was an innocent victim needing help. He finally agreed to teach the tea master what little swordsmanship he could in a day. The tea master bought a sword, and the two men began their practice that afternoon. But alas, the poor man was hopelessly inept. After several hours of watching the tea master struggle through hundreds of awkward practice cuts, he shook his head and sighed.

"Tomorrow, you are going to die," the swordsman said with calm conviction.

The tea master was crushed. He was physically and emotionally exhausted. He dropped his sword to his side and stood there staring at the ground, shoulders sagging and sword hanging loosely from his hand. The *samurai* pondered him for a moment then said, "Let's have tea." The tea master looked up in puzzlement, but he carefully sheathed his sword and began unpacking his tea set.

The two men settled beneath a tree, and the tea master began his familiar routine. The swordsman marveled as the man gracefully poured water into the bowl containing the bitter, green powder. As he artfully whisked the mixture into a frothy brew, the swordsman saw a remarkable transformation occur. Gone was the tired, broken man who stood before him only moments ago. Now the tea master's back was straight, his shoulders square, and his head erect. Before the swordsman now sat the solemn, dignified master of an ancient ritual.

The tea master poured the tea into a cup and, turning it in the ritual manner, offered it to the swordsman. His face was the picture of calmness, and looking into his eyes, the swordsman knew immediately the man was in *mushin*.

"Stop!" the swordsman said firmly. "Do you want to kill your enemy tomorrow?"

"You said I am going to die."

"You are, but do you want to die like a warrior? Do you want to kill your enemy?"

"Yes," the tea master said calmly.

"Then do what you are doing right now."

"But I'm doing nothing right now."

"Exactly! Your mind is empty. You neither desire life nor fear death. Tomorrow when you meet your enemy, I want you to empty your mind as you have now and raise you sword above your head. When he attacks, do nothing but cut and die."

The tea master, being a master, understood.

The next day the *ronin* was surprised to find the tea master standing in the road, waiting for him. When he approached and the man raised the sword above his head, the *ronin* chuckled to himself. But as he got closer, he began to feel uneasy. He expected to see the man shaking in fear, but the tea master's sword was still, and his face was grimly calm. He stopped a few paces away and searched the tea master's eyes. He saw nothing... only death.

The *ronin*'s mouth went dry. After a moment he said, "I cannot defeat you." He turned and walked away.

An aikijutsu man disarms a swordsman—an act only possible with a great deal of personal power.

This story perfectly illustrates power in its most naked form. The *ronin* began in a position of power. He knew he could kill the tea master, and he knew that he had frightened the man. That gave him power over his victim. But the master swordsman showed the tea master that he was ultimately more powerful than the *ronin*. You see, the *ronin* was a competent swordsman, but he was no master. The tea master, on the other hand, was inept at combat, but he was a true master. He discovered the secret of personal power.

Personal power is a quality few but warriors understand. It has little to do with physical strength or technical proficiency. Furthermore, it's a commodity separate from political power, economic power, or even military power, although people with personal power can usually achieve in those fields should they choose to. Personal power is quite simply the force that results from freeing yourself from the fear of failure, no matter what the consequences.

We all go through life making decisions by weighing the potential outcomes of our actions. But too often, people decide on a course of action based not on what they can achieve but on what fearful outcome they can avoid. As a result, individuals or circumstances that threaten these people with things they fear have power over them. Achieving personal power means finding the courage to drive ahead no matter what your opponent threatens. Whether the challenge be conflict with an employer, a legal confrontation, or personal combat, when you divorce yourself from any fear of consequences, your adversary no longer holds any power over you.

Man's greatest fear is death. But think of the power you have when you throw off any fear of dying. How threatening would the loss of a girlfriend, a job, or even financial ruin seem today if you knew you were going to die tomorrow. If you can kick that fear, then all the other calamities in life become trivial. So the first step to achieving personal power is to always assume you are going to die tomorrow. Face it... embrace it... savor it! Now go out and do today what you most need to achieve before you leave this world.

Warriors with personal power stand tall and strive for *shibumi* in everything they do. Why settle for anything imperfect or frivolous today when you are going to die tomorrow. You yearn to carve flaws out of your life. You just don't have time to waste on them.

Personal power leads the warrior to absolute dignity. A man who knows he will die tomorrow doesn't act like a clown; he doesn't make a fool of himself in public. A woman with personal power chooses her words carefully; she doesn't want some trivial nonsense to be remembered as her last utterance. When men and women of power speak, others listen. They can feel the power in their words and they know these people will stand behind what they say.

Yes, there are still those who quietly walk into crowded rooms and command attention simply by their presence. They stand straight and tall, and they move with a powerful grace that others envy. Since they expect to die, they have no time for anything short of *shibumi*. These people practice the arts of death, the ways of killing men. These are the men and women who live The Martial *Way*.

POINTS TO REMEMBER: THE WARRIOR STANDS ALONE

- Warriorship is a dignified calling. Its professional elite, whether they are military officers, law enforcers, or members of some other warrior vocation, move with a somber grace, an air of power.
- Dignity isn't something you can put on and off like a coat. It's a deeply-rooted behavior. It takes time to develop, and it can't be faked.

■ Posture is the currency of leadership. It's an unspoken language, a tool of command. Practice the principles of posture as often as possible. Make it an obsession.

■ Grace is an outward expression of physical and spiritual power. It is the product of confidence, strength, coordination, and perfect balance.

■ *Shibumi* is a sense of simple elegance, an aura of quiet perfection. Developing your sense of *shibumi* is a slow, deliberate process of carving away. You pare away everything in your technique, your conduct, and your manner that is imperfect or superfluous.

■ Personal power is the force that results from freeing yourself from the fear of failure, no matter what the consequences. The first step to achieving it is to always assume you are going to die tomorrow. Personal power leads to absolute dignity. Warriors with this quality stand tall and strive for *shibumi* in everything they do.

Chapter 12

MASTERY AND THE MARTIAL *WAY*

The Master said, "I will not be concerned at men's not knowing me, I will be concerned at my own lack of ability."

CONFUCIUS FROM THE *ANALECTS*

Have you fingered through the *Yellow Pages* lately? I travel a bit, and whenever I'm in a new town, I look to see who claims to be teaching what. Even when I'm home, I'll pull out the big yellow book when I'm feeling down and need some cheap entertainment. It never fails to get me laughing.

It's just amazing how much talent we have right here in the United States of America—at least, if these advertisements are to be believed. Every town and village of any size seems to be blessed with a drove of seventh and eighth degree black belts. Some even profess ninth and tenth degrees. Lots of these guys claim to be ex-head instructors for various armies, navies, and national police forces. Gosh, this country must be a virtual Mecca of martial arts experience and expertise. And look at the competitive records they advertise. There seem to be national champions from the United States, Japan, and Korea in every little burg in America. What's more, many towns can boast of their international, pan-American, and all-European champions.

But that's nothing compared to the various levels of mastery these people proclaim. Gone are the days when instructors considered it an honor simply to be called *sensei*, *sabum*, or *sifu*. Now they have to be masters, grand masters, international grand masters, or supreme grand masters. There are even a few professors around, which has always puzzled me since none of the ones I've met even had a baccalaureate degree, much less a doctorate or appointment to the faculty of an accredited university.* While all this posturing is mildly amusing to warriors and serious students, it raises a pointed question: just what constitutes a master in the martial arts?

This issue used to weigh heavily on my mind when I was much younger. I earned my first degree black belt when I was 21 years old. But while many of my peers moved on to other interests after realizing this ambition, I knew I was still a long way from any noteworthy achievement. About this time, I realized the martial arts would always be an important part of my life, so I began considering long-term goals and looking for role models to emulate. At first, I didn't have to look far. The fifth degree black belts in my organization were addressed as "master" and their fighting abilities seemed awesome. With a little research, I learned it normally took 15 to 20 years of training to reach that grade—a worthy challenge. So I made mastery my goal and set out on the road that I believed would lead me there.

But over the years that followed, I began to ponder the grounds of my quest. Doesn't the title "master" suggest the holder has mastered something, I wondered. And doesn't that mean he's learned it all? So, if fifth degree holders are masters, what more is there for them to learn to reach sixth and seventh degrees?

*I suspect the title "professor" became popular when martial artists first heard it used in reference to Jigoro Kano (founder of Judo) and Gichen Funakoshi (founder of Shotokan Karate-Do). However, both of these men were educators and earned the title in addition to their martial arts achievements, not because of them.

Perhaps the fifth degree master has mastered all the curriculum to that point, I reasoned. But if that is so, why isn't a first degree student a master of his level of training, a second degree a master of his, and so on?

Obviously, there was something more about this concept of mastery than I could grasp with the limited understanding my meager rank provided. At least, I thought so then.

My confusion finally reached a head after about ten years of training. At that point, I was still a low-ranking black belt, but being an Air Force officer, I had traveled quite a bit and trained with a number of people from various other martial arts and associations. This gave me a broader perspective on some issues than most of my peers, and having developed a degree of administrative skill and writing ability, I was appointed to work as a staffer for the executive council of my organization.

There I was, a second degree black belt sitting in the closed meetings of the highest ranking members of my association. I was in the company of men from all across the country, ranging in rank from fourth degree to our president, a seventh degree.* What an opportunity, I thought. Now I'll see firsthand how these masters really think and work. I saw it, all right... Boy did I see it!

Most of these meetings were pretty mundane. The council discussed items such as scheduling black belt testings and seminars, minor adjustments in curriculum, and publication of the latest version of the organization's official training manual. But one day several years later, I witnessed a historic meeting. I was there the day they proclaimed fourth degree black belts masters.

By that time, I held a third degree and was officially accepted as the lowest-ranking member of the council. This gave me the privilege of taking part in the debates and voting. So I was able to express my concerns when a fifth degree council member pro-

*During this period, there was also one woman on the council. Unlike most of the men, she maintained her dignity amid the squabbling that was to follow.

posed we realign black belt titles, conferring the honored designation of "master" at the fourth degree level rather than at fifth degree.

I was dumbstruck. How could a fourth degree black belt be a master? More to the point, how could a man or woman who wasn't a master yesterday, suddenly be one today with no additional knowledge or skill? My mind reeled with these questions, and I was only vaguely aware as the other members hotly debated whether the title "master" or "master instructor" sounded more important. As they fought on, I pondered my own situation. I was only two years from eligibility for testing for fourth degree, and I knew I was nowhere close to mastery. How can I master these skills with only two more years of practice? On the other hand,

Traditional Chinese arts were often taught in a dual-track system. Only the most trusted students learned the secret techniques, the system within the system.

how could I ever let students call me "master" before I'm certain I've truly mastered the art?

Finally, I found my voice and turned abruptly to face our president. "How can a fourth degree black belt be a master?" I said sharply. Everyone around the table fell silent in disbelief. The president glared at me for a moment, then he softened and the tension around the table diminished a bit. But I remained rigid as the president patiently explained that since black belts in our organization knew so much more than those from other groups, he had no qualm considering our fourth-degree members masters.

Once again, I was speechless. I had practiced with members of other organizations, and I knew that what the president said simply wasn't true. What's more, I had trained with nearly all these men, and while most of them were indeed better than me, I was already more skillful than some of the fourth-degree members present. Furthermore, my knowledge of martial arts history, tradition, and philosophy was second to no one in the room. Yet, I was not a master, nor was I anywhere close to being one.

But the issue was settled. The council ratified the motion with a nearly-unanimous vote; I dissented. Then, I sat back and watched them argue over how to best show the world they were masters.

"Let's wear a broad, gold stripe running the length of our belts."

"Yes, but only a broken stripe for fourth-degree masters and then, only if they teach."

"What? Masters who don't have students can't have stripes? That's discrimination!"

I watched in disgust as these men quibbled over stripes and patches. Tempers flared as they struggled to find the best ways to stroke their own egos. "Is this what mastery is all about?" I silently asked myself. "Is this what I want to be?"

I never tested for fourth degree black belt in that organization.

But that leads us back to the central issue: just what is a master in the martial arts? What should you, a warrior searching for your own martial destiny, aspire to be? This final chapter will answer those questions. It will compare modern and traditional concepts of mastery as they apply to the various martial arts. Then, you'll learn what true mastery is to warriors who live The Martial *Way*.

MASTERY IN THE MARTIAL ARTS AND WAYS

Before the twentieth century, the notion of mastery in the martial arts entailed learning nothing less than an entire system. Today, that standard is still observed in traditional arts where students are expected to learn not only the external system but also the inner or secret teachings before they can claim mastery.*

In feudal times, nearly all martial arts had two-part training programs. Among warriors, this traditional, dual-track system was used for only one purpose—to ensure survival. Defeat in combat meant death, and feudal warriors didn't want their enemies to learn details of their methods of fighting. So, like the systems of security classification modern governments now use to protect their military secrets, the traditional schools of warriorship only taught their most effective techniques and strategies to their most trusted members.

In China, teachers using this dual-track training method often took the approach of teaching the same sets of forms in two different ways. The "outer circle" of students, those not privy to the school's secret strategies, were taught the same techniques and patterns that the most privileged students were, but certain critical details and the principles behind them were deliberately omitted. Often, these students studied for years to master a system without

* Don't confuse this with the dichotomy between external arts, those which rely on physical strength, and internal arts, those which emphasize development of intrinsic energy.

ever knowing they weren't getting it all. Eventually, after learning all the external forms, they left the school thinking themselves masters.

But they quickly learned differently whenever they faced in actual combat a member of the school's "inner circle," those few trusted students handpicked by the *sifu* to learn the inner system, the system within the system. These students were taught the same forms as the other students and practiced them in the same ways in public. But when no one else was around, the *sifu* taught the inner circle subtle variations based on the school's secret principles and strategies. In some cases, the secrets involved forming the hands differently or attacking different targets. Others involved special footwork, varied timing, or slightly different angles of attack. In any event, students who failed, even after decades of study, to gain the teacher's trust never learned the secrets that would enable them to survive an encounter with the few who did.

In Japan, the dual-track training approach was even more formal. There, the martial arts were practiced by professional warriors, and the martial *ryu* were usually sanctioned and supported by the *daimyo* (warlords) whose warriors they trained. Secrecy was an issue of provincial security. Often, entire arts were kept secret. Even when they weren't, common soldiers were usually only taught the external versions of their respective martial arts, and only higher-ranking *samurai*, or those handpicked to become teachers, were taught the *okuden*, the "hidden teachings."

Throughout Asia and later the world, there have been proponents who only knew the external versions of their arts but professed to have mastered complete systems. Some were deliberate frauds, while others made these claims quite innocently, not knowing the arts they practiced included principles and strategies beyond the scope of their training. In either case, no practitioner can master a traditional martial art without having learned the entire system, internal as well as external.

Of course, the modern martial ways have no secret teachings.* That is true partially because the founders of many of the modern *budo* (martial way) systems weren't privy to the inner teachings of the traditional martial arts they studied. But the main reason there aren't any *okuden* in the modern martial ways is because there just isn't any need for them to have secrets. The main purpose for these systems has shifted from warfare to self development. Furthermore, secret techniques are contrary to the principles of sport competition, where ethics dictate that players should test their skills by competing on equal footing.

The problem with this situation is that it tends to dissolve the distinctions between masters and non-masters. Any student can pick up a book and learn all the same techniques and forms that even the highest ranked karate-do or taekwondo master performed at his final testing. You may argue that with the master's many years of training, he's developed skills vastly superior to his juniors. Often, that is the case. But there are many junior *yudansha* who have the youth and talent to execute forms far better than most of the supposed masters of their arts. I've seen dancers and gymnasts take up a martial way and perfect all the movements within a year or two. Should they be considered masters?

Of course, you'll contend that even though these people can imitate the movements, they usually can't fight like masters. However, that argument carries its own pitfall. Certainly, anyone professing to be a master should be able to defeat non-master students of his or her art. But I suspect few middle-aged masters of sport-oriented martial ways would fare well in single combat against even a low-ranking black belt if the junior is an accomplished tournament competitor in his prime. So, does that mean

*I've encountered one school of Japanese karate-do that teaches *okuden*. However, that school resides in a *dojo* that specializes in classical Japanese martial arts and seems to have incorporated traditional aesthetics into its training program.

we should declare champion fighters masters and reduce them in grade as their skills erode with age?* I think not.

Despite these problems, claims of mastery in the modern martial ways can only be credible after an individual learns the entire system and has been promoted to its highest technical grade. The reason some *budo* systems find themselves in such dilemmas is because they regard mastery as more of a title than an accomplishment.

As I cited earlier, there are organizations today that confer titles of mastery to grades below the highest awarded in their arts. This tendency may stem from the fact that once practitioners reach the intermediate black-belt grades, lacking *okuden* or a coherent system of strategy, there is very little left to teach them. Often they memorize a new form or two and test for each subsequent promotion. But each of these new patterns are usually little more than rearrangements of the same techniques used in earlier forms. In essence, once they reach the middle grades, they know just as much of the art as practitioners at the highest level.

But the main reason we see intermediate-grade *yudansha* called master is because modern martial artists tend to view the concept of mastery from a tradesman's perspective. My father was a sheet-metal skilled tradesman, a certified master journeyman. He earned those credentials by completing a series of schools and apprenticeships, working a specified number of years at lower levels, then successfully passing a trade-union-sanctioned test. Sound familiar? But does his title of "master journeyman" imply he knows everything there is to know about sheet-metal work? No.

Likewise, my air force vocation is space operations, and I wear the master space operations badge. I earned that distinction

*Bowing to these realities, some sport-oriented martial ways now promote students based on competitive records, and *sumo* goes so far as to reduce its former champions in grade when they lose their competitive rankings.

by graduating from a school, then working in the field for seven years. Does that imply I know all of space operations? Have I mastered my profession? Not even close.

In the tradesman's world, the title "master" is the highest in a series of technical certifications, but it never implies the holder has mastered anything. People certified as master carpenters, master plumbers, or master electricians are expected to be good; they've undergone a substantial amount of training and experience, and therefore command higher wages. But no one in those fields ever pretends to know it all, to be masters in the sense that mastery in the martial arts traditionally involves. They've simply met the last in a set of vocational benchmarks arbitrarily laid out by a governing body within their trade or profession.

Traditional Japanese arts still reserve the *okuden*, the "hidden teachings," for their most trusted members.

That approach is very different from how the term should be used in the martial arts. But if you apply the tradesman's mentality to martial arts titles, conferring the title of "master" to fifth-degree practitioners, or even to those at the fourth degree, makes perfect sense. After all, it doesn't mean they've really mastered anything. It just signifies they have reached an arbitrary benchmark set by a governing body.

Truly mastering a martial art or martial way is an admirable goal. It entails learning an entire system—all the techniques, forms, strategies, tactics, and the principles and philosophies behind them. Certainly, that is an objective worth devoting a considerable portion of your life to. But even that can be a dangerous trap. If you're chasing that goal as an end in itself, you're running headlong toward an empty shadow.

You must keep in mind that all systems are artificial; they are the limited creations of men seeking the best ways to teach followers the various methods of warfare. In other words, every system, good or bad, is nothing more than a framework. Technical mastery of the framework itself is certainly important. But if that alone is your goal, you will never see beyond it to what the system's founder really meant to teach you.*

True mastery in the martial arts goes beyond mastering any one specific system of fighting. The only goal truly worthy of a serious warrior's efforts is mastering The Martial *Way* itself.

MASTERY IN THE MARTIAL *WAY*

In every field of endeavor there are a few men and women who, while mastering the mechanics of their system, intuitively sense there is something more than technique, something beyond the mere physical maneuvers that others work so hard to perfect. These people sense and reach for a level of mastery most ordinary

*Of course, if the founder himself never discovered The Martial *Way*, then all he ever meant to teach was the framework. Sadly, that is the case with many modern systems.

people don't even know is possible. They move beyond technical mastery to touch the soul of their craft; they perceive and merge with the very essence of what makes their calling art.

The field of music offers us some of the best examples of this kind of mastery. We see men like Mozart, who could compose entire concertos in his mind, then visualize and dictate the complex musical scores for all the instruments simultaneously. And there was Beethoven, who created his most beautiful and complex orchestrations after he was totally deaf. These were men who stepped beyond mastering the technical details of music and moved naturally with the *tao*, the *do*, the *Way* of their art.

Traditional martial artists have long recognized this kind of genius. They know there are individuals who step beyond the mere technical mastery of artificial systems to touch the essence of personal warfare, the very soul of The Martial *Way*. People of this caliber do not study one art alone. Indeed, you can't perceive the *Way* by looking for it through the lens of one narrow system. Instead, they study personal combat as a whole, using systems of technique as vehicles toward mastery, not doctrinal cages to imprison them.

Once a student becomes one with the *Way*, the barriers of technical expertise fall aside and the root principles of many fields of endeavor become apparent and natural. The great Chinese strategist, Sun Tzu, was not only a master general but also a gifted administrator. Miyamoto Musashi, Japan's master swordsman, defeated sixty opponents in personal combat. But he was also an accomplished poet and painter, and he learned these arts without any instruction. As he explained in the introduction to his *Go Rin No Sho*, he simply took up his brush and did them.

> *...I studied morning and evening searching for the principle, and came to realize the Way of strategy when I was fifty. Since then I have lived without following any particular Way. Thus with the virtue of strategy I practice many arts and abilities—all things with no teacher.*

These are men who found the *Way*. But they didn't do it by burying themselves in the technical details of one system alone. They did it by taking a broad view of the *Way* and, thereby, seeing into its depths.

You can't find The Martial *Way* by focusing exclusively on one narrow system, any more than Mozart would have found the *Way* had he devoted his life to mastering the piccolo. And that is the failing of so many of the modern *budo*, where each proponent insists his is the one-and-only best method of fighting and, therefore, eschews all others. That is also why, traditionalists assert, there is an absolute lack of true masters among pure specialists of the modern *budo* forms, no matter what their degree of technical perfection (Draeger, 1969, p. 62).

The Japanese have a word for one who has mastered The Martial *Way*. They refer to him or her as a *meijin*, which simply means "master." To be called a *meijin* is the highest complement in the Japanese martial arts. But it isn't a title of address—you don't meet "Tanaka *Meijin*" or "Suzuki *Meijin*." Indeed, any true *meijin* is more than satisfied with the simple honorific *Sensei* or even *San*. Nor is this honor conferred by an organization, and no self-respecting warrior would ever think of proclaiming himself a *meijin*. But occasionally, ever-so-rarely, a man or woman emerges from the community of warriors whose wisdom is so profound and whose skill is so natural and pure that the *kaiden*, those who have mastered the various systems, look on in awe and say simply, "*meijin desu*," that is a master.

I am not a *meijin*. In fact, I haven't yet mastered a single system. But no matter what level of skill I eventually reach, you will never hear me introduce myself as "Master Morgan." Nor will I ever permit anyone to address me in that manner. Because if I allow people to call me that, I may start believing it, and that would be tragic. For to believe myself a master would be to say I've learned it all. Then, I would lose my direction. My progress in becoming one with the *Way* would stop.

No, I'm content being known as a simple warrior, a man-at-arms concerned only with living The Martial *Way*. I am an anachronism, a man devoted to studying arcane methods of warfare, a man bound by a rigid code of ethics made long obsolete in this world of shifting mores. But there is no shame in that, because warriorship is a noble endeavor, a powerful way of life. You will discover that too, if you haven't already. You see, warriorship is an elite calling; it's not for everyone. But if you live the warrior's life you will lift yourself above the masses of common men and women.

With the warrior mind-set, you'll pattern your life around the pursuit of excellence. Indeed, The Martial *Way* is a discipline devoted to the perfection of character. It's a very personal pursuit in which the student turns his attention inward. He evaluates the strength of his spirit and sets about polishing those facets that need work. So instead of being a carpenter or a lawyer who does a martial art as a hobby, you'll be a warrior, practicing both your career and your art to hone your spirit. With that approach, you can't help but achieve in your chosen vocation, whatever it may be.

Warriorship offers you other gifts. As a warrior, you learn to see through the guise of popular dogma to perceive the truth in any issue. You understand the role of doctrines—those sets of broad and general beliefs—and you realize that people who entrust their lives to a single doctrine tend to shut out ideas from other sources. In convincing themselves that theirs is the one true way, they become slaves to the very doctrines they profess. You, on the other hand, have learned to sort fact from belief. As a warrior, you evaluate doctrines objectively, extracting the useful portions of each and discarding the rest.

The ability to see through the guise of doctrine will guide your personal growth in all facets of your life, and as a warrior you'll know how to apply that insight most effectively though training. Whatever path you take, you will excel because you have learned to make training a daily regimen. When a challenge arises, you'll have the mettle to meet it. By employing *shugyo* in your training, not only have you accelerated your learning process, but you've hardened your spirit as well. Most importantly, you'll train effectively. You've learned that making a game of important issues is self defeating. As a result, you'll take a "*jutsu*" approach to training for anything in your life that is important.

More than anything else, warriors are strategists. As you live The Martial *Way*, you'll come to understand just how important the command of strategy is in your life. Whether choosing a place to live, planning your career, or pursuing a mate, strategy will guide your effort. You've learned to identify your objectives and collect information about your target. You also know how to study the environment, then program yourself for engagement. Even combat tactics will fare well in other channels of your life, for life itself is conflict.

This man has studied kung fu for 56 years. As head of a system, he is a legitimate *sigun*, or grand master, yet he has his students address him as "*sifu.*"

You will be amazed how important reading your opponent will be in business meetings, investments, even social encounters. And your sense of rhythm and timing will complement your skill in controlling the fighting range to give you an enormous advantage in closing deals or sealing alliances. But your repertoire of esoteric skills may be your greatest asset in dealing with the friends and adversaries around you.

Access to *aiki* and *kiai* gives you the resources to either harmonize with your opponents' spirits or crush them, which ever approach best serves your purposes. You are a different breed. Your peers and enemies are completely unprepared for an adversary with a centered, warrior's heart. They've never encountered one who can focus on an objective to the degree you can. And *mushin* will clear your mind to read the subtle nuances from those around you. In a crisis, it will leave you free to react with lightning speed, to focus your *zanshin* on dominating your unfortunate attacker, whether the threat be overt or the insidious kind more common in the business world.

But the force of warriorship doesn't function through conflict alone. One of your greatest strengths will be your sense of honor. As a warrior, you are a member of an elite fraternity. You are physically, intellectually, and spiritually superior to most of those around you. But these blessings bring with them responsibilities. You must recognize and meet your obligations. You must fulfill your *giri* to uphold justice. Most of all, you must live with courage.

Your associates will realize there is something different about you. They will come to know that you always stand behind your word. They will appreciate your courtesy, but they know it isn't a facade to hide weakness. They can sense you are a dangerous individual, restraining yourself for their safety. Most of all, both your superiors and your subordinates will know your loyalty is steadfast. That is your greatest strength. For no man or woman can stand alone, and your loyalty inspires the loyalty of those around you.

As you grow older, the superiority of your life style will become ever more apparent to you and those around you. You will see your friends and enemies fatten and decay with age, while your body remains firm and strong. You have learned the secrets of physical training. Your muscles will remain strong and durable, you'll stay long-winded, and you will have a supple body long past middle age. Non-warriors will look at you in envy and say you were blessed with good genes. But you know the secret.

Warriorship gives you an objectivity towards religion. You already understand the role doctrine plays in mainstream society. As you look at religious doctrine, you realize that exclusive thinking closes your mind to valuable truths from other sources. In understanding that nearly all religions can be approached as philosophies, you are free to consider and adopt their tenets without violating your own religious convictions.

Warriorship is a dignified calling, and whether or not you pursue a warrior vocation, living The Martial *Way* will teach you to move with a somber grace, an air of power. As a warrior, you know that dignity is a deeply-rooted behavior. It takes time to develop, and it can't be faked. But by constant attention you will eventually develop a strong current of personal power, the force that results from freeing yourself from the fear of failure, no matter what the consequences. Personal power leads to absolute dignity. Warriors with this quality stand tall and strive for *shibumi* in everything they do.

You don't have to study a classical martial art to live The Martial *Way*. Those who practice modern *budo* systems and even those who play at combat sports can study and live the warrior's life style. But you must always remember that all systems are artificial. That is to say, mastery of them is not an end in itself but only a vehicle towards that end. More importantly, you must subdue the external gratifications of rank, prestige, competitive victory, and ego in general for the truer rewards of personal development.

The Martial *Way* does not start and end at the door of the training hall. It is a way of life in which every action is done in the context of warriorship. It's a holistic discipline aimed at the pursuit of excellence, not just in the training hall, but in life. It is a *Way* of power, a life style of success. Its disciples strive to apply the *Way* in every vocation, and its adepts tend to be achievers in any field of endeavor.

The Martial *Way* is not for everyone, fellow warrior. You are a special individual, and that carries a heavy responsibility. Therefore, you must think, feel, and act as a warrior in every situation. You represent a select caste, a noble profession. In this world of pomp and shabby facade, you must be the tempered, the polished, the elite.

In martial cultures of the past, the warrior caste was occupied by a select few, usually chosen by birth. Today, true warriors are rarer still, but times have changed. Gone now are the days of

Technical mastery is an admirable achievement, but the only goal truly worthy of a serious warrior's efforts is mastering The Martial *Way* itself.

inherited status. To earn your rightful place in today's world, you must set yourself apart from the rest of society by your personal excellence. Where warriorship was once a birthright, it is now a calling.

Heed the call, warrior. Heed the call!

POINTS TO REMEMBER: MASTERY AND THE MARTIAL *WAY*

■ No one can master a traditional martial art without having learned the entire system, internal as well as external.

■ Typically, the modern martial ways have no secret teachings. This, and the lack of a coherent system of strategy, tends to dissolve the distinctions between masters and non-masters.

■ Conferring titles of mastery to individuals in ranks below a system's highest technical grade reflects a tradesman's mentality.

■ Claims of mastery in the modern martial ways can only be credible after an individual learns the entire system and has been promoted to its highest technical grade.

■ There are individuals who step beyond the mere technical mastery of artificial systems to touch the essence of personal warfare, the very soul of The Martial *Way*. But you can't achieve this kind of mastery studying one system alone. Remember, all systems are artificial. The only goal truly worthy of a serious warrior's efforts is mastering The Martial *Way* itself.

Appendix A

GLOSSARY

The following is a selected glossary of foreign words and martial arts terms used in *Living the Martial Way.*

AI: Blending, harmony, joining, or union. Also, to concentrate or focus. (Japanese)

AIKI: United spirit. The spiritual principle of destroying an adversary's will to fight, or the physical act of dominating an adversary by harmonizing with his force and redirecting it. (Japanese)

AIKIDO: Modern budo system derived from Daito Ryu Aikijujutsu: (Japanese)

AIKIJUJUTSU: Daito Ryu and the family of jujutsu systems descended from it emphasizing the development and use of aiki. (Japanese)

AIKIJUTSU: The art of aiki. (Japanese)

AI UCHI: Literally "harmonizing strikes." A circumstance of mutual killing in which two adversaries strike each other simultaneously. This concept is common to classical Japanese martial arts, particularly kenjutsu. (Japanese)

ANATMAN: "Nonsoulness." A Buddhist doctrinal tenet that proposes man does not possess a soul. (Indian)

BAKUFU: The administrative bureaucracy of Japan's Tokugawa Shogunate (1600-1868). (Japanese)

BODHISATTVA: Literally "enlightened being." A minor deity in Mahayana Buddhism. (Indian)

BUDO: Martial way. Originally referring to The Martial *Way*, a warrior way of life devoted to self development, but now more commonly used in reference to specific modern combative systems. (Japanese)

BUDO SHOSHINSHU: A 16th century treatise on Japanese warrior ethics and life style written by Daidoji Yuzan. (Japanese)

BUGEI: Literally "martial art." The classical methods of fighting developed by Japanese warriors for the sole purpose of real combat. (Japanese)

BUJUTSU: Same as bugei. (Japanese)

BUNKAI: Application. To practice forms or other solo training methods with a partner. (Japanese)

BUSHI: A warrior of the samurai caste. (Japanese)

BUSHIDO: Literally "*Way* of the Warrior." A feudal code of Japanese warrior ethics evolved from Confucian thought. (Japanese)

CH'AN: The Chinese meditative sect of Mahayana Buddhism. (Chinese)

CHI: Vital energy or spirit. (Chinese)

CHIN NA: Grappling art. (Chinese)

CHUNG DO KWAN: Blue Wave School. Taekwondo (originally Tae Soo Do) system founded in 1941 by Won Kook Yi. (Korean)

COMAULT: A drill command roughly meaning "snap to" or "form up at attention." (Korean)

DAIMYO: Literally "great name." A warlord in feudal Japan. (Japanese)

DAITO RYU: Great Eastern School. A school of classical martial arts dating from the Heian period and passed down to the Takeda family. Source of the family of aiki-arts. (Japanese)

DAN: Degree or grade. A category of rank often indicated by a black belt. (Japanese and Korean)

DESU: A relational in the Japanese language meaning "that is," "they are," etcetera. (Japanese)

DIM MAK: Purportedly, a Chinese system of strikes and touches that disrupt the victim's vital force, injuring organs to cause illness or death sometime later. (Chinese)

DO: A suffix meaning "way." (Japanese and Korean)

DOBOK: A training uniform. (Korean)

DOJANG: Training hall. (Korean)
DOJO: Literally "way place." A training hall. (Japanese)
DHYANA: The Indian meditative sect of Mahayana Buddhism. (Indian)
GI: A training uniform. (Japanese)
GIRI: Literally "right reason." A sense of obligation or duty. (Japanese)
GO RIN NO SHO: "A Book of Five Rings." The classical treatise on sword strategy and tactics written by Miyamoto Musashi in 1645. (Japanese)
GUP: Class. A category of rank for ungraded students, those who haven't reached the "dan" ranks. (Korean)
HAKAMA: Pleated, skirt-like pants worn by practitioners of the classical Japanese martial arts and some traditional budo systems. (Japanese)
HAKKO RYU: Eighth-Light School. Jujutsu system developed by Ryuho Okuyama in 1941 from Daito Ryu Aikijujutsu. (Japanese)
HANSHI: A master instructor or the headmaster of a ryu. (Japanese)
HANTACHI: Literally "half standing." A stance on one knee. Also, a training format in which one student is standing and the other kneeling. (Japanese)
HAPPO ZANSHIN: Keenly alert in eight directions. (see zanshin) (Japanese)
HARA: Literally "belly." The center of the body where one's soul resides. (Japanese)
HARAGEI: Belly art. The physical art of controlling and moving from one's center. Mental and spiritual connotations synonymous with intuition and courage. (Japanese)
HINAYANA: Literally "the smaller vehicle." A name by which the Mahayana Buddhists commonly refer to the Therevada sect. (Indian)
HWARANG: Literally "flower of manhood." A warrior society in the 6th century Korean kingdom of Silla. (Korean)
HWARANG-DO: The ethical code developed by warriors in the 6th century Korean kingdom of Silla. Also the name of a modern martial way founded by Joo Bang Lee. (Korean)
I: Mind. (Chinese)
IAIGOSHI: A ready posture kneeling on one knee. (Japanese)

IN: The soft, female, dark, or negative principle of nature. (Japanese)

IPPON SEOI NAGE: One-arm shoulder throw. A throw common to judo but used in some other arts as well. (Japanese)

ITTEN: Literally "one point." A point in the lower abdomen about three inches below the navel. (Japanese)

ITTO TENSHIN RYU: A school of kenjutsu from the late Edo period, founded by Kurosawa Kojiro. (Japanese)

JEET KUNE DO: A modern, eclectic combative system founded by Bruce Lee. (Chinese)

JINZA: A shrine. (Japanese)

JU: Suppleness, flexibility, or yielding.(Japanese)

JUDO: Yielding way. Modern budo and combative sport derived from jujutsu. Founded by Jigoro Kano in 1881. (Japanese)

JUJUTSU: Yielding art. General term for a wide range of hand-to-hand combat arts, usually emphasizing grappling and throwing, from feudal Japan. (Japanese)

JUTSU: Art or technique. (Japanese)

JUJUTSUKA: One who practices jujutsu. (Japanese)

KAIDEN: Literally "final teaching." The highest grade in some traditional Japanese arts. One who has mastered a system. (Japanese)

KAMI: A spirit as conceived in the Shinto religion.(Japanese)

KAMIZA: Literally "spirit seat." A shelf on the front wall of a Japanese style training hall where a shrine often resides.

KARATE: Empty hand. System of combat developed on Okinawa emphasizing striking. (Japanese)

KARATE-DO: Modern budo form of karate. (Japanese)

KATA: A formal, prearranged exercise. (Japanese)

KATSU: Victory. (Japanese)

KENJUTSU: Sword art. Classical Japanese swordsmanship. (Japanese)

KI: Spirit, breath, the life force. (Japanese and Korean)

KIAI: Focused or concentrated life force. Also a "spirit shout."

KIME: Focus—physical, mental, or spiritual. (Japanese)

KIRISUTE GOMEN: "Killing and going away." The legal right the shogun granted warriors to kill disrespectful commoners on the spot. (Japanese)

KOEN: A riddle with no logical answer used in the Rinzai sect of Zen to confound the conscious mind and allow the aspirant to achieve spontaneous enlightenment. (Japanese)

KOKORO: Heart or mental attitude. (Japanese)

KOKYU CHIKARA: Breath power. Internal power as opposed to physical strength. (Japanese)

KUNG FU: Generic name (Mandarin) for a wide range of Chinese combative systems. The Cantonese term is "gung fu." (Chinese)

KUZUSHI: To off-balance an opponent before executing a throw or some other technique. (Japanese)

KYUBA NO MICHI: "The *Way* of the bow and horse," a code of warrior ethics developed in the 12th century during the reign of Shogun Yoritomo Minamoto.(Japanese)

KUMITE: Freestyle practice in karate and other striking arts. (Japanese)

KYOSHI: A teacher. (Japanese)

KYU: Class. A category of rank for ungraded students, those who haven't reached the "dan" ranks.

LI: Strength. (Chinese)

LUN GAR PAI: Literally "Lun Family System." A system of Chinese kung fu originated in the Kun Lun Shan mountain region of western China. (Chinese)

MAHAYANA: Literally "the larger vehicle." A major sect of Buddhism. (Indian)

MAKE: Defeat. (Japanese)

MEIJIN: A great master. (Japanese)

MENKYO: A license or certificate. (Japanese)

MUSHIN: Mind-no-mind. Conscious but without thought.(Japanese)

NAJUNDE JIRUGI: A low punch. (Korean)

NAJUNDE MAKGI: A low block. (Korean)

NINJA: Stealth. A feudal Japanese group of spies and assassins. (Japanese)

OKUDEN: Hidden teachings. (Japanese)

ON: A debt, obligation, or favor. A burden.(Japanese)

PAHDO: A drill command meaning "stop and return to ready position. (Korean)

RANDORI: Freestyle practice in jujutsu and other grappling arts. (Japanese)

RENSHI: A trainer. A teaching certificate roughly equivalent to fourth or fifth dan. (Japanese)

RONIN: Literally "wave man." A masterless samurai. A rogue. (Japanese)

RYO: A feudal monetary measure of gold. (Japanese)

RYU: A style of an art. A school. (Japanese)

SABUM: A teacher. (Korean)

SAMURAI: Literally "one who serves." A warrior in feudal Japan. A member of the elite class in feudal Japan's four-caste (merchant, artisan, peasant, warrior) social order. (Japanese)

SAN: An honorific title meaning mister, missus, miss, etcetera. (Japanese)

SATORI: Sudden or spontaneous enlightenment. (Japanese)

SANCHIN: Literally "three battles." A breathing method designed to toughen the body, and also an ancient karate kata that employs it. (Japanese)

SANKIN KOTAI: The law of "alternate attendance," which required all daimyo to maintain residences for their families in Edo and to spend every other year in the feudal capital personally. (Japanese)

SEIKA TANDEN: The lower abdomen. (Japanese)

SENPAI: One's senior in the training hall. Often, a general title of address for graded students. (Japanese)

SENSEI: A teacher. (Japanese)

SEPPUKU: Ritual suicide by disembowelment. (Japanese)

SHIBUMI: Restrained elegance. (Japanese)

SHIHO NAGE: Four-directions throw. (Japanese)

SHIZOKU: Descendants from families of the samurai caste. Ex-samurai. (Japanese)

SHOGUN: The military governor of feudal Japan. (Japanese)

SHOTOKAN: House of Shoto. Original school of Japanese karate founded by Gichen Funakoshi in 1922. Shoto was the pseudonym under which Funakoshi wrote poetry. (Japanese)

SHUAI CHIAO: Chinese wrestling. (Chinese)

SHUGYO: Austere training. (Japanese)

SHULT: Drill command meaning "at ease." (Korean)

SIFU: A teacher. (Chinese)

SUMO: A modern sport-version of sumai, a grappling art dating from the 8th century. (Japanese)

TAEKWONDO: Way of smashing with feet and fists. A modern martial way and combative sport emphasizing high kicking and body punching. Also spelled "tae kwon do" and "taekwon-do." (Korean)

TAI CHI: Soft, internal art usually practiced in slow, graceful forms. Modern versions used mostly to promote health. (Chinese)

TAI OTOSHI: Leg drop. A commonly used judo throw. (Japanese)

TANDEN: The abdomen. (Japanese)

TANG SOO DO: China hand way ("tang" refering to China's T'ang Dynasty). Modern martial way and combative sport emphasizing foot fighting and punching. Also spelled "tang su do." (Korean)

TAO: The *Way*. (Chinese)

TAO TE CHING: The *Way of Changes*, a Chinese classic written by Lao Tzu around the 3rd century B.C. It is the fundamental text of Taoism. (Chinese)

TATAMI: Floor mats made of bundled straw. (Japanese)

TE: Hand. Old name for striking arts on Okinawa. (Japanese)

TENSHO: Okinawan karate kata employing dynamic tension and sanchin stance. (Japanese)

THERAVADA: Literally, "the tradition of the elders." A major sect of Buddhism. (Indian)

TORI: Defender. The person who applies the technique. (Japanese)

UKE: Attacker. The person who receives the technique. (Japanese)

UECHI RYU: Internal system of Okinawan karate founded by Uechi Kanbun (1877-1948) after he returned from studying kung fu in China. (Japanese)

UM: The soft, female, dark, or negative principle of nature. (Korean)

WA: The classical concept of nonresistance or fusion. (Japanese)

WAZA: A technique. (Japanese)

YAKUZA: The Japanese mafia. (Japanese)

YAMABUSHI: Literally "mountain warriors." Militant monks from the mystically-oriented Buddhist monasteries in the secluded mountains of feudal Japan. (Japanese)

YAMATE RYU: Mountain-Hand School. School of aikijutsu founded by Taro Yamada, circa 1920, from Daito Ryu Aikijujutsu. Originally Yamanote Ryu, or "Hand-of-the-Mountain School." (Japanese)

YANG: The hard, male, light, or positive principle of nature. (Chinese)

YIN: The soft, female, dark, or negative principle of nature. (Chinese)

YO: The hard, male, light, or positive principle of nature. (Japanese)

YUDANSHA: A graded student (First dan and above). (Japanese)

ZANSHIN: Literally "remaining spirit." A state of hyper-awareness that remains after executing a perfect technique. A sense of alert domination. Also called "the ideal of awareness" and "alertness-remaining-form."

ZAZEN: The seated meditation used in the Soto sect of Zen in which the aspirant sits in mushin and waits for satori. Also used in traditional martial arts to develop mushin. (Japanese)

ZEN: The Japanese meditative sect of Mahayana Buddhism. (Japanese)

Appendix B

SELECTED BIBLIOGRAPHY

I sincerely hope you will continue your study of The Martial *Way*. To that end, I offer this list of books I've found particularly helpful in understanding the history of the martial arts, warrior training, honor, and the warrior culture in general. Also, I have included several books that offer sound guidance in areas of warrior living—conditioning, nutrition, philosophy, etcetera.

I have organized the list into four groups: the first provides general background information on martial arts history and warrior culture. The remaining three correspond to the three parts of this book.

MARTIAL ARTS HISTORY AND WARRIOR CULTURE

Draeger, Donn F. *Classical Bujutsu*. New York: Weatherhill, 1973.

Draeger, Donn F. *Classical Budo*. New York: Weatherhill, 1974.

Draeger, Donn F. *Modern Bujutsu & Budo*. New York: Weatherhill, 1974.

Draeger, Donn F. and Smith, Robert W. *Comprehensive Asian Fighting Arts* (formerly *Asian Fighting Arts*). Tokyo: Kodansha International, 1969.

Harrison, E.J. *The Fighting Spirit of Japan*. 1912. Reprint. Woodstock, N.Y.: Overlook Press, 1955.

Kim, Richard. *The Classical Man*. Hong Kong: Masters Publication, 1982.

Minick, Michael. *The Wisdom of Kung Fu*. New York: William Morrow & Company, Inc., 1974.

Nelson, Randy F. (ed.). *The Overlook Martial Arts Reader*. Woodstock, N.Y.: Overlook Press, 1989.

Ratti, Oscar and Westbrook, Adele. *Secrets of the Samurai: A Survey of the Martial Arts of Feudal Japan*. Rutland and Tokyo: Charles E. Tuttle Co., 1973.

THE *WAY* OF TRAINING

Choi, Hong Hi, *Taekwon-Do*. Cedar Knolls, N.J.: Wehman Brothers, Inc., 1972.

Chun, Richard. *Advancing in Tae Kwon Do*. New York: Harper & Row, Publishers, 1982.

Funakoshi, Gichen. *Karate-Do Kyohan*. Tokyo: Kodansha International, 1973.

Funakoshi, Gichen. *Karate-Do, My Way of Life*. Tokyo: Kodansha International, 1975.

Hassel, Randall G. *The Karate Experience*. Rutland and Tokyo: Charles E. Tuttle Co., 1980.

Kano, Jigoro. *Kodokan Judo*. Tokyo: Kodansha International, 1986.

Lee, Bruce. *Tao of Jeet Kune Do*. Burbank, CA.: Ohara Publications, 1975.

Lovret, Fredrick J. *The Way and the Power: Secrets of Japanese Strategy*. Boulder, CO.: Paladin Press, 1987.

Lovret, Fredrick, *The Student's Handbook*. San Diego, CA: Taseki Publishing Co., 1989.

Maslak, Paul. *What the Masters Know*. Hollywood, CA.: Unique Publications, 1980.

Miyamoto, Musashi. *A Book of Five Rings: A Guide to Strategy*. Translated by Victor Harris. Woodstock, N.Y.: Overlook Press, 1974.

Oyama, Masutatsu. *The Kyokushin Way: Mas. Oyama's Karate Philosophy*. Tokyo: Japan Publications Inc., 1979.

Palumbo, Dennis G. *The Secrets of Hakkoryu Jujutsu Shodan Tactics*. Boulder, CO.: Paladin Press, 1987.

Palumbo, Dennis G. *The Secret Nidan Techniques of Hakkoryu Jujutsu*. Boulder, CO.: Paladin Press, 1988.

Son, Duk Sun and Clark, Robert J. *Black Belt Korean Karate*. Englewood Cliffs, N.J.: Prentice-Hall Inc., 1983.

Sun Tzu, *The Art of War*. Edited and foreword by James Clavell, New York: Dell Publishing, 1983.

Ueshiba, Kisshomaru. *The Spirit of Aikido*. Translated by Taitetsu Unno. Tokyo: Kodansha International, 1984.

Warner, Gordon and Draeger, Donn F. *Japanese Swordsmanship: Technique and Practice*. New York: Weatherhill, 1982.

Westbrook, A. and Ratti, O. *Aikido and the Dynamic Sphere*. Rutland and Tokyo: Charles E. Tuttle Co., 1970.

Wing, R.L. *The Art of Strategy: A New Translation of Sun Tzu's Classic, The Art of War*. New York: Doubleday, 1988.

THE *WAY* OF HONOR

Allyn, John. *The 47 Ronin Story*. Rutland and Tokyo: Charles E. Tuttle Co., 1970.

Nitobe, Inazo. *Bushido: The Soul of Japan*. 1905. Reprint. Rutland and Tokyo: Charles E. Tuttle Co., 1969.

Sadler, A.L. *The Code of the Samurai*. Rutland and Tokyo: Charles E. Tuttle Co., 1941.

Wilson, William Scott. *The Ideals of the Samurai: Writings of Japanese Warriors*. Burbank, CA.: Ohara Publications, 1982.

Yamamoto, Tsunetomo. *Hagakure: The Book of the Samurai*. Translated by William Scott Wilson. Tokyo: Kodansha International, 1979.

THE *WAY* OF LIVING

Cavendish, Richard. *The Eastern Religions*, New York: Arco Publications., 1980.

Castaneda, Carlos. *Journey to Ixtlan: The Lessons of Don Juan*. New York: Washington Square Press, Pocket Books, 1972.

Castaneda, Carlos. *Tales of Power*. New York: Pocket Books, 1974.

Cooper, Keneth H. *Aerobics*. New York: M. Evans and Company, Inc., 1968.

Confucius. *Confucian Analects*. New York: Penguin Books, 1979.

de Bary, W. T. (ed). *Sources of Japanese Tradition*, New York: Columbia University Press, 1958.

Deshimaru, Taisen. *The Zen Way to the Martial Arts*. Translated by Nancy Amphoux. New York: E.P. Dutton Inc., 1979.

Feibleman, J.K., *Understanding Oriental Philosophy: A Popular Account for the Western World*, New York: Horizon Press, 1976.

Fox. *Sports Physiology*. Philadelphia, PA: Saunders College Publications, 1979.

Haas, Robert. *Eat to Win: The Sports Nutrition Bible*. New York: Rawson Associates, 1983.

Hopfe, L. M., *Religions of the world*, Encino, CA: Glencoe Pub. Co., 1976.

Lao, Tzu. *Tao te Ching*. New York: Penguin Books, 1963.

Lao, Tzu. *Tao te Ching: A New Translation based on the recently discovered Ma-Wang-Tui Texts*. Translation, introduction, and commentary by Robert G. Henricks. New York: Ballantine Books, 1979.

McArdle, William D., Katch, Frank I., and Katch, Victor L. *Exercise Physiology: Energy, Nutrition, and Human Performance (2nd ed.)*. Philadelphia, PA.: Lea & Febiger, 1986.

Millman, Dan. *The Warrior Athlete: Body, Mind, & Spirit*. Walpole, N.H.: Stillpoint Publishing, 1979.

Rogers, David J. *Fighting to Win: Samurai Techniques for your Work and Life*. Garden City, N.Y.: Doubleday, 1984.

Soho, Takuan *The Unfettered Mind*. Translated by William Scott Wilson. Tokyo: Kodansha International, 1986.

Strauss, R.H. *Sports Medicine and Physiology*. Philadelphia, PA.: W.B. Saunders Co., 1979.

Vander, Sherman, and Luciano. *Human Physiology: The Mechanics of Body Function (3rd ed)*. New York: McGraw-Hill, 1980.

Van de Wetering, Janwillem. *The Empty Mirror: Experiences in a Japanese Zen Monestery*. New York: Washington Square Press, Pocket Books, 1973.